Entrée to Entrelac

to Entrelac

The definitive guide
from a *biased* knitter

Gwen Bortner

Photography by
Alexis Xenakis

8
Entrelac
Basics

- ◆ An overview
- ◆ Basic components
- ◆ Key concepts
- ◆ Flat versus seamless
- ◆ Projects
- ◆ Practice blocks
- ◆ Triangles
- ◆ Rectangles

Projects

Practice blocks

16

Classic entrelac
Classic entrelac in the mirror
Diamonds, zigzags, and argyles

Welcome

I was first introduced to entrelac in the mid-80s while working part-time in the local yarn shop. I had been hired because of my ability to apply math skills to yarn substitutions, pattern adjustments, and sweater design. An Anny Blatt design featuring entrelac caught my fancy, so I started experimenting with the technique. My first piece of entrelac was rectangular in shape, as were all pieces of entrelac I had ever seen. In the mid-80s, knitting yokes into sweatshirts was all the rage and I thought it would be fun to do this with entrelac — but how?

Moving from flat to circular and then from a cylinder to a cone were all problems I would have to solve. Calculating gauge on a piece of entrelac fabric presented the type of geometric and mathematical challenge I relished and this is how my love of entrelac began. Now I have the opportunity to share my love of entrelac through this book.

Whether you are new to entrelac, have dabbled some, or love it and just want more interesting designs to try, this book is for you. For knitters who have never tried entrelac (or tried without success), the book is designed to work as a series of skills and concepts, each building on the previous, with projects along the way to apply what you have learned. Knitters with some entrelac experience can review the basics and then learn options for shaping, seams, and joins. For those 'just here for the designs,' each chapter has projects. Finally, if you are completely addicted to entrelac and want try your hand at design, information is provided to assist in understanding the challenges associated with entrelac.

— *Gwen Bortner*

One last thing

In talking with knitters over the years, many of them students, I have found several common themes related to their success (or failure) with entrelac.

1 Learning entrelac is much easier by doing than by reading. Of course you will need to read, but do so with needles and yarn at hand. Because I believe this is the key to learning entrelac, most ideas will have an accompanying Practice Block. In addition, many key concepts will also be used in smaller projects that are quick to knit and reinforce the featured skills. If you become confused, give the Practice Block a try; hopefully it will solidify your understanding.

2 When you begin, you have to be a bit of a blind follower; just do what the instructions state and don't overthink them. If you follow — stitch by stitch, row by row — they will work! The fabric may look misshapen, but keep going, it will straighten itself out in the end.

3 Knitting in both directions (or knitting backwards as it is commonly known) is the key for most knitters to enjoy entrelac. It becomes more efficient and less confusing the more you practice. I was able to cut more than one-third of my knitting time by eliminating the need to turn my work. Practice the technique early and it will become second nature in no time. You will even start using it in other projects, thinking about it, and approaching your knitting differently.

4 Entrelac is much easier to knit than it looks. With a little bit of practice and understanding, it can become your 'mindless knitting.' I know this is hard to believe, but many of my students can verify this.

5 Once the basic concepts of entrelac are understood, working from a diagram is easy for most knitters. This is even true for knitters who avoid charts. For the more complex projects, diagrams are a necessity so become familiar with them as you work all the projects.

Yes, that was more than one more thing, but these things are important to remember. If you remember nothing else, remember to enjoy the process as you enter the entrelac world — knitting entrelac is fun!

Guidelines from a Biased Knitter

Both as a knitter and as an instructor, I try to have as few absolutes as possible. Even so, I have strong preferences for some of the key techniques used in entrelac.

Selvedge stitches

For entrelac fabric, I prefer that every edge stitch be worked on every row — usually in stockinette. (If a project requires slipping edge stitches or any other special treatment, we will note that in the instruction.) An edge where every stitch is worked is firmer than a slipped-stitch edge. And when more than 1 stitch needs to be picked up for every 2 rows, it is much easier. In addition, it is possible to pick up through only half a stitch (my preference) and still maintain a firm edge.

Picking up stitches

PUP and PUK Entrelac requires picked-up stitches. Because it is a frequent requirement, I strongly recommend you learn to both pick up and knit (we call this PUK) and pick up and purl (we call this PUP) — without the use of a crochet hook. When creating entrelac fabric, approximately half of the picked-up stitches will be worked as PUP stitches with the wrong side facing. With a little practice, you will soon be comfortable picking up both ways.

The knot I recommend picking up through only half a stitch along the selvedge edge. The firmest part of the fabric edge is what I have termed 'the knot.' For standard entrelac, there are the same number of knots as there are stitches to be picked up: 1 knot for every 2 rows of knitting. Picking up through the knot tends to result in fewer gaps, a consistent line, and less bulk on the wrong side of the fabric.

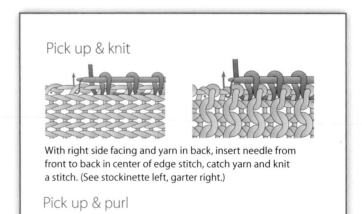

Pick up & knit

With right side facing and yarn in back, insert needle from front to back in center of edge stitch, catch yarn and knit a stitch. (See stockinette left, garter right.)

Pick up & purl

With wrong side facing and yarn in front, insert needle from back to front in center of edge stitch, catch yarn, and purl.

As we begin to build on the multi-directional possibilities of entrelac, a temporary cast-on is often the answer. Temporary cast-ons use waste yarn to hold the loops that form between stitches under the needle. When this waste yarn is removed, the loops can be placed on a needle and a row of stitches is available to join or knit in another direction. I prefer the temporary crochet cast-on.

One of the comments I hear when someone sees an entrelac project is, "Oh, there must be a thousand ends to weave in." In most cases, this is not true, but there are 1 or 2 at the beginning and end of each tier. Even so, I make a habit of catching the tails or weaving in the ends as I go. By taking the few extra moments to deal with the ends at the beginning of each tier, my finishing time is greatly reduced.

Temporary crochet cast-on

1 Using waste yarn and leaving a short tail, make a slipknot on crochet hook. Hold hook in right hand; in left hand, hold knitting needle on top of yarn and behind hook. With hook to left of yarn, bring yarn through loop on hook; yarn goes over top of needle, forming a stitch.

2 Bring yarn under point of needle and hook yarn through loop forming next stitch. Repeat Step 2 until 1 stitch remains to cast on. Slip loop from hook to needle for last stitch.

Picking up loops from a temporary cast-on

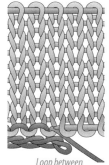

There will seem to be 1 fewer loops than cast-on stitches. Pick up the last loop in the loop between the last stitch of the first row of knitting and the first stitch of the second row of knitting.

Loop between stitches

Weaving-in tails

The tail is woven alternately above and below the working yarn on the purl side of the work. Weaving the carries results in a firmer fabric than stranding does.

From the knit side
To weave the tail above a knit stitch: Insert needle into stitch and under woven yarn, then knit the stitch as usual.

To weave the tail below a knit stitch: Insert needle into stitch and over woven yarn, then knit the stitch as usual.

From the purl side
To weave the tail above a purl stitch: Insert needle into stitch and under woven yarn, then purl the stitch as usual.

To weave the tail below a purl stitch: Insert needle into stitch and over woven yarn, then purl the stitch as usual.

5 steps for learning to knit from left to right

Step 1: Turn your work to the WS and insert your needle as if to purl.

Step 2: Without changing your needles, turn your work to the RS and note the position of the inserted needle. While still looking at the RS, pull the needle out and reinsert it to make sure you understand the motion.

Step 3: Turn your work back to the WS. Wrap your yarn around the needle without pulling up a loop.

Step 4: Without changing the position of the yarn (holding the wrap in place), turn your work to the RS and note the position of the yarn and the direction of the wrap. While still looking at the RS, slowly unwrap and rewrap the yarn to make sure you understand the direction of the wrap.

Step 5: With the RS of the work facing you, pull the loop that is wrapped around your needle toward you.

Repeat these steps until you are familiar with the correct positioning of the needle and wrap direction of the yarn. Note that the yarn wraps around the needle in the same direction whether you knit from left to right or right to left.

Knitting in both directions

A majority of the students in my Learn to Knit Entrelac classes think that learning to knit in both directions (also known as knitting backwards) is one of the coolest techniques they have ever learned. And everyone who takes the time to learn agrees that the time is greatly reduced by knitting in both directions.

Knitting in both directions will speed up the process because at the end of the right-side rows you will not turn your work, but knit in the opposite direction (backwards) — working the stitches from the right-hand needle onto the left-hand needle. You eliminate swapping the needles and fiddling with the yarn. Since entrelac is made up of many short rows, knitting in both directions is a skill worth learning.

I believe the easiest way to learn to knit in the other direction is to watch yourself purl from the wrong side.

When you first learn to work this way, it may be slower than turning and purling. But remember that learning to knit from left to right is much like learning to knit from right to left; it takes practice.

Until you become comfortable with the process, your tension may be inconsistent. With repetition, an uneven tension will smooth out. Also be aware that even when your tension is consistent, your gauge when knitting in both directions may not be the same as your gauge when turning the work for alternating right-side and wrong-side rows of knit and purl.

First you're knitting in both directions…

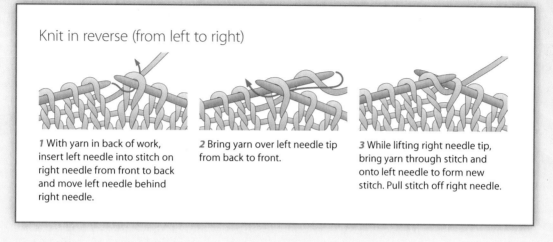

Knit in reverse (from left to right)

1 With yarn in back of work, insert left needle into stitch on right needle from front to back and move left needle behind right needle.

2 Bring yarn over left needle tip from back to front.

3 While lifting right needle tip, bring yarn through stitch and onto left needle to form new stitch. Pull stitch off right needle.

…then purling in both directions…

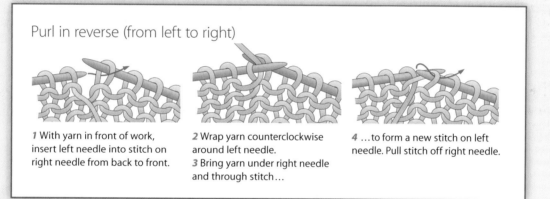

Purl in reverse (from left to right)

1 With yarn in front of work, insert left needle into stitch on right needle from back to front.

2 Wrap yarn counterclockwise around left needle.
3 Bring yarn under right needle and through stitch…

4 …to form a new stitch on left needle. Pull stitch off right needle.

…and soon you'll want to learn much more.

Here are directions for the common wrong-side decrease, increase, and pick-up — now shown worked on the right side, so you needn't turn the work. If you come across another wrong-side maneuver and wonder how to do it from the right-side, just apply our 5 steps for learning to knit from left to right.

P2tog

1 Insert right needle into first 2 stitches on left needle.

2 Purl these 2 stitches together as if they were 1.
The result is a right slanting decrease.

P2tog worked in reverse

1 Insert left needle into first 2 stitches on right needle as shown (left needle is behind).

2 Bring yarn over left needle tip from back to front and pull yarn through these 2 stitches (as if they were 1). Pull both stitches off right needle.

Purl into front and back worked in reverse (pf&b)

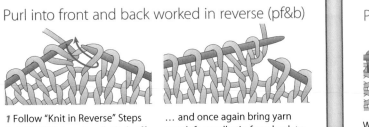

1 Follow "Knit in Reverse" Steps 1–3 EXCEPT do not pull stitch off right needle. *2* Insert left needle back into this stitch as shown…

… and once again bring yarn over left needle tip from back to front and pull yarn through stitch onto left needle. Pull stitch off right needle.

Pick up & purl in reverse (PUP)

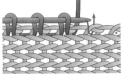

With right-side facing and yarn in back, insert needle from front to back in center of edge stitch, catch yarn, and knit a stitch.

The worrisome bits

In any 'learn to entrelac' class, there are a number of questions that I wait to answer until near the end of class. They are detailed, 'make-the-fabric' perfect concerns that slow students down. It is important that you first have a basic understanding of how entrelac fabric is formed. Try not to get to hung up on these notes as you begin, but know the information is waiting here when you need it.

◆ I almost always pick up in the center of a stitch as shown in the drawings on page viii. But whether you pick up through half stitch or a whole stitch, the most important thing to remember is to be consistent. The goal is a straight, even line of stitches. You will also see from the drawings that I pick up through the tighter turning stitch along the edge of the fabric (the knot). By picking up there, I am less likely to get holes. There is always 1 turning stitch for every 2 rows — the correct number of pick up points in most cases.

◆ Holes at the intersection point where 4 units meet, if small, are just the nature of entrelac — my entrelac fabric has those holes too. Large holes are usually the result of either not starting the pick-up close enough to the top of the edge or not picking up the last stitch close enough to the previous tier. If one intersection hole happens to be a little too big, just use the tail or extra yarn and whip-stitch it closed on the back!

◆ A big worry for many knitters is the fact that the color from the previous tier sometimes peeks through at the join. This, too, is the nature of entrelac and is not nearly as visible at 'normal' viewing distance as when we are creating the fabric in our lap. Some yarns will have a stronger tendency toward showing this than others. If it is a real concern, work a color-change row between tiers as in Prussian Jewels (page 59). But note, out of all the projects in the book, I used this technique only once as a color solution, and once again to form the decorative welts on the Chullo sampler (page 115).

Working with the book

The Project

A Brief Intro
Each project is explained in an intro that gives background and Gwen's design thoughts.

The UNITS in this project and the **Base stitches** for size of each rectangle (or triangle) unit.

Notes
These notes will help you complete the project with minimal interruptions by addressing points that need attention BEFORE you stumble on them.

Here you will find vital information on *Level of* **difficulty.**

Size
Fit (when applicable) and finished measurements.

Note that you can find complete row-by-row instructions for the basic UNITS on page 158.

The rucksack demonstrates what will happen when stripes are added to felted entrelac fabric. The lightning bolt is created by strategically placing stripes of color within each entrelac unit. Since the contrasting color (B) is only used for a few rows, the main color (A) can be carried from unit to unit. Color B can be carried up along the joining selvedge, minimizing the number of ends.

Lightning bolt rucksack

Bottom
Tier 1, base rectangles [With waste yarn and crochet cast-on, cast on 11. With A, work Unjoined LR] 4 times — 44 stitches, 4 rectangles. Cut A. *Tier 2,* b With WS facing, slip live stitches from last rectangle to right needle and PUP11 along its selvedge. Work 3 RR. PUP11 and remove waste yarn from Rectangle 1, placing stitches on left needle. Work RR, joining to stitches from temporary cast-on. c Removing waste yarn and joining to stitches from temporary cast-on, work 3 RR along bottom of Tier 1 rectangles — d 88 stitches, 8 RR.

Main Bag
e Continue working entrelac in the round, carrying color B along the join. *Tier 3* Work 8 LR. *Tier 4* Work 8 RR. *Tiers 5–10* Repeat last 2 tiers 3 more times. *Tier 11* Cut B. With A only, work 8 LR, binding off all stitches on Row 22.

Finishing
f Fold points of last 8 units to outside of bag and stitch where indicated by red dots to form casing for strap.

Straps *Each strap should measure approximately 1 yard after felting. Felting will reduce length by one-quarter to one-third.*

Twisted cord g Cut one 8-yard length of A and two of B; hold A and B together for each cord. Make 4.

h Carefully remove knots from 2 cords and knot them together; repeat for other pair of cords. Insert cords from inside to outside of bag between stitches at points shown, pulling knot snug against inside of bag and secu...

Felt bag to desired size. Shape as necessary and air dry.

i, j Insert cords in casing, beginning above attachment point and taking cords from each pair in opposite directions around to other side of bag t... Adjust to desired length; knot ends together; trim excess cord.

notes
◆ See page 152 for any unfamiliar techniques.
◆ Project is worked in seamless entrelac.
◆ Join new length of B in each unit of first tier; carry B along join from tier to tier. Cut A at end of each tier when changing direction.
◆ When binding off stitches on final tier, lift last stitch bound-off for unit over the first stitch picked up for the next unit.

Intermediate
20" high x 17" wide before felting
14½" high x 11½" wide after felting

10cm/4"
2B
1B
Tier stockinette stitch before felting

1 2 3 **4** 5 6
Medium weight
A 490 yds
B 160 yds

5.5mm/US9, or size to obtain gauge, 60cm (24") or longer

&
extra dpn
crochet hook
waste yarn

110

Guage

Here you will find vital information on *Level of* **difficulty.**

Yarn used
Thickness and yardage of each needed.

Needles

& etc.
Additional tools and notions.

Glowing UNITS are modified from the basic UNITS. Each instance will be explained in the project.

---

the UNITS

LBT Left-leaning Base Triangle
LST Left-leaning Starting Triangle
LR Left-leaning Rectangle
LET Left-leaning Ending Triangle
LTT Left-leaning Top Triangle

RBT Right-leaning Base Triangle
RST Right-leaning Starting Triangle
RR Right-leaning Rectangle
RET Right-leaning Ending Triangle
RTT Right-leaning Top Triangle

159

Chart key

Techniques
Clear, additional techniques and how-tos wherever you need them are on page 152!.

3 Fold cord in half, smoothing as it twists on itself. Pull knot through original fold to secure.

the
UNITS
se number
1 stitches

and R Pic-up
es and work first
s (18 rows) with A
change to B and
lete unit.

LR

SSK   P2K

RR

PUP   P2tog

unjoined LR

PUP   P2K

For row-by-row
instructions,
see page 158

Entrée
Entrelac

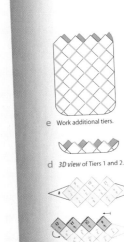

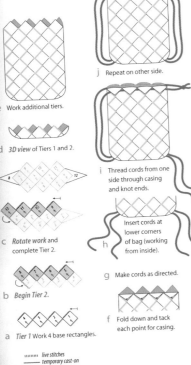

j Repeat on other side.

e Work additional tiers.

d *3D view* of Tiers 1 and 2.

i Thread cords from one side through casing and knot ends.

Insert cords at lower corners of bag (working from inside).

h

c *Rotate work* and complete Tier 2.

g Make cords as directed.

b *Begin Tier 2.*

f Fold down and tack each point for casing.

a *Tier 1* Work 4 base rectangles.

ıııııı *live stitches*
———— *temporary cast-on*
∿∿∿ *joined edge*
———— *picked-up stitches*
———— *column B row*

➜ *direction of work*

BROWN SHEEP COMPANY Nature Spun Worsted in colors N04W Z (A), and 308W (B)

111

This book was designed as a instructional/reference book that also has a variety of intriguing patterns. Each section builds upon the prior one.

Entrelac basics covers an overview of entrelac, the general directions for the 10 basic entrelac units, the differences of working entrelac flat or seamlessly and a number of starter projects.

Simple shapes and seams is where entrelac begins to get interesting. Topics include methods for shaping entrelac fabric, an introduction to diagrams, and alternative seaming methods.

Intriguing constructions takes shaping and seaming entrelac to another level. Fully integrated pockets, entrelac fabric in all shapes and sizes, and 3-dimensional gussets are just a few of the topics explored.

Color, texture, and other interesting fabrics asks (and answers) the 'what if' questions. The more creative projects are found within this section as entrelac is combined with other knitting techniques to produce something wonderful and unique.

Designing with entrelac covers the various aspects of gauge, designing with a bias fabric, and walks you through the steps of creating an entrelac design from scratch.

Yarn
The yarn used in each photographed project

Practice blocks prepare you for upcoming projects,

ıııııı *live stitches*
———— *temporary cast-on*
∿∿∿ *joined edge*
———— *picked-up stitches*
———— *column B row*

➜ *direction of work*

Entrelac Basics

Entrelac is quite simple, it's not much more than knits, purls, picked-up stitches, increases, and decreases. Even so, the resulting fabric looks tremendously complex. Because its simplicity can be explored, enhanced, and developed in new ways, it seems the more I know, the more there is to learn. Let's start with the basics.

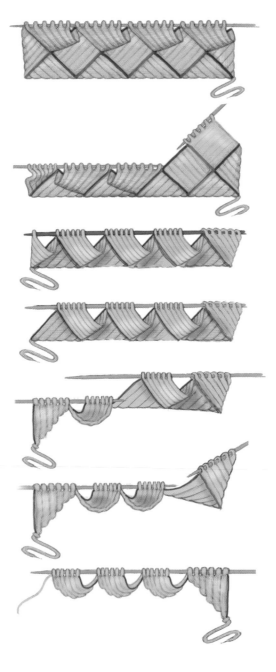

An overview

Entrelac, the French word for interlaced, is a technique that is worked in small sections that are joined as they are worked. When completed, entrelac fabric looks like strips of knitting woven together on the bias.

This technique is distinct in both the construction and the finished product, with limitations as well as unique opportunities for creative and alternative solutions.

These factors combined with my love of math have made entrelac my passion. (Others might say obsession.)

The first entrelac projects I saw were interesting, but seemed to follow an unwritten rule that shapes created with entrelac must be rectilinear. We dress our bodies in rectangles, but cylinders, cones, and curves are more flattering. Once I understood the basics of entrelac, I focused on eliminating seams. Working cylinders, cones, and curves followed. Methods of increasing and decreasing in entrelac led to more interesting shapes. As I worked on this book, additional applications developed.

Basic components

Entrelac is composed of triangles and rectangles. What appear to be diamonds are actually knit as rectangles. Triangles are typically used along the edges, while the body of the fabric is made of rectangles. Interestingly, there are only 2 basic variations of rectangles and 8 variations of triangles.

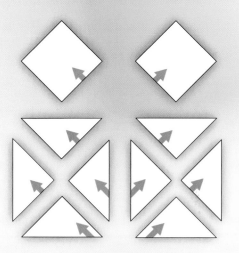

In entrelac diagrams, arrows point in the direction a rectangle or triangle is worked, and in the direction it leans in the fabric: to the left in a left-leaning shape, to the right in a right-leaning shape. The 2 generic terms for rectangles are right-leaning rectangle (RR) and left-leaning rectangle (LR). There are 4 positions for triangles: base triangles, starting triangles, ending triangles, and top triangles. Triangles in each position can be left-leaning or right-leaning, hence the 8 options.

We will present basic instructions for each of the 10 units in stockinette stitch. A multitude of combinations are possible once you understand their basic construction.

Key concepts

The knitting skills for entrelac are basic; even new knitters can learn the technique. Just follow the directions (somewhat blindly and with a little trust) until you get a broader understanding of the process. Then 'ah-ha', it all comes together.

Before jumping into the 'how' of entrelac, a brief overview of key concepts is in order.

Units

- A unit is a single triangular or rectangular shape. Within patterns, these shapes will be identified by an abbreviation and an icon.

- Typically, each unit is completed before beginning the next unit.

- Units are composed of rows of knitting, worked back and forth.

- Most units will include twice as many rows as stitches.

- In the fabric, individual units will appear to lean either to the left or right; this is indicated by a green arrow on the diagrams.

- Units are worked flat (knit back and forth in rows).

Tiers

- A tier is a series of consecutively created units all leaning in the same direction.

- In most cases, the units within a tier will be the same size.

- Tiers can be worked flat or seamlessly, but in seamless entrelac, the tiers are joined at the edges forming a cylinder as they are worked.

Base numbers

- When creating a unit, the key is to know the base number of stitches. The base number of stitches is the number of stitches picked up at the base of rectangles and some triangles, and the number of stitches in the full width of other triangles that increase from a single stitch.

- The larger the base number of stitches, the larger the entrelac unit will be. In designs with graduated sizes of units, the concept of base number minus 1 (Base – 1) is used.

Process

- Most units begin with a row of stitches being picked up along the selvedge of a unit from the previous tier.

- The pink arrow at the base of a unit indicates the direction of the pick-up.

- The direction of the pink arrow also indicates the type of pick-up. For left-pointing arrows, pick up and knit (PUK); for right-pointing arrows, pick up and purl (PUP).

- As a unit is worked, it is joined to the live stitches from an adjacent unit in the previous tier. On our diagrams this joined edge is represented by a jagged blue line.

- Decreases join a stitch of the current unit together with 1 or more stitches from the unit in the previous tier.

- The only seaming required within a project will be joining the pieces together. Units join to units and tiers to tiers as the fabric is worked.

Technique

- When picking up stitches, start as close to the top point of the selvedge (near the needle) as possible, work toward the previous tier, and space stitches evenly.

- In most cases, pick up 1 stitch for every 2 rows.

- When creating left-leaning units, the pick-up selvedge is immediately below the right-hand needle and for right-leaning units, the pick-up selvedge is immediately below the left-hand needle (when viewing your work from the right side).

- Tiers of left-leaning units are worked from right to left (as you view the right side of the work). Tiers of right-leaning units are worked from left to right. As such, when working flat, the point where a tier ends is the starting point for the next tier.

Flat versus seamless

Whether the entrelac fabric is created flat or seamlessly, the individual units are worked in the same manner. Having an understanding of both fabrics is important.

Knit flat

In most cases, when entrelac is knit flat, starting and ending triangles are required. They are also used every other tier to create vertical edges. Assuming no shaping is occurring, tiers with edge triangles will have one fewer rectangular unit than the tier without edge triangles.

Knit seamlessly

When entrelac is knit seamlessly, the resulting fabric is a tube. There is no need for starting and ending triangles. They are eliminated; the first rectangle is picked up along the last rectangle of the previous tier and joined to the first rectangle of the previous tier. This means that the yarn must be cut between tiers even when using the same yarn. Each tier will have the same number of rectangular units, and tiers of left-leaning rectangles alternate with tiers of right-leaning rectangles. Unlike knitting in the round, at the end of each tier of seamless entrelac, the following tier is worked in the opposite direction as if working flat.

Projects

Entrelac, even in its most basic form, can be used to create a variety of interesting projects. Practice Blocks will be spread throughout the book; a basic overview and the first 7 blocks are in this section. In addition to the Practice Blocks, other projects — perfect for gifts or to keep for yourself — provide a great introduction to the world of entrelac.

The practice blocks

The practice blocks are designed to give you quick, hands-on experience with a new skill or concept. Each completed block should be very close in size to all other blocks.

The blocks are shown in 2 contrasting colors, light gray and charcoal gray. A number of projects can be created out of the blocks. A single block can become a felted trivet or hot pad. Five blocks? They'll make a cute bag. Join 6 blocks and felt for a great placemat. Make 9 or more blocks into a pillow. If you make all 18, you'll have enough for a small throw. Even more blocks joined together can be an interesting afghan or felted to form a rug.

Basic UNITS

Triangles

Base triangles are used to start entrelac and establish the diagonals — to create the peaks and valleys that the next tier's units fit into. The directions can seem confusing, but when you realize that you are basically forming the angle by working short rows, it starts to make sense.

Starting and ending triangles produce straight edges along the sides of a flat piece of fabric. These triangles are not used for seamless entrelac.

Starting triangles are created by increasing 1 stitch along the selvedge of the fabric every other row and joining to the unit on the previous tier. An *ending triangle* is the other half of the starting triangle. Stitches for ending triangles are picked up, then decreased along the selvedge every other row. Upon completion of an ending triangle, 1 stitch remains. When the same yarn is used in the next tier, the last stitch does not need to be secured, but instead can be used as the first picked-up stitch for the next tier. *Top triangles*, sometimes known as finishing triangles, create a horizontal edge, filling in the peaks of the previous tier and bringing the fabric back to square.

Base Triangles (BTs)

If the base triangles can be created in a manner similar to the starting edge triangle stitches already on the needle, we call these Increase LBTs or Increase RBTs.

inc LBT

Increase LBT (Left-leaning Base Triangle) With RS facing, cast on 1. *Row 1* (WS) P1 (cast-on stitch). *Row 2* (RS) Knit in front and back of stitch (kf&b). *Row 3* Purl stitches worked on previous row. *Row 4* Knit to last stitch, kf&b. Repeat last 2 rows to base number of stitches, end with a RS row.

Increase RBT
(Right-leaning Base Triangle)

inc RBT

With WS facing, cast on 1. *Row 1* (RS) K1 (cast-on stitch). *Row 2* (WS) Purl in front and back of stitch (pf&b). *Row 3* Knit stitches worked on previous row. *Row 4* Purl to last stitch, pf&b. Repeat last 2 rows to base number of stitches, end with a WS row.

The following directions are used when there are stitches on the needle before Tier 1 is worked. Either stitches have been cast on or another knitted fabric, like ribbing, is below the entrelac fabric.

Base Triangles from live stitches (LBTs)

Join LBT (Left-leaning Base Triangle) *Row 1* (RS) K1 (existing stitch). *Row 2 and all WS rows* Purl stitch(es) worked on previous row. *Row 3* Knit stitch(es) worked on previous row, k2tog (2 existing stitches). *Row 5* Knit stitches worked on previous row, k1 (existing stitch). Repeat last 4 rows to base number of stitches, end with a RS row.

join LBT

Join RBT (Right-leaning Base Triangle) This triangle is the visual opposite of a LBT and its process is mirrored: RBTs work the joining decrease on wrong-side rows as a p2tog. *Row 1* (WS) P1 (existing stitch). *Row 2 and all RS rows* Knit stitch worked on previous row. *Row 3* Purl stitch(es) worked on previous row, p2tog (2 existing stitches). *Row 5* Purl stitches worked on previous row, p1 (existing stitch). Repeat last 4 rows to base number of stitches, end with a WS row.

join RBT

Entrée to Entrelac

Starting Triangles (STs)

RST (Right-leaning Starting Triangle)
With RS facing, cast on 1 (next to last stitch worked on previous tier). *Row 1* (WS) P2tog to join (cast-on stitch with stitch from previous tier). *Row 2* (RS) Kf&b. *Row 3* Purl to last stitch of unit, p2tog to join. *Row 4* Knit to last stitch, kf&b. Repeat last 2 rows until all stitches from unit in previous tier have been joined, end with a WS row — base number of stitches.

LST (Left-leaning Starting Triangle)
With WS facing, cast on 1 (next to last stitch worked on previous tier). *Row 1* (RS) SSK to join (cast-on stitch with stitch from previous tier). *Row 2* (WS) Pf&b. *Row 3* Knit to last stitch of unit, SSK to join. *Row 4* Purl to last stitch, pf&b. Repeat last 2 rows until all stitches from unit in previous tier have been joined, end with a RS row—base number of stitches.

Ending Triangles (ETs)

RET (Right-leaning Ending Triangle)
With WS facing, pick up and purl base stitches along edge of unit in previous tier (PUP). *Row 1* (RS) Knit stitches worked on previous row. *Row 2* (WS) Purl to last 2 stitches, p2tog. Repeat last 2 rows until 1 stitch remains. *Next row* (RS) K1, fasten off.

LET (Left-leaning Ending Triangle)
With RS facing, pick up and knit base stitches along edge of unit in previous tier (PUK). *Row 1* (WS) Purl stitches worked on previous row. *Row 2* (RS) Knit to last 2 stitches, SSK. Repeat last 2 rows until 1 stitch remains. *Next row* (WS) P1, fasten off.

Top Triangles (TTs)

dec LTT

Decrease LTT
(Left-leaning Top Triangle)
With RS facing, pick up and knit base stitches along edge of unit in previous tier (PUK). *Row 1* (WS) Purl base stitches. *Row 2* (RS) Knit to last stitch of unit, SSK to join (last stitch with stitch from previous tier). *Row 3* Purl to last 2 stitches, p2tog. Repeat last 2 rows until all stitches from unit in previous tier have been joined and 1 stitch remains. Purl this stitch together with last stitch of Row 1 as you work on next unit OR fasten off on final unit of tier.

Decrease RTT
(Right-leaning Top Triangle)
With WS facing, pick up and purl base stitches along edge of unit in previous tier (PUP). *Row 1* (RS) Knit base stitches. *Row 2* (WS) Purl to last stitch of unit, p2tog to join (last stitch with stitch from previous tier). *Row 3* Knit to last 2 stitches, SSK. Repeat last 2 rows until all stitches from unit in previous tier have been joined and 1 stitch remains. Knit this stitch together with last stitch of Row 1 as you work on next unit OR fasten off on final unit of tier.

dec RTT

Our diagrams and the unit icons always represent the right side of the work. In some patterns, we use a modified block (perhaps in garter, seed, or another stich pattern). These are shown as glowing icons.

Icon key

live stitches

 **PUP**
pick up and purl stitches in direction of arrow

PUK
pick up and knit stitches in direction of arrow

joined edge

 direction of work

Bound-off LTT
(Left-leaning Top Triangle)
Work same as Decrease LTT EXCEPT *Row 3*
Purl to last stitch, turn work. *Row 4* K1, pass
previously unworked stitch over (BO 1), knit
to last stitch of unit, SSK to join with previous
tier. Repeat last 2 rows. Fasten off last stitch or
bind off over first stitch on Row 2 of next unit.

Bound-off RTT
(Right-leaning Top Triangle)
Work same as Decrease RTT EXCEPT *Row 3*
Knit to last stitch, turn work. *Row 4* P1, pass
previously unworked stitch over (BO 1), purl to
last stitch of unit, p2tog to join with previous
tier. Repeat last 2 rows. Fasten off last stitch or
bind off over first stitch on Row 2 of next unit.

When working a top triangle with a bound-off edge, it is important to bind off loosely. Because the triangle's top edge is a short row, it is very easy to bind off too tightly resulting in a puckered edge along the top of the entrelac fabric.

Tops with live stitches

Live-stitch LTT
(Left-leaning Top Triangle)
Work same as Decrease LTT EXCEPT *Row 3*
Purl 1 stitch fewer than worked on previous
row. If desired, wrap next stitch, then turn
work. When all stitches from unit in previous
tier have been joined, base number of stitches
remain on needle.

Live-stitch RTT
(Right-leaning Top Triangle)
Work same as Decrease RTT EXCEPT *Row 3*
Knit 1 stitch fewer than worked on previous
row. If desired, wrap next stitch, then turn.
When all stitches from unit in previous tier
have been joined, base number of stitches
remain on needle.

Rectangles

All the rest of entrelac fabric is made of rectangles and there are 2: right-leaning and left-leaning. In the diagrams, they are drawn as squares and often set on point like diamonds, although they are knit as rectangles. The basic directions assume a stockinette fabric but entrelac can be done in any number of fabrics which we explore later in the book. The join used matches the direction the rectangle leans: a right-leaning rectangle uses a right-leaning decrease (usually a p2tog) and a left-leaning rectangle uses a left-leaning decrease (usually an SSK). For right-leaning rectangles, the pick-up is done on the wrong side as a pick up and purl (PUP) and the joins to the previous tier are made on wrong-side rows. Again, the left-leaning rectangle is the visual opposite of the right-leaning rectangle with pick up and knit (PUK) and join on right-side rows.

RR (Right-leaning Rectangle)
With WS facing, pick up and purl base stitches along edge of unit in previous tier (PUP). *Row 1* (RS) Knit base stitches. *Row 2* (WS) Purl to last stitch of unit, p2tog to join (last stitch with stitch from previous tier). Repeat last 2 rows until all stitches from unit in previous tier have been joined — base number of stitches.

LR (Left-leaning Rectangle)
With RS facing, pick up and knit base stitches along edge of unit in previous tier (PUK). *Row 1* (WS) Purl base stitches. *Row 2* (RS) Knit to last stitch of unit, SSK to join (last stitch with stitch from previous tier). Repeat last 2 rows until all stitches from unit in previous tier have been joined — base number of stitches.

Unjoined Rectangle

Unjoined rectangles may be used at the end of a tier instead of the end triangles. They can be worked with a regular or temporary cast-on. See the Market Scarf (page 22) where the Unjoined rectangles produce a zig-zag edge. In the Baby's First Entrelac (page 130) and Family of Mittens (page 80), the unjoined rectangles are worked with temporary cast-ons for a seamless construction.

Unjoined RR
PUP OR purl into existing stitches and work stockinette stitch with no edge joins (knit on RS rows and purl on WS rows) until unit has twice as many rows as base stitches.

Unjoined LR
PUK OR knit into existing stitches and work stockinette stitch with no edge joins (knit on RS rows and purl on WS rows) until unit has twice as many rows as base stitches.

Double-join Rectangles

The double-join provides even more options for fit and construction. This rectangle is joined to the adjacent units at the end of every row.

Double-join LR
PUK or knit into existing stitches. *Row 1* (WS) Purl to last stitch of unit, p2tog to join (last stitch with stitch from adjacent left-leaning unit). *Row 2* (RS) Knit to last stitch of unit, SSK to join (last stitch with stitch from previous tier).

Double-join RR
PUP or purl into existing stitches *Row 1* (RS) Knit to last stitch of unit, SSK to join (last stitch with stitch from adjacent right-leaning unit). *Row 2* Purl to last stitch of unit, p2tog to join (last stitch with stitch from previous tier).

Entrée
to
Entrelac

15

the UNITS

Base number
6 stitches

Most entrelac patterns begin with left-leaning base triangles. Note that when 4 triangle units are worked together, they form a square. Use cotton for this practice block and work the units in garter stitch to make a great dishcloth.

Icon key

live stitches

PUP
pick up and purl stitches in direction of arrow

PUK
pick up and knit stitches in direction of arrow

joined edge

direction of work

All Practice Blocks are shown in BROWN SHEEP Lamb's Pride in colors 03 Grey Heather (A) and 06 Deep Charcoal (B). Unless noted otherwise, they were worked on 5.5mm /US 9 needles at a gauge of 5 stitches and 7 rows to 1" over stockinette stitch.

inc LBT Increase Left-leaning Base Triangle

With A, cast on 1. **Row 1** (WS) P1. **Row 2** (RS) Knit in front and back of stitch (kf&b). **Row 3** Purl stitches worked on previous row. **Row 4** Knit to last stitch, kf&b. Repeat last 2 rows to 6 (24) stitches, end with a RS row.

LR Left-leaning Rectangle

With A and RS facing, pick up and knit 6 stitches along edge of unit in previous tier (PUK6). **Row 1** (WS) P6. **Row 2** (RS) K5, SSK to join (last stitch of unit with stitch from previous tier). Repeat last 2 rows until all 6 stitches from previous tier have been joined — 6 stitches.

dec LTT Decrease Left-leaning Top Triangle

With A and RS facing, PUK6 **Row 1** (WS) Purl. **Row 2** (RS) Knit to last stitch of unit, SSK to join with previous tier). **Row 3** (WS) Purl to last 2 stitches, p2tog. Repeat last 2 rows until all 6 (24) stitches from previous tier have been joined and 1 stitch remains. Purl this stitch together with last stitch of Row 1 as you work on next unit OR fasten off on final unit of tier.

RST Right-leaning Starting Base Triangle

With B, make a slip knot and place on needle next to last stitch worked. **Row 1** (WS) P2tog to join (slip knot with stitch from previous tier). **Row 2** (RS) Kf&b. **Row 3** Purl to last stitch of unit, p2tog to join. **Row 4** Knit to last stitch, kf&b. Repeat last 2 rows until all 6 (24)stitches from previous tier have been joined, end with a WS row — 6 (24) stitches.

RR Right-leaning Rectangle

With B and WS facing, pick up and purl 6 stitches along edge of unit in previous tier (PUP6) **Row 1** (RS) K6. **Row 2** (WS) P5, p2tog to join (last stitch of unit with stitch from previous tier). Repeat last 2 rows until all 6 stitches from previous tier have been joined — 6 stitches.

RET Right-leaning Ending Triangle

With B and WS facing, PUP6. **Row 1** (RS) Knit stitches worked on previous row. **Row 2** (WS) Purl to last 2 stitches, p2tog. Repeat last 2 rows until 1 stitch remains. Next row (RS) K1, fasten off.

notes

◆ See page 152 for any unfamiliar techniques.

◆ Cut yarn at end of tier; join new yarn at beginning of tier.

Classic entrelac

You can also make a square using just the 4 triangles and working them with a base number of 24 stitches.

Tier 3 Work LTT.

Tier 2 Work RST, RET.

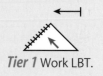

Tier 1 Work LBT.

Tier 4–8 Repeat Tiers 2 and 3 twice, then Tier 2 once.

Tier 3 Work 4 LR.

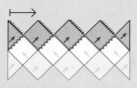

Tier 2 Work RST, 3 RR, RET.

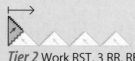

Tier 1 Work 4 LBT.

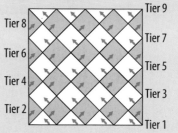

Tier 9
Tier 8
Tier 7
Tier 6
Tier 5
Tier 4
Tier 3
Tier 2
Tier 1

Tier 9 Work 4 LTT.

Color key
- ☐ A
- ▨ B

17

the UNITS

Base number
6 stitches

As the mirror opposite of Classic entrelac blocks, these start with right-leaning base triangles instead of left-leaning base triangles. By working both versions, you come to understand both the similarities and the differences between the units..

Icon key

▮▮▮▮
live stitches

▭ PUP ▭
pick up and purl stitches in direction of arrow

▭ PUK ▭
pick up and knit stitches in direction of arrow

∿∿∿∿∿∿
joined edge

↗
direction of work

LST Left-leaning Starting Triangle

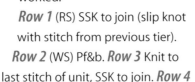

With B, make a slip knot and place on needle next to last stitch worked.
Row 1 (RS) SSK to join (slip knot with stitch from previous tier).
Row 2 (WS) Pf&b. *Row 3* Knit to last stitch of unit, SSK to join. *Row 4* Purl to last stitch, pf&b. Repeat last 2 rows until all 6 (24) stitches from previous tier have been joined — 6 (24) stitches.

LET Left-leaning Ending Triangle

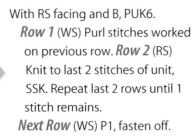

With RS facing and B, PUK6.
Row 1 (WS) Purl stitches worked on previous row. *Row 2* (RS) Knit to last 2 stitches of unit, SSK. Repeat last 2 rows until 1 stitch remains.
Next Row (WS) P1, fasten off.

LR Left-leaning Rectangle

With RS facing and B, pick up and knit 6 stitches along edge of unit in previous tier (PUK6).
Row 1 (WS) P6. *Row 2* (RS) K5, SSK to join (last stitch of unit with stitch from previous tier). Repeat last 2 rows until all 6 stitches from previous tier have been joined — 6 stitches.

inc RBT Increase Right-leaning Base Triangle

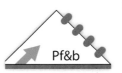

With A, cast on 1. *Row 1* (RS) K1.
Row 2 (WS) Purl in front and back of stitch (pf&b). *Row 3* Knit stitches worked on previous row. *Row 4* Purl to last stitch, pf&b. Repeat last 2 rows to 6 (24) stitches.

dec RTT Decrease Right-leaning Top Triangle

With WS facing and A, PUP6. *Row 1* (RS) Knit.
Row 2 (WS) Purl to last stitch of unit, p2tog to join (last stitch of unit with stitch from previous tier). *Row 3* Knit to last 2 stitches, SSK. Repeat last 2 rows until all 6 (24) stitches from previous tier have been joined and 1 stitch remains. Purl this stitch together with last stitch of Row 1 as you work next unit OR fasten off on final unit of tier.

RR Right-leaning Rectangle

With WS facing and A, pick up and purl 6 stitches along edge of unit in previous tier (PUP6). *Row 1* (RS) K6. *Row 2* (WS) P5, p2tog to join (last stitch of unit with stitch from previous tier). Repeat last 2 rows until all 6 stitches from previous tier have been joined — 6 stitches.

notes

◆ *See page 16 for vitals for practice blocks; see page 152 for any unfamiliar techniques.*

◆ *Cut yarn at end of tier; join new yarn at beginning of tier.*

Classic entrelac in the mirror

You can also make a square using just the 4 triangles and working them with a base number of 24 stitches.

Tier 3 Work RTT.

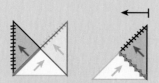

Tier 2 Work LST, LET.

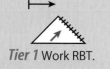

Tier 1 Work RBT.

Tier 4-8 Repeat Tiers 2 and 3 twice, then Tier 2 once.

Tier 3 Work 4 RR.

Tier 2 Work LST, 3 LR, LET.

Tier 1 Work 4 RBT.

Tier 9   Tier 8
Tier 7   Tier 6
Tier 5   Tier 4
Tier 3   Tier 2
Tier 1

Tier 9 Work 4 RTT.

Color key
- ☐ A
- ▨ B

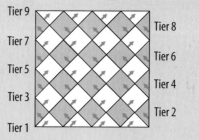

19

Base number
6 stitches

These three blocks are
created in the same
manner as the Classic
entrelac block. The only
difference is in the use
of color within each tier.
Note: When working
subsequent tiers in the
same solid color, take
care not to work too
many or too few stitches
in the first rows of
each unit.

Icon key

live stitches

PUP

pick up and purl stitches
in direction of arrow

PUK

pick up and knit stitches
in direction of arrow

joined edge

direction of work

Inc LBT Increase Left-leaning Base Triangle

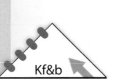

Cast on 1.
Row 1 (WS) P1 (cast-on stitch.
Row 2 (RS) Knit in front and
back of stitch (kf&b). ***Row 3*** Purl
stitches worked on previous row.
Row 4 Knit to last stitch, kf&b. Repeat last
2 rows to 6 stitches, end with a RS row.

LR Left-leaning Rectangle

With RS facing, pick up and knit
6 stitches along edge of unit in
previous tier (PUK6).
Row 1 (WS) P6.
Row 2 (RS) K5, SSK to join (last
stitch with of unit stitch from
previous tier).
Repeat last 2 rows until all 6
stitches from previous tier have been joined — 6
stitches.

dec LTT Decrease Left-leaning Top Triangle

With RS facing, PUK6
Row 1 (WS) Purl.
Row 2 (RS) Knit to last stitch of
unit, SSK to join with previous
tier.
Row 3 Purl to last 2 stitches,
p2tog. Repeat last 2 rows until all 6 stitches from
previous tier have been joined and 1 stitch remains.
Purl this stitch together with last stitch of Row 1 on
next unit OR on final unit of tier, fasten off.

notes

◆ *See page 16 for vitals for practice blocks; see*
page 152 for any unfamiliar techniques.

◆ *When color changes between units or tiers, cut*
yarn at end of tier; join new yarn at beginning
of tier.

RST Right-leaning Starting Triangle

Make a slip knot and place on needle
next to last stitch worked.
Row 1 (WS) P2tog to join (slip knot
with stitch from unit in previous tier).
Row 2 (RS) Kf&b.
Row 3 Purl to last stitch of unit,
p2tog to join.
Row 4 Knit to last stitch, kf&b.
Repeat last 2 rows until all 6 stitches
from previous tier have been joined, end with a
WS row — 6 stitches.

RR Right-leaning Rectangle

With WS facing, pick up and
purl 6 stitches along edge of
unit in previous tier (PUP6).
Row 1 (RS) K6.
Row 2 (WS) P5, p2tog to
join (last stitch of unit with
stitch from previous tier).
Repeat last 2 rows until all 6 stitches from
previous tier have been joined — 6 stitches.

RET Right-leaning Ending Triangle

With WS facing, PUP6.
Row 1 (RS) Knit stitches worked
on previous row.
Row 2 (WS) Purl to last 2 stitches,
p2tog. Repeat last 2 rows until 1
stitch remains.
Next row (RS) K1, fasten off.

Diamonds (Zigzag)

Tier 1 With A, work 4 LBT. *Tier 2* With B (A), work RST, 3 RR, RET. *Tier 3* With A (B), work 4 LR. *Tier 4* With A (B), work RST, 3 RR, RET. *Tier 5* With B (A), work 4 LR. *Tier 6* With A (A), repeat Tier 4. *Tier 7* Repeat Tier 3. *Tier 8* With B (B), repeat Tier 2. *Tier 9* With A, work 4 LTT.

Argyle

Tier 1 With A, work 4 LBT 4 times. *Tier 2* With A, work RST; with B, work RR; with A, work RR; with B, work RR; with A work RET. *Tier 3* With B, work 4 LR. *Tier 4* Repeat Tier 2. *Tier 5* With A, work 4 LR. *Tier 6* Repeat Tier 2. *Tier 7* Repeat Tier 3. *Tier 8* Repeat Tier 2. *Tier 9* With A, work 4 LTT.

Work contrast color as shown on diagram.

Chain St Crochet

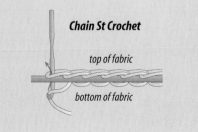

top of fabric

bottom of fabric

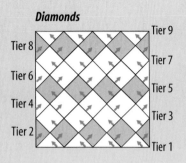

Diamonds

Tier 9 · Tier 8 · Tier 7 · Tier 6 · Tier 5 · Tier 4 · Tier 3 · Tier 2 · Tier 1

ZigZag

Tier 9 · Tier 8 · Tier 7 · Tier 6 · Tier 5 · Tier 4 · Tier 3 · Tier 2 · Tier 1

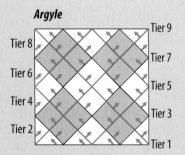

Argyle

Tier 9 · Tier 8 · Tier 7 · Tier 6 · Tier 5 · Tier 4 · Tier 3 · Tier 2 · Tier 1

Color key
- ☐ A
- ▨ B

— Chain stitch embroidery or crochet in opposite color (A on B and B on A).
➡ direction of work

21

Market scarf

As I design, I often think about projects in terms of instructional value. This design was created solely as an instructional project that did not use any triangles in the fabric. The exclusive use of rectangles produce a zigzag edge on all sides, simplifying the pattern while adding a design element.

notes

- ◆ See page 152 for any unfamiliar techniques.
- ◆ Checker board (as in stockinette scarf) cut yarn at end of each tier and join new yarn at beginning of tier.
- ◆ Either scarf can be expanded into a shawl by adding 9 units to each tier and working it to 60–72". Multiply yarn requirement amounts by 10 to determine how much you will need.

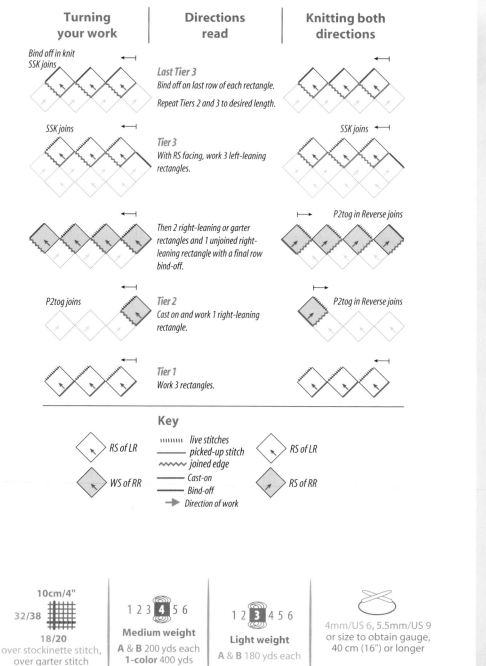

Turning your work	Directions read	Knitting both directions

Turning your work: Bind off in knit / SSK joins

Knitting both directions: SSK joins

Last Tier 3
Bind off on last row of each rectangle.
Repeat Tiers 2 and 3 to desired length.

SSK joins

Tier 3
With RS facing, work 3 left-leaning rectangles.

SSK joins

Turning your work: (unlabeled)

Then 2 right-leaning or garter rectangles and 1 unjoined right-leaning rectangle with a final row bind-off.

P2tog in Reverse joins

Turning your work: P2tog joins

Tier 2
Cast on and work 1 right-leaning rectangle.

P2tog in Reverse joins

Tier 1
Work 3 rectangles.

Key

- ◇ RS of LR
- ◈ WS of RR
- ⁙⁙⁙⁙ live stitches
- —— picked-up stitch
- ∿∿∿ joined edge
- —— Cast-on
- —— Bind-off
- → Direction of work
- ◇ RS of LR
- ◈ RS of RR

Easy
Approximately 6" x 60"

10cm/4"
32/38
18/20
over stockinette stitch, over garter stitch

1 2 3 **4** 5 6
Medium weight
A & B 200 yds each
1-color 400 yds

1 2 **3** 4 5 6
Light weight
A & B 180 yds each

4mm/US 6, 5.5mm/US 9 or size to obtain gauge, 40 cm (16") or longer

the
UNITS

Base number
6 stitches

LR
SSK / PUK

unjoined LR
PUK

unjoined RR
PUP

RR
PUP / P2tog

For row-by-row instructions see page 158

Entrée to Entrelac

22

Shown in MALABRIGO Merino Worsted in color 72 Apricot (A) and 42 Garnet (B)

Stockinette stitch scarf

Tier 1 Using cable cast-on, * cast on 6 stitches. Beginning with a purl row, work 12 rows of stockinette. Repeat from * 2 more times to complete Tier 1.

Tier 2 Cast on 6 stitches. Beginning with Row 2, work 1 RR; work 2 RR. Work 1 Unjoined RR, binding off on last row. *Tier 3* Work 3 LR.

Repeat Tiers 2 & Tier 3 to desired length, ending with odd tier and binding off last row of each unit.

Shown in KOLLAGE YARNS Temptation in Lagoon (A) and Lime Sorbet (B)

Knit in reverse (from left to right)

1 With yarn in back of work, insert left needle into stitch on right needle from front to back and move left needle behind right needle.

2 Bring yarn over left needle tip from back to front.

3 While lifting right needle tip, bring yarn through stitch and onto left needle to form new stitch. Pull stitch off right needle.

Purl in reverse (from left to right)

1 With yarn in front of work, insert left needle into stitch on right needle from back to front.

2 Wrap yarn counterclockwise around left needle.
3 Bring yarn under right needle and through stitch…

4 …to form a new stitch on left needle. Pull stitch off right needle.

Pick up & knit

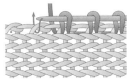 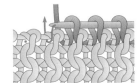

With right side facing and yarn in back, insert needle from front to back in center of edge stitch, catch yarn and knit a stitch. (See stockinette left, garter right.)

Pick up & purl

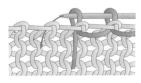

With wrong side facing and yarn in front, insert needle from back to front in center of edge stitch, catch yarn, and purl.

Pick up & purl in reverse (PUP)

With right-side facing and yarn in back, insert needle from front to back in center of edge stitch, catch yarn, and knit a stitch.

P2tog

1 Insert right needle into first 2 stitches on left needle.

2 Purl these 2 stitches together as if they were 1. The result is a right slanting decrease.

P2tog worked in reverse

1 Insert left needle into first 2 stitches on right needle as shown (left needle is behind).

2 Bring yarn over left needle tip from back to front and pull yarn through these 2 stitches (as if they were 1). Pull both stitches off right needle.

Garter stitch scarf

Work in garter stitch (knit all rows or purl all rows).

Tier 1 * Cast on 6 stitches. Work 12 rows of garter stitch over 6 stitches, ending on a RS row. Repeat from * 2 more times to complete Tier 1.

Tier 2 Cast on 6 stitches. Beginning with Row 2, work 1 RR; work 2 RR, 1 Unjoined RR. *Next row* Bind off to last stitch; pass stitch over first stitch picked up in next tier.

Tier 3 Work 3 RR.

Repeat Tiers 2 & 3 to desired length, ending with odd tier and binding off in pattern on last row of each unit.

Working entrelac in garter

Turning your work	OR	Working in both directions
Knit every row with SSK joins in any unit.	OR	Knit right to left, and purl left to right; with SSK joins in left-leaning units or p2tog in reverse joins in right-leaning units.
Purl every row with p2tog joins in any unit.	OR	Purl right to left, and knit left to right; with p2 tog joins in left leaning units, and SSK in reverse joins in right leaning units.

25

Inspired by the cardboard versions you find at your neighborhood coffee house. The felted sleeve uses only three of the basic units and is created seamlessly. Top triangles with bound-off stitches make the diameter slightly smaller than the base triangle edge, forming the tapered shape. Add a few rows to form beverage cozies. The Pointed Opening Edge Option starts with rectangles and are lined with craft boxes from the craft store, while the bottles, can, and glass cozies begin with triangles..

notes

◆ See page 152 for any unfamiliar techniques.

◆ Both projects are worked top down, from opening to base, in seamless entrelac.

Shown in BROWN SHEEP COMPANY Lamb's Pride Worsted in 2 colors

Java sleeve

Tier 1 With A, work 4 Inc LBT — 1 per dpn, 24 stitches. Cut yarn.

Tier 2 With B, work 3 RR, picking up stitches for first RR along edge of last LBT. For last RR PUP along first LBT and join to last LBT, making sure piece is not twisted. Cut yarn. **Tier 3** With RS facing and A, work 4 BO LTT, picking up stitches for first LTT along edge of first RR. Felt to desired size.

Tier 3

Tier 2

Tier 3
Tier 2
Tier 1

Tier 1

Easy

Sleeve 10" circumference by 2½" high
Cuppa Tall Height 3¼ (5½, 6½, 9)"
Cuppa Circumference measured after felting 8 (9¼, 13, 16)"

10cm/4"

24

17
over stockinette stitch

1 2 3 **4** 5 6
Medium weight
A, B 15 yds each for Sleeve
35 (50, 95, 120) yds for Cuppa

5.5mm/US 9, or size to obtain gauge, set of 5 dpns

the
UNITS
Base numbers
Cozy
6 stitches
Cuppa
5 (7, 9, 11) stitches

join LBT

K1•K2tog

Inc LBT
Kf&b

LR
SSK   PUK

bo LTT
BO
SSK   PUK

live LTT

SSK   PUK

RR

PUP   P2tog

live RTT

PUP   P2tog

For row-by-row instructions, see page 158.

Entrée
to
Entrelac

KNIT ONE CROCHET TOO Paint Box in color 10
below: BROWN SHEEP COMPANY, INC Lanaloft Worsted in color LL333W

Cuppa Joe

Work either flat or pointed opening.

Flat Opening With A, cast on 28 (40, 52, 64) and arrange evenly on 4 dpn; join and mark beginning of round. Purl 3 rounds. *Tier 1* Work 4 Join LBT.

Pointed Opening *Tier 1* *With empty dpn, cast on base number of stitches. Beginning with a WS row, work in stockinette stitch for 10 (14, 18, 22) rows. Continuing with attached yarn, repeat from * 3 more times — 4 rectangles. Join for seamless entrelac at beginning of next tier, making sure work is not twisted as you pick up for first RR along edge of first Tier 1 rectangle.

Body

Tier 2 Work 4 RR. *Tier 3* Work 4 LR.

Short Cup Only *Tier 4* Work 4 Live RTT — 20 (28, 36, 44) stitches.

Tall Cup Only *Tier 4* Work 4 RR. *Tier 5* Work 4 Live LTT — 20 (28, 36, 44) stitches.

Bottom Purl 1 round, using pf&b to increase 2 (3, 4, 5) stitches in each unit — 28 (40, 52, 64) stitches. Purl 1 round. *Next round* [Knit to last 2 stitches on dpn, k2tog] to end of round. Repeat last round until 4 stitches remain, 1 per dpn. Cut yarn and pull through last 4 stitches; fasten off. Felt to desired size.

Color key
- ☐ A
- ▩ B

⑈⑈⑈⑈ *live stitches*
——— *picked-up stitches*
∿∿∿ *joined edge*
➜ *Direction of work*

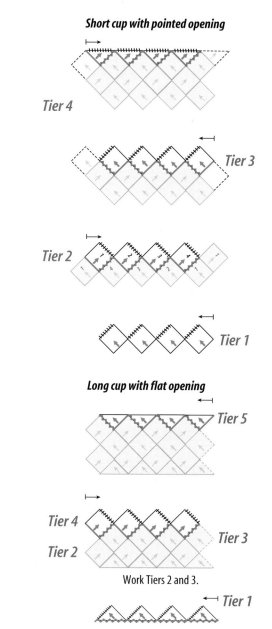

Short cup with pointed opening

Tier 4

Tier 3

Tier 2

Tier 1

Long cup with flat opening

Tier 5

Tier 4

Tier 3

Tier 2

Work Tiers 2 and 3.

Tier 1

Joined points hat

Where the Cuppa Joe provided an example of starting with rectangles, this hat shows what can be done by ending with rectangles. This is the first of 3 projects in the Family series providing options for the whole family.

notes

- ◆ See page 152 for any unfamiliar techniques.
- ◆ Hat is worked in seamless entrelac from rib to crown.
- ◆ Cut yarn after each tier.
- ◆ When binding off, pull last stitch of a unit over the first stitch of the following unit.
- ◆ For 1-color version, ignore A and B references.

Hat

With A, cast on 72 (78, 90) stitches. Join, mark beginning of round, and work in k2, p1 rib for 5". **Tier 1** Continuing with A, work 6 Join LBT — 48 (54, 60) stitches. **Tier 2** With B, work 6 RR. **Tier 3** With A, work 6 LR. **Tier 4** With B, work 6 RR, binding off on final row.

Finishing

Fold points to center and seam bound-off stitches of one unit to rows of the adjacent unit at the crown. Block to shape.

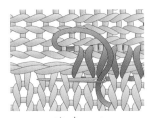

seam stitches to rows
Pick up 2 row bars (as shown) for every 1 stitch of cast-on.

the
UNITS
Base number
8 (9, 10) stitches

join LBT

K1•K2tog

LR

SSK   PUK

RR

PUP   P2tog

For row-by-row instructions see page 158

Easy	10cm/4"	1 2 3 **4** 5 6		&
S (M, L)		**Medium weight**		marker
Circumference 17½ (19¾, 22)"	26 **18** over stockinette stitch	**A** 75 (100, 125) yds **B** 40 (55, 65) yds OR 115 (155, 190) yds for one-color version	5mm/US 8, or size to obtain gauge, 40cm (16") or shorter	

BROWN SHEEP COMPANY, INC Lanaloft-Worsted **Small** in colors LL92 (**A**) and LL33 (**B**); **Large** in colors LL36 (**A**) and LL100 (**B**) OR for 1-color versions **Medium** in color LL333

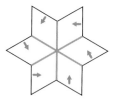

Sew stitches of 1 unit to rows of next unit at crown.

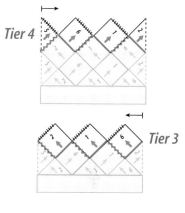

Tier 4

Tier 3

Tier 2

Tier 1

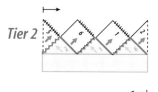

|||||| live stitches
——— picked-up stitches
∿∿∿ joined edge
——— seam
——— bind-off
➜ Direction of work

29

Harlequin slippers

These slippers are a fabulous starter project that would make a great gift. The garter stitch short-row heel is perfect for entrelac. The felting makes the finished socks durable and hides any minor inconsistencies associated with a first project.

Cuff and Ankle

With A, cast on 24 (28, 36, 40). Divide evenly over 4 dpn; join and mark beginning of round. [Knit 1 round, purl 1 round] 3 times. *Tier 1* Continuing with A, work 4 Join LBT — 16 (20, 24, 28) stitches. *Tier 2* With B, work 4 RR.

Heel and Instep

Begin Tier 3 With A, work 2 Live LTT. Turn work; purl stitches from these units onto 1 dpn, increasing 4 (4, 6, 6) stitches evenly across row — 12 (14, 18, 20) stitches. Do not cut yarn.

Short-row heel With B, k11 (13, 17, 19); bring yarn to front, slip 1, bring yarn to back, slip stitch back to left needle, turn work (W&T). *Decreasing short rows* [Knit 1 fewer stitch than previous row, W&T] 7 (9, 11, 13) times — 4 (4, 6, 6) center stitches unwrapped. *Increasing short rows* *When you come to a wrap on a following row, do not work it together with the stitch it wraps.* [Knit 1 more stitch than last row, W&T] 6 (8, 10, 12) times. Place final slipped stitch on needle with heel stitches — 12 (14, 18, 20) stitches. Cut B. Divide these stitches evenly between 2 dpns. *Complete Tier 3* Continuing with attached A and working around, work 2 Join LBT across heel stitches, then 2 LR.

Foot

Tier 4 With B, work 4 RR. *Tier 5* With A, work 4 LR. *Tier 6* With B, work 4 RR. *Tier 7* With A, work 4 Live LTT.

notes

◆ *See page 152 for any unfamiliar techniques.*

◆ *Except for short-row heel, cuff, and toes, socks are worked in seamless entrelac from cuff to toe.*

◆ *Break yarn after each tier.*

◆ *Work the same number of units for all sizes, but use a different base number (number of stitches and rows for each unit): 4 (5, 6, 7) stitches.*

the
UNITS
Base number
4 (5, 6, 7)

join LBT

K1•K2tog

LR

SSK   PUK

live LTT

SSK   PUK

RR

PUP   P2tog

For row-by-row instructions see page 158.

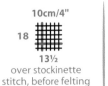

Intermediate

Toddler (Child, S–M Adult, M–L Adult)

Cuff Circumference
7 (9, 11, 14)", 6 (8, 10¼, 12)"

Foot Length (heel to toe)
6 (7, 10, 13½)", 5 (5½, 9½, 11)"

Approximate measurements before felting, after felting

10cm/4"
18
13½
over stockinette stitch, before felting

1 2 3 4 **5** 6
Bulky weight
A 40 (60, 110, 150) yds
B 40 (55, 100, 130) yds

8mm/US 11, or size to obtain gauge, set of 5

Entrée to Entrelac

Toe

Knit one round, increasing 8 (8, 12, 12) stitches — 24 (28, 36, 40) stitches, 6 (7, 9, 10) per needle. Cut A. *Round 1* With B, [k1, SSK, knit to end of needle; knit to last 3 stitches of next needle, k2tog, k1] twice. *Round 2* Knit. Repeat last 2 rounds until 2 (3, 3, 3) stitches remain on each needle.

Finishing & Felting

Slip stitches from first needle onto second needle; turn sock inside out. Slip all stitches from third to fourth needle and work 3-needle bind-off across all stitches. Turn right side out. Felt socks, checking size on actual foot while still damp; air dry.

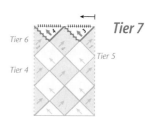

Toe

Tier 7

Complete Tier 3

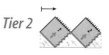

Continue Tier 3

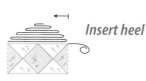

Insert heel

Begin Tier 3

Tier 2

Tier 1

BROWN SHEEP
COMPANY
Shepherd's Shades
Toddler colors
SS283 (**A**) and SS281
(**B**) **Child** colors
SS743 (**A**) and SS741
(**B**) **S–M Adult**
colors SS541 (**A**) and
SS542 (**B**)

Color key
- ☐ A
- ▨ B
- ⑉⑉⑉⑉ *live stitches*
- —— *picked-up stitches*
- ∿∿∿ *joined edge*
- —— Bind-off
- → Direction of work

Argyle bolero

Argyle designs seem to be made for entrelac. Careful placement of colors and accent lines prove a liitle entrelac goes a long way.

Body

Entrelac border *Tier 1* With A, work 16 Inc LBT — 96 (112, 128, 144, 160) stitches. *Tiers 2, 4* Beginning with A and alternating colors across units, work RST, 15 RR, RET. *Tier 3* With B, work 16 LR. *Tier 5* With A, work 16 Live LTT. *Next row* (WS) With A, work [p1, inc1, p1] — 144 (168, 192, 216, 240) stitches.

Entrelac border

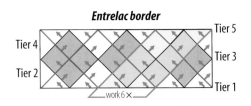

Tier 4
Tier 5
Tier 3
Tier 2
Tier 1
work 6 ×

Color key
□ A
▨ B

—— Chain stitch embroidery or crochet in opposite color (A on B and B on A).
→ direction of work

notes

◆ See page 152 for any unfamiliar techniques.

◆ Yarn is held double throughout.

◆ Units alternate color in Tier 2 and 4. When color changes, cut yarn.

◆ Argyle lines in and around diamond shapes are added after work is complete.

Chain St Crochet

top of fabric

bottom of fabric

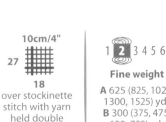

Slip stitch crochet as shown in chart, working in opposite color along entrelac joins.

Easy +
Standard Fit

XS (S-M, M-L, 1X, 2X)
A 32 (37¼, 42¾, 48, 53¼)"
B 11½ (13, 14½, 16, 16¾)"
C 12 (14¼, 16¼, 18½, 20)"

10cm/4"
27
18
over stockinette stitch with yarn held double

1 **2** 3 4 5 6
Fine weight
A 625 (825, 1025, 1300, 1525) yds
B 300 (375, 475, 600, 700) yds

4.5mm/US 7, or size to obtain gauge, 60cm (24") or longer

4mm/US F

1 large button

inc LBT

Kf&b

LR

SSK   PUK

live LTT

SSK   PUK

RST

Kf&b
P2tog

RR

PUP
P2tog

RET

P2tog
PUP

For row-by-row instructions see page 158

Divide at underarms **Next row** (RS) K33 (38, 43, 46, 50), put on hold for Right Front, bind off 6 (8, 10, 16, 20) for underarm, k66 (76, 86, 92, 100), put on hold for back, bind off 6 (8, 10, 16, 20) for underarm, k33 (38, 43, 46, 50).

Left Front *Shape armhole* Work in stockinette stitch, decreasing 1 stitch at beginning of every RS row 3 (4, 6, 8, 11) times — 30 (34, 37, 38, 39) stitches. Work even until 5¼ (5¼, 6¼, 6¼, 6½)" from underarm bind-off, end with a RS row.

Shape neck Bind off 8 (9, 10, 11, 11). Decrease 1 stitch at end of every RS row 8 (9, 10, 11, 11) times — 14 (16, 17, 16, 17) stitches. Work even until 7¾ (8, 9¼, 9¾, 10)" from underarm bind-off end with a WS row.

Shape shoulder Bind off 5 (5, 6, 6, 6) stitches at beginning of next 2 RS rows, then bind off remaining stitches next RS row.

Right Front Place Right Front stitches from hold onto needle. With WS facing, join A at armhole, and purl 1 row. Work as for Left Front EXCEPT shape armhole at end of RS rows and neck at beginning of RS rows.

Back Place Back stitches from hold onto needle. With WS facing, join A and work stockinette stitch, decreasing 1 stitch at beginning and end of every RS row 3 (4, 6, 8, 11) times — 60 (68, 74, 76, 78) stitches. Work even until piece measures 11¾ (13, 14¾, 16¼, 17)" from beginning. Bind off.

Sleeves

With B, cast on 54 (58, 62, 70, 82) stitches; work k2, p2 rib (beginning and ending with a k2) for 3 rows. Cut B, join A and continue in rib for 5 more rows. Work in stockinette stitch until piece measures 5¼ (6¼, 6¾, 7¾, 8¼)" from beginning.

Shape cap Bind off 3 (4, 5, 8, 10) stitches at beginning of next 2 rows. Decrease 1 stitch at each end of every RS row 12 (13, 15, 11, 12) times and every 4 rows 4 (4, 4, 7, 7) times. Bind off remaining stitches.

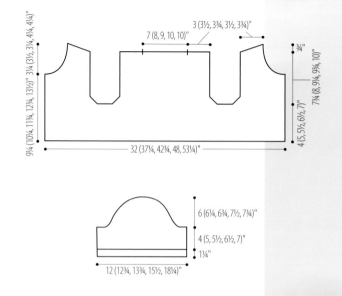

Finishing

Sew shoulder and sleeve seams; set in sleeve caps.

Bands *Front bands* With RS facing and A, and working along Left Front edge, PUK5 for every 7 rows of stockinette, then 18 (21, 24, 27, 30) stitches along the triangles; adjust count to a multiple of 4 + 2 as you work next row. Work 5 rows k2, p2 rib. Cut A, join B, and continue in rib for 2 more rows. Bind off in pattern on next row. Repeat for Right Front edge, EXCEPT on Row 3, work 2-stitch buttonhole on 3rd and 4th stitch from neck edge. *Neckband* With RS facing and B, and beginning at right front band, PUK6 across front band, then 1 stitch for every stitch around neck, and 6 across left front band. Work reverse stockinette stitch (purl on RS, knit on WS) for 5 rows, binding off in pattern on last row. *Bottom band* With RS facing and B, and beginning at left front band, PUK6 along edges of front bands and 18 (21, 24, 27, 30) stitches for every 2 triangles around hem. Work same as neckband. Attach button.

Painted diamonds

Placing the hand-painted yarn every third tier demonstrates how entrelac, even in its most basic form, can be easily manipulated to create visual interest.

Small: KNIT ONE CROCHET TOO Wick in colors 533 (**A**) and 565 (**B**)

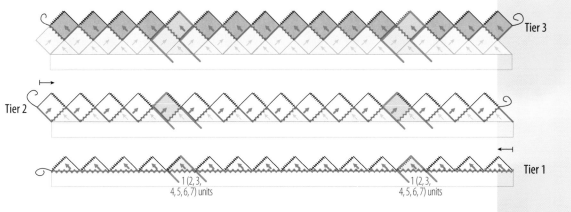

Tier 3

Tier 2

Tier 1

1 (2, 3, 4, 5, 6, 7) units   1 (2, 3, 4, 5, 6, 7) units

Although both Tier 1 and Tier 2 are worked in color A, you will cut A at the end of Tier 1 (at the bottom of the triangle) and rejoin A for Tier 2 (at the top of the triangle).

Border

With longer needle and A, cast on 72 (81, 90, 99, 108, 117, 126). Beginning with a WS row, work 8 rows in Seed Stitch. Place stitches on hold; cut yarn. Make second border, leaving stitches on needle and yarn attached.

Body

Return border stitches from hold to left needle. *Tier 1* Place marker for beginning of round. Work 8 (9, 10, 11, 12, 13, 14) Join LBT across each border — 96 (108, 120, 132, 144, 156, 168) stitches, 16 (18, 20, 22, 24, 26, 28) LBT. Cut A. *Tiers 2, 4* Rejoining A, work 16 (18, 20, 22, 24, 26, 28) RR. *Tier 3* With B, work 16 (18, 20, 22, 24, 26, 28) LR. *Tiers 5, 7* With A, work 16 (18, 20, 22, 24, 26, 28) LR . *Tier 6* With B, work 16 (18, 20, 22, 24, 26, 28) RR. *Tiers 8–12* Repeat Tiers 2–6.

SIZES XS–1X ONLY *Tier 13* Repeat Tier 7. *Tier 14* Repeat Tier 2. *Last Tier* With A, work 16 (18, 20, 22, 24) Live LTT.

SIZES 2X (3X) ONLY

Tiers 8–12 Repeat Tiers 2–6. *Last Tier* With A, work 26 (28) Live LTT.

FOR ALL SIZES

Increase round [K1, M1, k1] around — 144 (162, 180, 198, 216, 234, 252) stitches. Place marker at beginning of round and after 72 (81, 90, 99, 108, 117, 126) stitches.

Yoke *Separate Front and Back* [Work Seed Stitch to 3 (3, 4, 4, 5, 6, 7) stitches before marker, bind off 6 (6, 8, 8, 10, 12, 14)] 2 times, placing last 66 (75, 82, 91, 98, 105, 112) stitches on hold for Front.

stitches

SEED STITCH
OVER AN EVEN NUMBER OF STITCHES
WS rows [K1, p1] to end of row.
RS rows [P1, k1] to end of row.

SEED STITCH
OVER AN ODD NUMBER OF STITCHES
All rows [K1, p1] to last stitch, k1.

notes

◆ *See page 152 for any unfamiliar techniques.*

◆ *The body is worked in seamless entrelac between the bottom border and armhole.*

◆ *Cut yarn after each tier.*

the
UNITS
Base number
6 stitches

join LBT

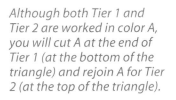
K1·K2tog

LR

SSK   PUK

live LTT

SSK   PUK

RR

PUP   P2tog

For row-by-row instructions see page 158

Easy +
Standard Fit
XS (S, M, L, 1X, 2X, 3X)
A 32 (36, 40, 44, 48, 52, 56)"
B 23 (23½, 24, 24½, 25, 25, 25)"

10cm/4"
36
18
over Seed Stitch

1 2 3 **4** 5 6
Medium weight
A 600 (700, 800, 900, 1000, 1100, 1175) yds
B 150 (175, 200, 225, 250, 275, 300) yds

4mm/US 6, or size to obtain gauge, 40cm (16") and 60cm (24") or longer

&
stitch holder, marker

Entrée
to
Entrelac

Back Continue in Seed Stitch, decreasing 1 stitch at each armhole edge every RS row 4 (6, 7, 10, 11, 12, 13) times — 58 (63, 68, 71, 76, 81, 86) stitches. Work even until armhole measures 6¾ (7½, 8, 8½, 9, 11, 11)". Bind off in pattern.

Front Join A and work as for back. AT SAME TIME, when piece measures 1½ (2, 2, 2½, 3, 4, 4)" from armhole, begin neck shaping on RS row: work 23 (25, 27, 28, 30, 32, 34) stitches, place remaining stitches on hold.

Left Front Continuing in pattern, decrease 1 stitch at end of every RS row 6 (7, 8, 8, 9, 8, 9) times. Work even until armhole measures 6¾ (7½, 8, 8½, 9, 11, 11)", ending on a WS row.

Shape shoulder **Next row** (RS). Bind off 6 (6, 6, 6, 7, 8, 8) stitches at beginning of next 2 RS rows, then bind off remaining stitches on the next row.

Right Front With RS facing and A, bind off 12 (13, 14, 15, 16, 17, 18) stitches for neck; work remaining 23 (25, 27, 28, 30, 32, 34) stitches as for Left Front, reverse shaping by working neck decreases at beginning of RS rows and binding off shoulder at beginning of WS rows.

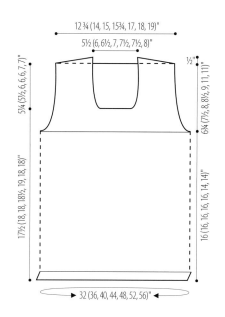

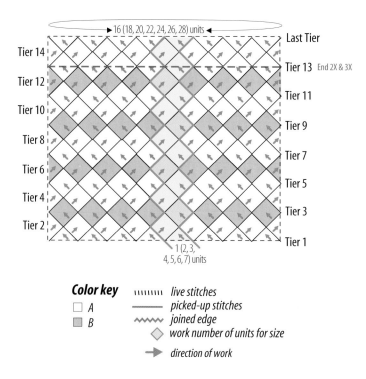

Finishing

Seam shoulders.

Armhole edging With RS facing, 16" circular needle, and A, begin at underarm and PUK1 for each stitch or 1 stitch for every 2 rows around armhole. Purl 1 round. With B, knit 1 round, purl 1 round. With A, [knit 1 round, purl 1 round] 2 times. Bind off.

Neck edging Work as for Armhole edging, beginning at center back neck. Block.

Spruce & ivory

Start with traditional entrelac fabric in two contrasting colors and then reduce the size of each unit to it's smallest dimension to create something slightly unexpected, yet totally wonderful. Small units allow variable sizing and gentle curves at the armholes and neck to be produced effortlessly. Change the colors to two similar shades and another look is achieved.

stitches

WORK UNIT WITH BIND-OFF
Bind off stitches on last row of unit.

notes

◆ *See page 152 for any unfamiliar techniques.*

◆ *When binding off on last row of a triangle or rectangle and working another shape on same tier must be worked immediately after, pass stitch remaining after bind-off over first picked-up stitch of next shape. Otherwise, fasten off last stitch.*

◆ *Entrelac is worked seamlessly to underarm; cut yarn after each tier.*

Body

With 24" needle and A, cast on 180 (204, 228, 252, 276). Do not turn; do not cut A. *Begin k2, p2 rib: Rnd 1* Place marker, join B and, being careful not to twist cast-on, k1, then bring A over B before continuing with B, k1, [p2, k2], to last 2 stitches, p2. Cut B. With A, work in rib until piece measures 1" from beginning. Remove marker.

Begin entrelac Work all left-leaning tiers in A, all right-leaning tiers in B.
Tier 1 Work 30 (34, 38, 42, 46) Join LBT — 120 (136, 152, 168, 184) stitches.
Tier 2 Work 30 (34, 38, 42, 46) RR. *Tier 3* Work 30 (34, 38, 42, 46) LR. Work last 2 tiers 9 (9, 10, 10, 11) more times.

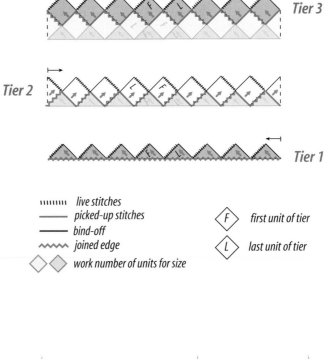

Tier 3

Tier 2

Tier 1

⟋⟍⟋⟍ live stitches
—— picked-up stitches
▬▬ bind-off
∿∿∿ joined edge
◇◇ work number of units for size

◇F first unit of tier
◇L last unit of tier

the
UNITS
Base number
4 stitches

join LBT

K1•K2tog

LR

SSK PUK

RR

PUP p2tog

dec RTT

SSK
PUP p2tog

For row-by-row instructions see page 158.

Intermediate

STANDARD FIT
S (M, L, 1X, 2X)

A 35 (40, 44½, 49, 54)"
B 19 (19½, 21, 21½, 23)"

10cm/4"
32
20
over stockinette stitch

1 2 3 **4** 5 6
Medium weight
A 480 (550, 700, 735, 860) yds
B 445 (515, 610, 685, 795) yds

4mm/US 6, or size to obtain gauge, 60cm (24") and 40cm (16") long

&
marker

12 (14, 14, 16, 18) RR on hold for Front

Left Underarm

13 (15, 15, 17, 19) RR for Back

Right Underarm

5 (7, 7, 9, 11) RR

2 (2, 4, 4, 4) RTT

5 (7, 7, 9, 11) RR

2 (2, 4, 4, 4) RTT

Divide for back and front **Next tier** Work 12 (14, 14, 16, 18) RR and place on hold for Front; work RR with bind-off; work 2 (2, 4, 4, 4) Dec RTT; work 13 (15, 15, 17, 19) RR, binding off last RR; work 2 (2, 4, 4, 4) Dec RTT. Piece measures approximately 12 (12, 13, 13, 14)" from beginning to top of RTTs.

Body

→ 30 (34, 38, 42, 46) units ◄

9 (9, 10, 10, 11) ✗

Tier 2

Tier 1

5 (7, 7, 9, 11) units

Small Shown in KOLLAGE YARNS Cornucopia in colors #6002 Aspen Green (**A**) and #6001 Antique Lace (**B**)

39

2X

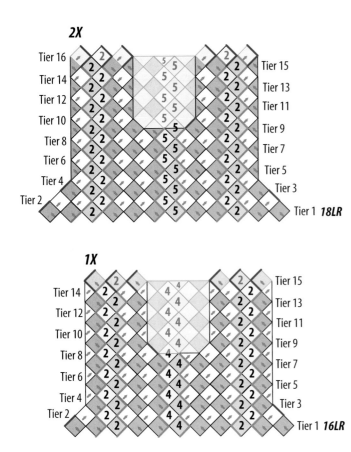

Tier 16 · Tier 15
Tier 14 · Tier 13
Tier 12 · Tier 11
Tier 10 · Tier 9
Tier 8 · Tier 7
Tier 6 · Tier 5
Tier 4 · Tier 3
Tier 2 · Tier 1 **18LR**

1X

Tier 14 · Tier 15
Tier 12 · Tier 13
Tier 10 · Tier 11
Tier 8 · Tier 9
Tier 6 · Tier 7
Tier 4 · Tier 5
Tier 2 · Tier 3
Tier 1 **16LR**

Back

Shape armholes Tier 1 Begin at top of last RR and work 12 (14, 14, 16, 18) LR, binding off last LR.

SIZES S (L) ONLY **Tier 2** Work 11 (13) RR. **Tier 3** Work LST, work 10 (12) LR, work LET. **Tiers 4–11** Repeat last 2 tiers 4 times. SIZE S ONLY **Tier 12** Work 3 RR with bind-off; work 5 Dec RTT; work 3 RR with bind-off. SIZE L ONLY **Tier 12** Repeat Tier 2. **Tier 13** Work LST with bind-off; work 3 LR with bind-off; work 6 Dec LTT; 3 LR with bind-off; work LET.

SIZES M (1×) ONLY **Tier 2** Work 13 (15) RR, binding off last RR. **Tier 3** Work 12 (14) LR. **Tier 4** Work RST, 11 (13) RR, RET. **Tier 5** Work 12(14) LR. **Tiers 6-11 (6–13)** Repeat last 2 tiers 3 (4) times. **Tier 12 (14)** Repeat Tier 4. **Tier 13 (15)** Work 3 (4) LR with bind-off; work 6 Dec LTT, work 3 (4) LR with bind-off.

SIZE 2× ONLY **Tier 2** Work 17 RR binding off last RR. **Tier 3** Work 16 LR binding off last LR. **Tier 4** Work 15 RR. **Tier 5** Work LST, 14 LR, LET. **Tiers 6–15** Repeat last 2 tiers 5 times. **Tier 16** Work 4 RR with bind-off; work 7 Dec RTT; work 4 RR with bind-off.

Front

Shape armholes Work as for Back through Tier 5 (6, 6, 7, 8) — 15(17,19, 21,23) units.

SIZE S ONLY **Tier 6** Work 4 RR binding off last RR; work 3 Dec RTT; work 4 RR. Armhole measures approximately 3" to top of RTTs. **Continue Left Front Tier 7** Work LST; work 3 LR, binding off last LR. **Tier 8** Work 3 RR. **Tier 9** Work LST, 2 LR, LET. **Tier 10** Repeat Tier 8. **Tier 11** Work LST with bind-off; work 2 LR with bind-off; work LET. **Continue Right Front Tier 7** Work 3 LR, LET. **Tiers 8–11** Work as for Left Front.

SIZE M ONLY **Tier 7** Work 4 LR, binding off last LR; work 4 Dec LTT; work 4 LR. Armhole measures approximately 3¾" to top of LTTs. **Continue Right Front Tier 8** Work RST; work 3 RR, binding off last RR. **Tier 9** Work 3 LR. **Tier 10** Work RST, 2 RR, RET. **Tier 11** Repeat Tier 9. **Tier 12** Work RST with bind-off; work 2 RR with bind-off; work RET. **Continue Left Front Tier 8** Work 3 RR, RET. **Tiers 9–12** Work as for Right Front.

SIZE L ONLY **Tier 7** Work LST; work 4 LR, binding off last LR; work

the
UNITS
Base number
4 stitches

dec LTT

LST

LET

RST

RET

For row-by-row instructions, see page 158

Entrée to Entrelac

40

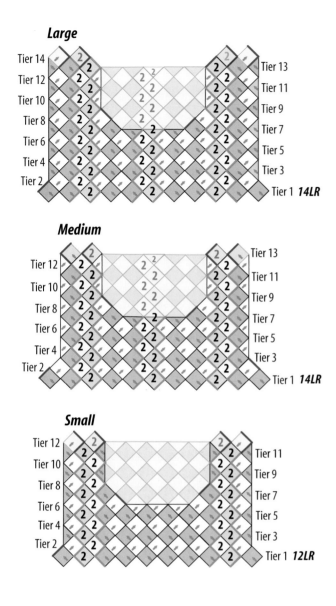

Large

Tier 14 ... Tier 13
Tier 12 ... Tier 11
Tier 10 ... Tier 9
Tier 8 ... Tier 7
Tier 6 ... Tier 5
Tier 4 ... Tier 3
Tier 2 ... Tier 1 **14LR**

Medium

Tier 12 ... Tier 13
Tier 10 ... Tier 11
Tier 8 ... Tier 9
Tier 6 ... Tier 7
Tier 4 ... Tier 5
Tier 2 ... Tier 3
... Tier 1 **14LR**

Small

Tier 12 ... Tier 11
Tier 10 ... Tier 9
Tier 8 ... Tier 7
Tier 6 ... Tier 5
Tier 4 ... Tier 3
Tier 2 ... Tier 1 **12LR**

4 Dec LTT, 4 LR, LET. Armhole measures approx 3¾" to top of LTTs. **Continue Right Front** *Tier 8* Work 4 RR, binding off on last RR. *Tier 9* Work 3 LR, LET. *Tier 10* Work 3 RR, RET. *Tiers 11 and 12* Repeat Tiers 9 and 10. *Tier 13* Repeat Tier 9. *Tier 14* Work 3 RST with bind-off; work 3 RR with bind-off. **Continue Left Front** *Tier 8* Work 4 RR. *Tier 9* Work LST, work 3 LR. *Tier 10* Work RST, work 3 RR. *Tiers 11 and 12* Repeat last 2 tiers. *Tier 13* Repeat Tier 9. *Tier 14* Work 2 RR with bind-off.

SIZE 1× ONLY *Tier 8* Work RST; work 4 RR, binding off last RR; work 5 Dec RTT, 4 RR, RET. Armhole measures approximately 4¼" to top of RTTs. **Continue Left Front** *Tier 9* Work 4 LR. *Tier 10* Work RST, 3 RR, RET. *Tiers 11 and 12* Repeat Tiers 9 and 10. *Tier 13* WRepeat Tier 9. *Tier 14* Work 3 RST with bind-off; work 3 RR with bind-off, work RET. **Continue Right Front** Work as for Left Front.

SIZE 2× ONLY *Tier 9* Work LST; work 4 LR, binding off last LR; work 6 Dec LTT, 4 LR, LET. Armhole measures approximately 4¾" to top of LTTs. **Continue Right Front** *Tier 10* Work 4 RR. *Tier 11* Work LST, 3 LR, LET. *Tiers 12 and 13* Repeat Tiers 10 and 11. *Tier 14* Repeat Tier 10. *Tier 15* Work LST with bind-off; work 3 LR with bind-off; work LET. **Continue Left Front** Work as for Right Front.

Finishing

Block vest, using damp towel. Join shoulders, folding points of highest tier of back rectangles into V between rectangles on other shoulder. (Fold line is at top of back shoulder.)

Neckband With RS facing, 16" needle, and A, begin at shoulder fold line and PUK 88 (100, 108, 120, 132) evenly around neck edge. Place marker, join, and work in k2, p2 rib for 6 rounds. Work 1 round B, 1 round A. Bind off in pattern with A.

Armhole band Work as for neckband, picking up 88 (100, 108, 120, 132) evenly around armhole edge.

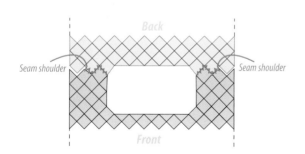

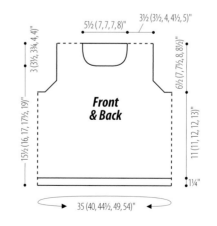

5½ (7, 7, 7, 8)"

3½ (3½, 4, 4½, 5)"

3 (3½, 3¾, 4, 4)"

6½ (7, 7½, 8, 8½)"

15½ (16, 17, 17½, 19)"

Front & Back

11 (11, 12, 12, 13)"

1¼"

35 (40, 44½, 49, 54)"

Zigzag vest

Zigzag lines are easy to create in entrelac. Turn the fabric on its side and you have vertical lines. Felt the finished product for a seasonal vest, when a coat is just a little too much.

Left Front *Tier 1* With longer needle and A, work 5 Inc LBT — 35 (40, 45) • 50 (55, 60, 65, 70) stitches. *Tier 2* Using cable cast-on, cast on base number of stitches. Beginning first unit on Row 2, work 5 RR and RET. *Tier 3* With B, work 5 LR. PUK along left edge of RR in tier below. Beginning with a WS row, work base number of rows in stockinette stitch. *Tier 4* Work RST, 5 RR, RET.

Left Armhole *Tier 5* With A, work 4 LR, binding off last LR; work 2 Dec LTT. *Tier 6* Joining A and beginning along right edge of last LR worked in previous tier, work 3 RR, RET. *Tier 7* Work 3 LR, LET. *Tier 8* Work 3 RR, RET. *Tier 9* Work 3 LR. PUK base number along left edge of RR in tier below. Beginning with a WS row, work base number of rows in stockinette stitch. Work 2 Inc LBT.

Back *Tier 10* With B, work RST, 5 RR, RET. *Tier 11* Work 6 LR. *Tiers 12 and 14* With A, work RST, 5 RR, RET. *Tier 13* Work 6 LR. *Tier 15* With B, work 6 LR. *Tier 16* Work RST, 5 RR, RET.

Right Armhole *Tier 17–21* Repeat Tiers 5–9.

Right Front *Tier 22* Repeat Tier 10. *Tier 23* Repeat Tier 11, binding off last LR. *Tier 24* With A, work 5 RR, RET. *Tier 25* Work 5 Dec LTT.

Finishing
Seam shoulders.

Bands With RS facing and A, PUK1 for each stitch and every 2 rows along rectangles and 2 stitches for every 3 rows along triangles. *Armhole* With shorter needle, purl 4 rounds; bind off in purl. *Bottom band* With longer needle, work in reverse stockinette stitch (knit on WS, purl on RS) for 8 rows; bind off in purl. *Front and neck band* With longer needle, work in reverse stockinette stitch; bind off in purl.

Felt vest to desired size and firmness. *Optional* Attach zipper.

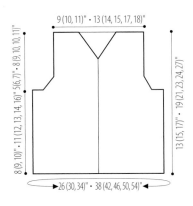

9 (10, 11)" • 13 (14, 15, 17, 18)"

8 (9, 10)" • 11 (12, 13, 14, 16)" 5 (6, 7)" • 8 (9, 10, 10, 11)"

13 (15, 17)" • 19 (21, 23, 24, 27)"

►26 (30, 34)" • 38 (42, 46, 50, 54)"◄

approximate measurements, after felting

notes

◆ *See page 152 for any unfamiliar techniques.*

◆ *Vest is worked in one piece from center front to center front.*

Easy +

Children's • Adult's
4–6, (8–10, 12–14) • S (M, L, 1X, 2X)
A 26 (30, 34)" • 38 (42, 46, 50, 54)"
B 13 (15, 17)" • 19 (21, 23, 24, 27)"
Approximate measurements after felting

10cm/4"

26 (30)

18 (20)

over stockinette stitch, before (after) felting

1 2 3 **4** 5 6

Worsted weight
A 250 (325, 425) • 525 (625, 750, 875, 1025) yds
B 100 (125, 150) • 175 (225, 250, 300, 350) yds

6mm/US 10 or size to obtain gauge, 40cm (16") and 60cm (24") or longer

&
1 separating zipper
10 (12, 14)"
16 (18, 20, 22, 24)"
or longer

the
UNITS
Base number
7 (8, 9) 10 (11, 12, 13, 14) stitches and
14 (16, 18) 20 (22, 24, 26, 28) rows

inc LBT

RST

LR

RR

dec LTT

RET

LET

For row-by-row instructions see page 158

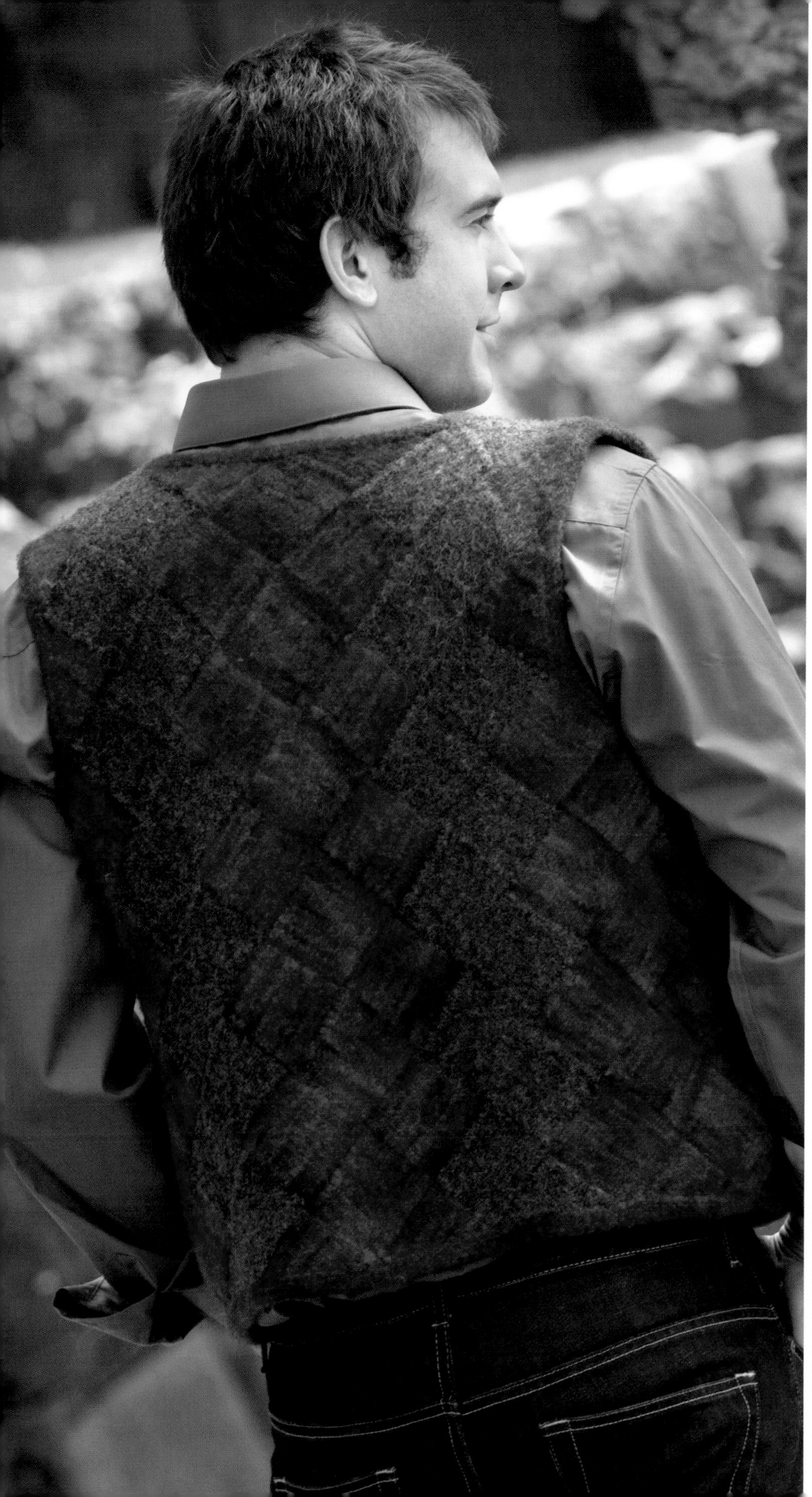

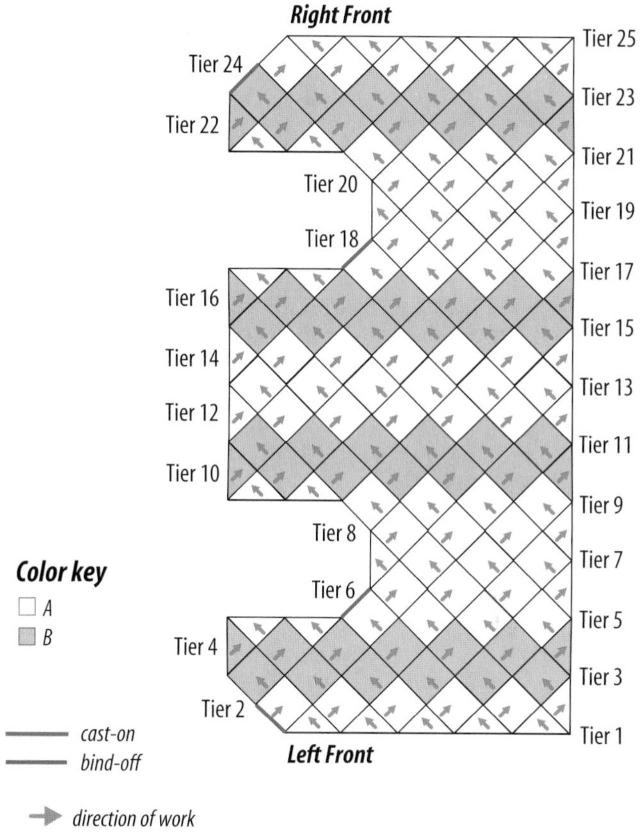
Right Front
Tier 25
Tier 24
Tier 23
Tier 22
Tier 21
Tier 20
Tier 19
Tier 18
Tier 17
Tier 16
Tier 15
Tier 14
Tier 13
Tier 12
Tier 11
Tier 10
Tier 9
Tier 8
Tier 7
Tier 6
Tier 5
Tier 4
Tier 3
Tier 2
Tier 1
Left Front
Color key
A
B
cast-on
bind-off
direction of work

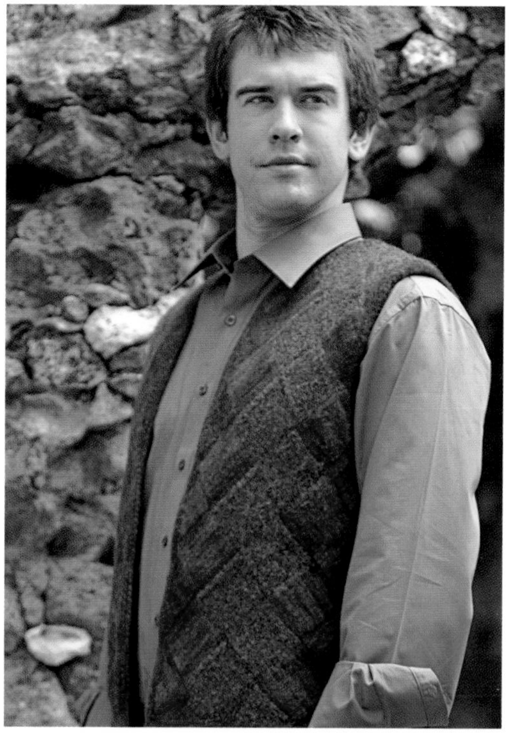

Large BROWN SHEEP COMPANY Lanaloft Worsted in colors LL222 (A) and LL18 (B)

Simple shapes
& zigzag seams

Diagonal lines and zigzag edges, difficult to create in other knitting techniques, are what entrelac does best. Considering these characteristics as opportunities instead of challenges, creates a realm of new possibilities.

Top downs for everyone page 64

When I first discovered entrelac, all the patterns I encountered were made up of flat squares or rectangles seamed together. Often, the seams were not attractive and the garment shapes were rectangular with boat necks and bloused sleeves. The unique construction of entrelac was not being used to its advantage. I knew if these constraints could be eliminated, more attractive garments could be knit.

An overview

My first design project in entrelac was a sweatshirt yoke (yes, this was in the mid-80's). Eliminating side seams was the first thing I tackled, and the result was seamless entrelac. I realized that if each tier had one fewer base number of stitches, it would pull in naturally. Shaping could be achieved by increasing or decreasing the size of each entrelac unit. Seams, when necessary, could follow the natural entrelac line. These 2 concepts solved the problem of knitting a yoke in entrelac.

And, this was just the tip of the entrelac iceberg.

Basic shaping

In entrelac, shaping occurs in two ways: changing the size of the units (the rectangles or triangles) on a given tier or following the lines formed by the units. One of the simplest ways to change the size of the unit is to pick up more or fewer base stitches than on the previous tier.

When increasing the base number of stitches, the 2-rows-to-1-stitch ratio will not be maintained on that tier without, on the previous tier, increasing the stitch count on the final row of each unit. If the current tier has a base number of 5 stitches and the next tier needs a base number of 7, it is necessary to increase 2 stitches on the last row of each unit. If the difference is 2 or more, I will always do the increases. In cases where the difference in the base numbers is 1 stitch, I may do the increase or just settle for a tier of units that are 2 rows short.

When decreasing the base number, it is necessary to join *2 stitches* from the

Hobo bag page 54

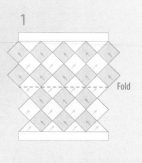

previous tier with *1 stitch* from the current tier to maintain the 2-rows-to-1-stitch ratio. For example, on a left-leaning unit, the first joining decrease is an SSSK (slip 1 stitch from the last stitch of the current entrelac unit and 2 stitches from the joining unit, then knit those 3 stitches together). For a right-leaning unit, the decrease is a p3tog.

Repeat this process a number of times equal to the difference between the base number of stitches in the current unit and the joining unit. So if the previous tier used 8 stitches as the base number and the current tier has a base number of 6 stitches, use an SSSK or p3tog join on the first and second join rows of each unit. In the entrelac panels of the Hobo bag, each tier is reduced by 1 stitch, so the SSSK or p3tog is worked only on the first join row.

Just as there is more than one way to change unit size, there are also several ways to change the number of units on a tier. Changing the unit count will usually result in an angled edge. The simplest method is either to cast on stitches and work a rectangle as the first unit of a new tier (instead of working a starting triangle) or to work an unjoined rectangle as the last unit of a tier and bind off stitches on its final row (instead of working an ending triangle).

Binding off all stitches on the final row of the last rectangle of a tier forms a 45° angle. Eliminating edge triangles and working 1 fewer rectangle each tier brings the piece to a point.

By casting on stitches at the beginning of each tier, eliminating edge triangles, and working 1 *more* rectangle each tier, the piece grows from a point. Examples of both adding units within a tier and subtracting units within a tier can be seen in the Diamond yoke jacket. This example also demonstrates how this technique can be used to shape a neckline.

Diamond yoke jacket page 69

1
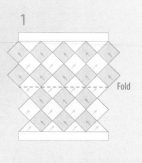
Fold

2
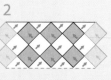

3

Eyeglass case page 53

46

Unique edges

The unique structure of entrelac can become a wonderful design feature. The simplest examples can be seen when we begin or end a project with rectangles instead of triangles.

But, what if you wanted a similar look along a vertical edge for a cardigan opening? By creating rectangles in place of triangles along the edge, a zigzag edge is fashioned. Place a button loop at each point and a unique cardigan closure is formed, one that does not interrupt the pattern created by the entrelac stitch.

The zigzag — available as either a horizontal or vertical edge — also integrates with knitted fabrics that naturally form a scalloped edge. Ripple stitch, Feather and Fan, and many lace patterns scallop as a result of the placement of increases and decreases within the fabric. It is easy to move back and forth between entrelac and these other fabrics while avoiding unattractive puckering at the point of transition.

Sample of grid page 147

Other shapes and lines can also be formed. By using 45° and 90° grid graph paper, it is easy to visualize any number of shapes or lines by outlining entrelac units on the grid. This is often how I begin working through the details of an entrelac design, by sketching necklines, armhole shapes, and any other edge I want, while following the natural shape of entrelac.

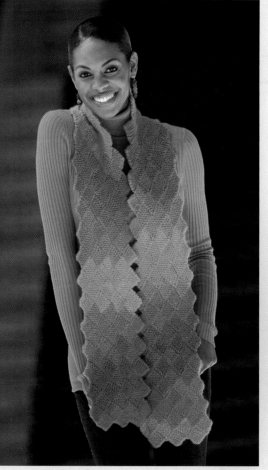

Market scarf page 22

Entrée
to
Entrelac

Base number
6 stitches

Rippled patterns are easy to combine with entrelac. Increases are placed at the points and decreases are made in the valleys.

When working entrelac on point, you can form a square by adding or subtracting a unit in every tier. Using two contrasting colors results in a checkerboard effect.

Icon key

●●●●
live stitches

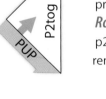

PUP
pick up and purl stitches in direction of arrow

PUK
pick up and knit stitches in direction of arrow

~~~~~~~~
joined edge

↗
direction of work

inc LBT Increase Left-leaning Base Triangle

Cast on 1. (Cast-on stitch).

Row 1 (WS) P1 (cast-on stitch).

Row 2 (RS) Knit in front and back of stitch (kf&b).

Row 3 Purl stitches worked on previous row.

Row 4 Knit to last stitch, kf&b. Repeat last 2 rows to 6 stitches, end with a RS row.

LR Left-leaning Rectangle

With RS facing, pick up and knit 6 stitches along edge of unit in previous tier (PUK6).

Row 1 (WS) P6.

Row 2 (RS) K5, SSK to join (last stitch of unit with stitch from previous tier). Repeat last 2 rows until all 6 stitches from previous tier have been joined — 6 stitches.

dec LTT Decrease Left-leaning Top Triangle

With RS facing, PUK6.

Row 1 (WS) Purl.

Row 2 (RS) Knit to last stitch of unit, SSK to join with previous tier.

Row 3 (WS) Purl to last 2 stitches, p2tog. Repeat last 2 rows until all 6 stitches from previous tier have been joined and 1 stitch remains. Purl this stitch together with last stitch of Row 1 on next unit OR fasten off on final unit of tier.

unjoined LR Unjoined Rectangle

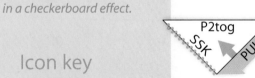
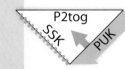

Work same as LR EXCEPT *Row 2* (RS) K6. Repeat Rows 1 and 2 until unit has twice as many rows as base stitches.

RST Right-leaning Starting Triangle

Make a slip knot and place on needle next to last stitch worked.

Row 1 (WS) P2tog to join (slip knot with stitch from previous tier).

Row 2 (RS) Kf&b.

Row 3 Purl to last stitch of unit, p2tog to join.

Row 4 Knit to last stitch, kf&b. Repeat last 2 rows until all 6 stitches from previous tier have been joined, end with a WS row — 6 stitches.

RR Right-leaning Rectangle

With WS facing, pick up and purl 6 stitches along edge of unit in previous tier (PUP6).

Row 1 (RS) K6.

Row 2 (WS) P5, p2tog to join (last stitch of unit with stitch from previous tier). Repeat last 2 rows until all 6 stitches from previous tier have been joined — 6 stitches.

RET Right-leaning Ending Triangle

With WS facing, PUP6.

Row 1 (RS) Knit stitches worked in previous row.

Row 2 (WS) Purl to last 2 stitches, p2tog. Repeat last 2 rows until 1 stitch remains. *Next row* (RS) K1, fasten off.

unjoined RR Unjoined Rectangle

Work same as RR EXCEPT *Row 2* (WS) P6. Repeat Rows 1 and 2 until unit has twice as many rows as base stitches.

notes

◆ *See page 16 for vitals for practice blocks; see page 152 for any unfamiliar techniques.*

◆ *Cut yarn at end of tier; join new yarn at beginning of tier.*

◆ *For Entrelac on point: Cast-on counts as Row 1 of rectangle; begin first LR or RR of tier with Row 2.*

Ripple stitch

Tier 1 With B, work 4 LBT.

Ripple Insert With WS facing and A, [p6, PUP6] 4 times.

Row 1 (RS) [K2tog, k3, (M1), k2, M1, k3, SSK] 4 times. *Row 2* (WS) Purl. Repeat last 2 rows 4 more times; repeat Row 1.

Tier 2 With B, work live stitches. Work 1 RST, 3 RR, 1 RET. *Tier 3* With A, work 4 LR. *Tier 4* Repeat Tier 2.

Ripple Insert With RS facing and A, [PUK6, k6] 4 times.

Row 1 (WS) [P1, M1, p3, p2tog, SSP, p3, M1, p1] 4 times.

Row 2 (RS) Knit. Repeat last 2 rows 4 more times; repeat Row 1.

Tier 5 With B, work live stitches. Work 4 LTT. Weave in remaining ends; block.

Incl yarn over With into back of yarnover on next row.

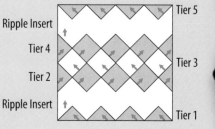

Color key

- ☐ A
- ▨ B

—— bind-off
—— cast-on
➔ direction of work

Entrelac on point

Tier 1 With A, cast on 6. Beginning with a WS row, work 11 rows in stockinette stitch (St st).

Tier 2 With B, cast on 6. Work 1 LR, 1 Unjoined LR.

Tier 3 (5) With A, cast on 6. Work 2 (4) RR, 1 Unjoined LR.

Tier 4 (6) With B, cast on 6. Work 3 (5) LR, 1 Unjoined LR. On Tier 6, bind off Unjoined LR.

Tiers 7–11 Bind off on last row of last unit.

Tier 7 (9, 11) With A, work 5 (3, 1) RR.

Tier 8 (10) With B, work 4 (2) LR.

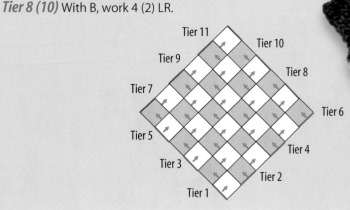

49

A simple card case demonstrates how easily you can create a triangular flap. Note that a crochet seam on the outside becomes a decorative element.

notes

◆ *See page152 for any unfamiliar techniques.*

◆ *For one-color version, ignore A and B references.*

◆ *Cut yarn after each tier*

Card case

Tier 1 With A, work 2 Inc LBT. **Tier 2** With B, work RST, 1 RR, RET. **Tier 3** With A, work 2 LR. **Tiers 4–6** Repeat last 2 tiers once, then Tier 2 once. **Tier 7** With A, work 2 LR, binding off last LR. **Tier 8** With B, work 1 RR with bind-off.

Finishing

With crochet hook and B, work slip stitch crochet (ss) around piece as shown on schematic. **Side seam** With WS together, work 14 half double crochet through slip stitches at each side. **Edging & button loop** Starting at seam, work half double crochet around top edge and flap using slip stitch as a guide; placing a chain of 4-6 stitches at point of flap. Attach button at base of card case to correspond to button loop.

Easy +

Approximate Measurements

Bag 4½" high x 6½" circumference
Eyeglass Case 4" high x 7½" wide
Card Case 3" high x 4½" wide
Cell Phone Case 6" high x 8" circumference

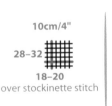

10cm/4"

28–32

18–20
over stockinette stitch

1 2 3 **4** 5 6

Medium weight +

2 balls of either yarn will make a set

4mm/US 6, or size to obtain gauge, set of 5 dpn

&

Eyeglass Case 6 (8)"
Ghees Hex Open Purse Frames
Card Case crochet hook 4mm
Cell Phone Case Size 3 snap waste yarn crochet hook

☻

Card Case one 18mm (¾") buton

---

the
UNITS

Base numbers

Card Case: 6 stitches
Cell Phone: 6 or 5 stitches as specified

Inc LBT

LR

bo LTT

RR

RST

RET

Unjoined RR

For row-by-row instructions see page 158.

*Entrée
to
Entrelac*

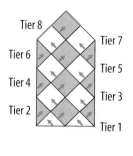

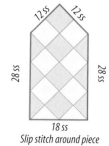

Half double crochet to join sides

Card case

18 ss

12 ss 12 ss

28 ss 28 ss

Slip stitch around piece

Cell phone case

Bottom rectangle With waste yarn and using temporary crochet cast-on, cast on 6. With A, work Unjoined LR 1. Cut yarn.

Body

Tier 1 Working each pick-up with B and a new dpn: PUP6 along left edge of LR 1; work Unjoined RR 2. PUP6 along right edge of RR 2; work RR 3. PUP6 along right edge of LR 1; work Unjoined RR 4. PUP6 along right edge of RR 4; remove waste yarn from LR 1 and place stitches on new dpn; work RR 5. Continue in seamless entrelac with 6 base stitches. *Tiers 2, 4* With A, work 4 LR. *Tier 3* With B, 4 RR. *Tier 5* With B, work four 5-stitch RR, working p3tog on first joining row of each unit (last stitch of unit with 2 stitches from unit in previous tier) — 4 stitches decreased and base number reduced to 5. *Tier 6* With A, work Bo LTT; work 1 LR, binding off all stitches of unit on final row; work Bo LTT; work 1 LR.

Finishing

Bind off 2 stitches. Work 3-stitch I-cord for 5". Work 2 rows stockinette stitch, increasing 1 stitch each row — 5 stitches. Bind off. Sew 1 half of snap at the end of the I-cord and other half on point of other rectangle.

Cell phone case

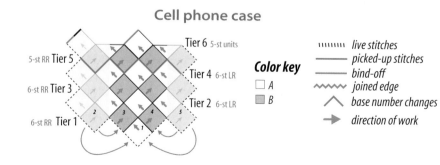

5-st RR **Tier 5**

6-st RR **Tier 3**

6-st RR **Tier 1**

Tier 6 5-st units

Tier 4 6-st LR

Tier 2 6-st LR

Color key
- ☐ A
- ▨ B

live stitches
picked-up stitches
bind-off
joined edge
base number changes
direction of work

RR 5

RR 4

RR 3

RR 2

LR 1

Surround a single rectangle at the center bottom with a 4-rectangle tier, then go from there. Entrelac worked seamlessly to the top is quick and rewarding. Perfect for using up that half ball of multicolor yarn.

notes

◆ *Cell case is worked in seamless entrelac, with decreasing unit sizes for shaping.*

Mini drawstring bag

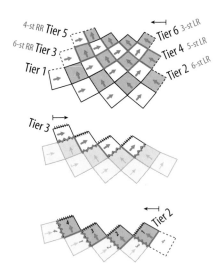

This bag is similar to the Cuppa Joe, but uses decreasing tiers to form the bottom of the bag. Create a larger bag by adding more tiers, starting with larger units, or adding more units per tier.

notes

◆ See page 152 for any unfamiliar techniques.

◆ Bag is worked in seamless entrelac from top to bottom.

◆ Bag is shaped by reducing the base number of stitches picked up. When base number is reduced by 1 stitch, joining 2 stitches from previous tier with 1 stitch from current unit maintains the 2:1 ratio of rows to stitches.

Mini drawstring bag

Tier 1 * With A and empty dpn, cast on 6 stitches. *Row 1 and all RS rows* Knit. *Row 2* (WS) Purl. *Row 4* P2, yo, p2tog, p2. *Rows 6, 8, 10, 12* Purl. Continuing with attached yarn, repeat from * 3 more times — 4 rectangles, 1 per dpn. *Tier 2* With B, work 3 LR, picking up stitches for first LR along edge of last rectangle. For last LR, PUP along first rectangle and join to last rectangle, making sure piece is not twisted. *Tier 3* With A, work four 6-stitch RR. *Tier 4* With B, work four 5-stitch LR, working SSSK on first joining row of each LR (last stitch of unit with 2 stitches from unit in previous tier). *Tier 5* With A, work four 4-stitch RR, working p3tog on first joining row. *Tier 6* With B, ork four 3-stitch LR, working SSSK on first joining row.

Finishing

Cut yarn, leaving 8 – 10" tail. Thread tail through 12 remaining stitches and pull tight to close bottom of bag. Fasten off.

Straps (Make 2) Knit a 2-stitch I-cord, 24" long. Lace through eyelets as shown in illustration on page 111.

the
UNITS

Base number
Bag: 6, 5, 4, or 3 stitches as specified

Eyeglass Case: 6 stitches

LR

unjoined LR

join RBT

RR

live RTT

unjoined RR

For row-by-row instructions see page 158.

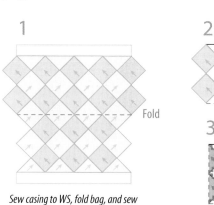

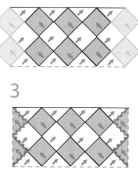

Sew casing to WS, fold bag, and sew zigzag seams, seaming stitches to rows and rows to stitches.

Eyeglass case

Casing With A, cast on 36. Work k1, p1 rib for 6 rows. ***Turning row*** Purl.

Body

Tier 1 Work 4 Join RBT, binding off last row of last unit. ***Tiers 2, 4*** With B, work 3 LR. ***Tier 3*** With A, cast on 6. Work 3 RR; work 1 Unjoined RR, binding off last row. ***Tier 5*** With A, cast on 6. Work 3 RR, 1 Unjoined RR. ***Tiers 6, 8*** With B, cast on 6. Work 4 LR; work 1 Unjoined LR, binding off last row. ***Tier 7*** With A, work 4 RR. ***Tier 9*** With A, work 4 Live RTT. ***Casing*** [P1, M1, p1] to end (turning row) — 28 stitches. Work k1, p1 rib for 6 rows. Bind off in pattern.

Finishing

Fold casings to WS at turning row, sew edge to inside. Fold at red dashed line; work zigzag seam, joining points as shown (Illustrations 1–3). Insert spring metal closures in casing so opposite ends meet. Insert pins into hinges at either end (you may need pliers to complete this step).

The eyeglass case creates vertical zigzag edges through the use of cast-on and bound-off rectangles. What a great opportunity to try zigzag seams!

notes

◆ *Cast-on at beginning of tier counts as Row 1 of unit; begin first LR or RR of tier with Row 2.*

◆ *Casing is designed for spring metal closure; bag can also be finished with small zipper or hook and loop tape.*

,,,,,,,,,	live stitches
——	picked-up stitches
——	bind-off
——	cast-on
∿∿∿	joined edge
∧	base number changes
→	direction of work

Color key
□ A
▨ B

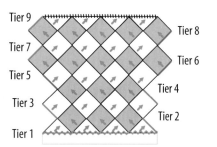

Tier 9
Tier 7
Tier 5
Tier 3
Tier 1
Tier 8
Tier 6
Tier 4
Tier 2

Hobo bag

Front and back panels

Panel 1 *Tier 1* Work six 11-stitch Inc LBT. *Tier 2* Work 10-stitch units: RST, 5 RR, RET, working p3tog on first joining row of each (last stitch of unit with 2 stitches from previous tier). *Tier 3* Work six 9-stitch LR, working SSSK on first joining row. *Tiers 4–8* Repeat last 2 tiers twice, then Tier 2 once, decreasing 1 base stitch/unit in each tier. *Tier 9* Work six 3-stitch Live LTT, working SSSK on first joining row. Place stitches on hold—18 stitches.

Panel 2 Work same as Panel 1 EXCEPT work right-leaning units for left-leaning units and left-leaning for right-leaning.

Finishing the panels

Decide which panel you would like for the front. **Front panel** *Next row* K1 [yo, k2] 8 times, yo, k1—27 stitches. Bind off. **Back panel** *Work button tab* **Row 1** K1 [yo, k2] 8 times, yo, k1. Bind off 9 stitches and work to end. **Row 2** Bind off 9 stitches and work to end—9 stitches. Knit 24 rows. **Next row** K3, work 1-row buttonhole over 3 stitches, k3. Knit 4 rows. Decrease 1 stitch at beginning of each row until 3 stitches remain, bind off.

Joining the panels *With RS facing, PUK 42 along side, 100 along bottom, and 42 along other side of one panel;* cast on 11. Repeat * to * along other panel, beginning at top of second panel with second needle. Stitches are now picked up on 3 sides of each panel with 11 cast-on stitches connecting them.

Side and bottom strip Fold wrong sides together. Working only with the 11 cast-on stitches, join yarn and work as follows: *All rows* K10, SSK to join (last stitch of strip with panel stitch). Work down side, across bottom and up other side, joining to each stitch of both panels. Bag is now joined on 3 sides.

Strap Continue in garter stitch on 11 stitches approximately 33" or until desired length. *Felting shrinks length of garter stitch only slightly.* Bind off; seam to cast-on edge. Felt bag to desired thickness. Attach button on front panel corresponding to button tab.

The bag shaping is done by reducing the base number of stitches by one for each tier. The felted fabric creates structure and the long-repeat yarn keeps the fabric interesting.

notes

◆ *See page 152 for any unfamiliar techniques.*

◆ *A single strip, joined to the front and back panels as it is worked, forms the sides, bottom, and strap.*

◆ *Bag is shaped by reducing the base number of stitches picked up.*

◆ *When base number is reduced by 1 stitch, joining 2 stitches from previous tier with 1 stitch from current unit maintains the 2-rows-to-1-stitch ratio.*

---

the
UNITS
Base number
11 stitches reduced to 3

inc LBT

LR

live LTT

LST

LET

Button

Entrée
to
Entrelac

Intermediate
9 (7½)" deep, 19 (14)" across base, 8 (6½)" across opening
2½ (1½)" x 33" strap
Before (after) felting

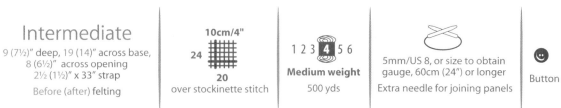

10cm/4"
24
20
over stockinette stitch

1 2 3 **4** 5 6
Medium weight
500 yds

5mm/US 8, or size to obtain gauge, 60cm (24") or longer
Extra needle for joining panels

Button

RST

Kf&b

P2tog

RR

PUP

P2tog

RET

PUP

P2tog

inc RBT

Pf&b

live RTT

PUP

P2tog

For row-by-row instructions see page 158.

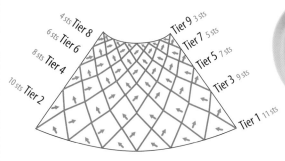

4 sts **Tier 8**
6 sts **Tier 6**
8 sts **Tier 4**
10 sts **Tier 2**

Tier 9 3 sts
Tier 7 5 sts
Tier 5 7 sts
Tier 3 9 sts
Tier 1 11 sts

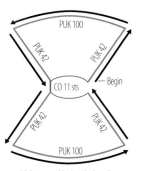

PUK 100

PUK 42   PUK 42

CO 11 sts — Begin

PUK 42   PUK 42

PUK 100

Pick up and knit stitches for side and bottom strip.

—— *picked-up stitches*

⋀ *base number changes*

— *cast-on*

➜ *direction of work*

JOJOLAND Rhythm
in color M01

55

The trapeze shape was inspired by one of my favorite designers, Deborah Newton. The entrelac fabric blends from one color to the next like a watercolor. Created with 3 strands of a lace-weight yarn, the color change is gradual with only 1 strand changing each tier.

stitches

REVERSE STOCKINETTE STITCH
RS rows Purl. **WS rows** Knit.

INC 1 Yo; on next row, work into back of yo.

notes

◆ See page 152 for any unfamiliar techniques.

◆ Coat is worked with 3 strands held together: for bodice and sleeves all 3 are the same color (DDD); in the skirt, 1 changes each tier (AAB, ABB, ABC, etc).

◆ Skirt is shaped by decreasing the base number in the units of right-leaning tiers. On RST and RR, work p3tog for first decrease (last stitch with 2 stitches from unit in previous tier); on RET, purl last 3 stitches together.

◆ Button and buttonhole bands are worked in intarsia.

Watercolor coat

Skirt *Begin border* With AAA, cast on 360 (384, 408, 432). Beginning with a RS row, work 4 rows of reverse stockinette stitch.
Tier 1 [Work LR over base number of stitches, beginning on Row 2 and joining to border stitches] 12 times. *Tier 2* With AAB, change to base number minus 1 (Base −1) and work RST, 11 RR, RET. *Tier 3* With ABB, work 12 LR. *Tier 4* Change to Base −2 and ABC, work RST, 11 RR, RET. *Tier 5* With BBC, work 12 LR. *Tier 6* Change to Base −3 and BCC, work RST, 11 RR, RET. *Tier 7* With BCD, work 12 LR. *Tier 8* Change to Base −4 and CCD, work RST, 11 RR, RET. *Tier 9* With CDD, work 12 LR. *Tier 10* With DDD, and working p2tog instead of p3tog on first WS row, work RST, 11 RR, RET. *Tier 11* With DDD, work 12 Dec LTT—132 (144, 156, 168) stitches.

Bodice Continue with DDD. *Next row* (WS) [K1, inc1, k1] to end— 198 (216, 234, 252) stitches. *Eyelet increase row* P7 (8, 1, 2) [yo, p8] 23 (25, 29, 31) times, yo, p7 (8, 1, 2) — 222 (242, 264, 284) stitches. *Next row* (WS) Knit,

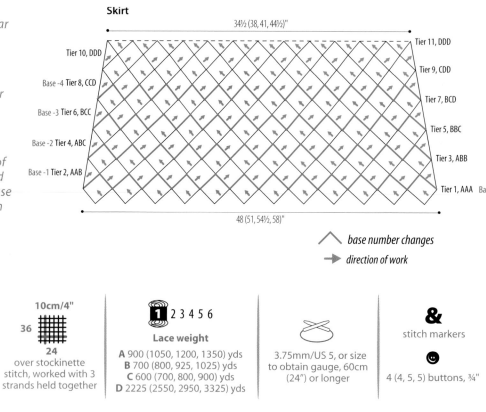

Skirt

34½ (38, 41, 44½)"

Tier 10, DDD
Base -4 Tier 8, CCD
Base -3 Tier 6, BCC
Base -2 Tier 4, ABC
Base -1 Tier 2, AAB

Tier 11, DDD
Tier 9, CDD
Tier 7, BCD
Tier 5, BBC
Tier 3, ABB
Tier 1, AAA Ba

48 (51, 54½, 58)"

⌃ base number changes
➡ direction of work

Right column diagrams

LR
dec LTT
RST
RR
RET

For row-by-row instructions see page 158.

Bottom info bar

Intermediate

STANDARD FIT
S (M, L, 1X)
A 37 (41, 45, 49)"
B 29 (31½, 33¾, 36¼)"
C 29 (30, 31, 32)"

10cm/4"
36
24
over stockinette stitch, worked with 3 strands held together

1 2 3 4 5 6
Lace weight
A 900 (1050, 1200, 1350) yds
B 700 (800, 925, 1025) yds
C 600 (700, 800, 900) yds
D 2225 (2550, 2950, 3325) yds

3.75mm/US 5, or size to obtain gauge, 60cm (24") or longer

&
stitch markers
☺
4 (4, 5, 5) buttons, ¾"

knitting into front of each yarn-over. *Next row* (RS) Purl. Beginning and ending with a WS row, work in stockinette stitch for 4 (4½, 5, 5½)", end on a WS row.

Divide for Fronts and Back Next row Work 49 (52, 56, 59) stitches and place on hold for right front, bind off 14 (18, 20, 24) for right underarm, work 96 (102, 112, 118) stitches and place on hold for back, bind off 14 (18, 20, 24) for left armhole, work remaining 49 (52, 56, 59) stitches for left front.

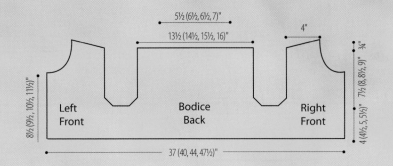

Continue Left Front Decrease 1 stitch at armhole edge every RS row 7 (8, 10, 11) times. Work even until armhole measures 4½ (5, 5½, 6)". End with a RS row.

Shape neck Next row At neck edge, bind off 9 (10, 10, 11). Decrease 1 stitch every RS row at neck edge 9 (10, 11, 12) times — 24 (24, 25, 25) stitches. Work even until armhole measures 7½ (8, 8½, 9)" from armhole bind-off, end with a RS row.

Shape shoulder Next row Work to 5 stitches from armhole edge, wrap next stitch and turn work (W&T); work 1 row even. Work to 11 stitches from armhole edge, W&T; work 1 row even. Work to 17 stitches from armhole edge, W&T; work 1 row even. Work across all stitches, hiding wraps. Bind off.

Continue Right Front Beginning on a WS row, join yarn and work 49 (52, 56, 59) stitches of Right Front as for Left Front, EXCEPT shape armhole at end of RS rows and neck. Shape neck and shoulder at beginning of RS rows.

Continue Back Beginning on a WS row, join yarn and work 96 (102, 112, 118) stitches of Back. Decrease 1 stitch at each armhole edge every RS row 7 (8, 10, 11) times —82 (86, 92, 96) stitches. Work to same length as Front to beginning of shoulder shaping. Bind off.

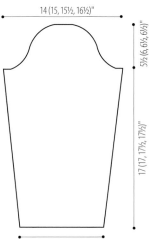

14 (15, 15½, 16½)"

5½ (6, 6½, 6½)"

17 (17, 17½, 17½)"

8½ (9, 10, 10½)"

Sleeves With DDD, cast on 52 (54, 60, 64) stitches. Beginning with a RS row, work 4 rows of reverse stockinette stitch. Continuing in stockinette stitch, increase 1 stitch each end of this row and every 8th row 15 (17, 16, 17) times — 84 (90, 94, 100) stitches. Work even until piece measures 17 (17, 17½, 17½)" from beginning.

Shape cap Bind off 7 (9, 10, 12) stitches at beginning of next two 2 rows. Decrease 1 stitch each edge every RS row 7 (8, 10, 11) times, every other RS row 1 (2, 3, 5) times, and every RS row 15 (14, 12, 9) times. Bind off 8 stitches at the beginning of the next 2 rows; bind off remaining 8 (8, 8, 10) stitches.

Finishing

Join shoulder seams. Set in sleeves. Sew sleeve seams.

Button band With RS facing and DDD, and starting at neck edge of left front, PUK 53 (58, 66, 71) stitches to first triangle. Pick up stitches along edge triangles of skirt as follows: Place marker (pm), change 1 strand of D to C (CDD), PUK16 (18, 19, 21). Pm, change 1 D to C (CCD), PUK 16 (18, 19, 21). Pm, change 1 D to B (BCC), PUK 18 (19, 21, 22). Pm, change 1 C to A (ABC), PUK 19 (21, 22, 24). Pm, change 1 C to A (AAB), PUK 21 (22, 24, 25). Working in colors as established, and interlocking the changing strands at markers on wrong side, work 4 rows in Reverse stockinette stitch. On next WS row, bind off in pattern to 3 stitches before last marker, purl to end of row — 56 (61, 69, 74) stitches. Knit 1 row. Work 4 rows in Reverse stockinette stitch. Bind off in pattern.

Buttonhole band With WS facing and DDD, and starting at neck edge of right front, PUP and work 4 rows as for button band. *Buttonhole row* (RS) Bind off in pattern to 3 stitches before last marker; knitting across remainder of row, evenly space 4 (4, 5, 5) [k2tog, yo] buttonholes, working first buttonhole just after marker and last buttonhole 5 stitches from the end of the row. Purl 1 row. Work 4 rows in Reverse stockinette stitch. Bind off in pattern.

Neckband With RS facing and DDD, PUK 15 (16, 16, 17) stitches along right front neck, 17 (18, 19, 20) stitches to shoulder, 38 (42, 44, 48) stitches along back neck, 17 (18, 19, 20) stitches to front neck and 15 (16, 16, 17) stitches along left front neck — 102 (110, 114, 122) stitches. Work 4 rows in Reverse stockinette. Bind off in pattern.

Attach buttons. Work 70" twisted cord with 2 strands of each color and lace, thru eyelets.

Prussian jewels

Entrelac and ripple stitch patterns are the perfect marriage of knitted fabrics — each flows seamlessly into the other. Decreasing entrelac shapes the waist and a color change avoids any chance of color showing between tiers.

stitches

WS CC ROW With new color, [PUP base number of stitches along edge of unit in previous tier, then purl same number from needle] to end. Do not turn unless directed.

RS CC ROW With new color, [knit base number of stitches then PUK base number along edge of unit in previous tier] to end. Do not turn unless directed.

WORK UNIT WITH BIND-OFF Bind off on last row of unit.

notes

◆ *See page 152 for any unfamiliar techniques.*

◆ *Body is worked circularly in entrelac and chart pattern. At underarm, Front and Back worked separately.*

◆ *Sleeves are worked circularly to beginning of cap, then cap is worked in rows.*

◆ *For ease of working, mark RS of first rectangle of Tier 1.*

◆ *Color-change (CC) Rows are worked between tiers to prevent preceding color from showing through. Work rectangles into stitches picked up on CC rows.*

◆ *Cut old yarn at each color change.*

Prussian jewels

Body

Work 20 (22, 24, 26) units each tier. **Tier 1** With longer circular needle and C, cast on 320 (352, 384, 416). Join, [work 8-stitch LGR, joining to next 8 cast-on stitches] around. *Use removable marker to mark next 8 stitches.* **Tier 2** Work WS CC row with B: [PUP8, p8] to end. [Work 8-stitch RGR, joining to next 8 stitches] around.

Work RS CC row with A, [k8, PUK8] to end. Do not turn. ***Begin Chart A:*** *Round 1* Place marker (pm) for beginning of round, work 16-stitch repeat of Chart A 20 (22, 24, 26) times. Work pattern through Round 16, then repeat Rounds 15 and 16 four more times. Do not turn. **Tier 3:** *CC Round* With RS facing and D, knit 1 round, ending 8 stitches before marker. Remove marker, [work 8-stitch LRs, joining to next 8 stitches] around. **Tier 4** Work WS CC row with B: [PUP7, p2tog, p6] to end — 280 (308, 336, 364) stitches. [Work 7-stitch RRs, joining to next 7 stitches] around. **Tier 5** Work RS CC row with C: [PUK6, SSK, k5] to end — 240 (264, 288, 312) stitches. [Work 6-stitch LRs, joining to next 6 stitches] around. **Tier 6** Work WS CC row with E: [PUP5, p2tog, p4] to end — 200 (220, 240, 260) stitches. [Work 5-stitch RRs, joining to next 5 stitches] around.

Chart B Work RS CC row with A: [k5, PUK5] to end. Pm and work Chart B until piece measures 15½ (16, 16½, 17)" from beginning. End with Round 2, 5 stitches before marker.

Chart A

16-st rep

Stitch Key

☐ Knit on RS, purl on WS
▨ Purl on RS
◉ Yarn over (yo)
◥ SSK
◪ K2tog
◙ K1 through back loop (tbl) on RS, p1 tbl on WS
▣ P1 tbl on RS

Chart B

10-st rep

the
UNITS

Base number
8, 7, 6, 5 stitches as specified

LR

LGR
Work as LR EXCEPT knit WS rows.

LST

LET

bo LTT

Experienced

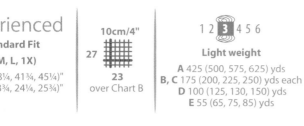

Standard Fit
S (M, L, 1X)

A 34¾ (38¼, 41¾, 45¼)"
B 22½ (23¾, 24¼, 25¾)"

10cm/4"
27
23
over Chart B

1 2 **3** 4 5 6
Light weight
A 425 (500, 575, 625) yds
B, C 175 (200, 225, 250) yds each
D 100 (125, 130, 150) yds
E 55 (65, 75, 85) yds

4.5mm/US 7, or size to obtain gauge, 40cm (16") and 74cm (29") long

One set 4.5mm/US 7

&
markers

RR

RGR
Work as RR EXCEPT begin with a WS row AND purl RS rows.

bo RTT

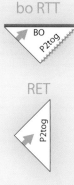

RET

RST

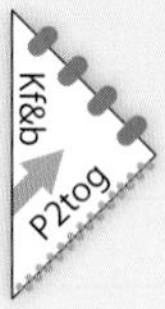

For row-by-row instructions see page 158.

Glow indicates a modified unit.

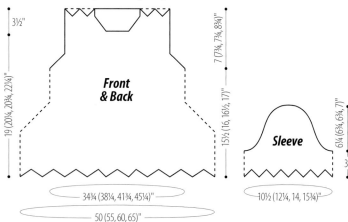

6½ (6½, 8, 8)"   3¼ (4, 4, 4¾)"

3½"

Front & Back

19 (20¼, 20¾, 22¼)"

15½ (16, 16½, 17)"

7 (7¾, 7¾, 8¾)"

Sleeve

6¼ (6¾, 6¾, 7)"

3"

34¾ (38¼, 41¾, 45¼)"

50 (55, 60, 65)"

10½ (12¼, 14, 15¾)"

Shown in BERROCO Bonsai in colors #4134 Sumi Ink (**A**), #4103 Bamboo (**B**), #4121 Raku Brown (**C**), #4110 Shibui Clay (**D**), and #4101 Tofu (**E**).

Divide for Front and Back

Next row (RS) Bind off 10 stitches for underarm, removing marker (knit last yo of round tbl before binding off); knit until 90 (100, 110, 120) stitches are on right needle, place them on hold for Front; bind off 10 for underarm, knit to end — 90 (100, 110, 120) on needle for Back.

Color key
- A
- B
- C
- D
- E

⋁⋁⋁⋁ live stitches

F first

L last

→ direction of work

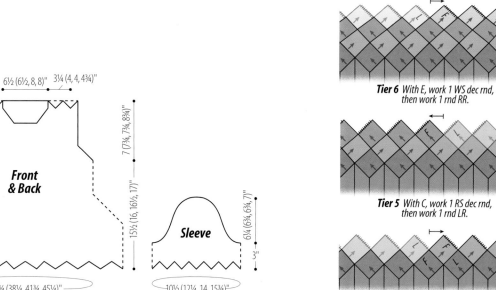

Tier 6 *With E, work 1 WS dec rnd, then work 1 rnd RR.*

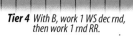

Tier 5 *With C, work 1 RS dec rnd, then work 1 rnd LR.*

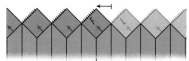

Tier 4 *With B, work 1 WS dec rnd, then work 1 rnd RR.*

rnd marker
Tier 3 *K1 RS rnd with D, ending 8 sts before rnd marker, then work 1 rnd LR.*

Chart A *(b) Work Chart A for 24 rnds.*

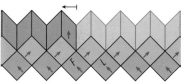

Chart A *(a) Work a RS color change rnd.*

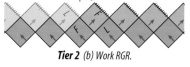

Tier 2 *(b) Work RGR.*

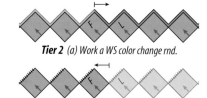

Tier 2 *(a) Work a WS color change rnd.*

Tier 1 *Work LGR.*

61

Base number for all remaining units is 5 stitches; each unit is joined to next 5 CC stitches. **Back yoke** *Tier 7* (WS) With D, purl. Work 9 (10, 11, 12) LR, binding off last LR. Do not turn, slide work to other end of needle (slide). *Tier 8* Work RS CC row with B: [k5, PUK5] to end — 80 (90, 100, 110) stitches. Work 8 (9, 10, 11) RR, joining to CC row. Slide. *Tier 9* With WS facing and C: [PUP5, p5 from left needle] to end, PUP1 in corner of last unit from previous tier — 81 (91, 101, 111) stitches. Work LST, 7 (8, 9, 10) LR, LET. ***Tiers 10–13 (10–13, 10–13, 10–15)*** [Repeat Tiers 8 and 9] 2 (2, 2, 3) more times (pick up last group of stitches along LET on RS CC rows and follow yoke diagram for color sequence). Slide. Work RS CC row with E (E, E, B): [k5, PUK5] to end (pick up last group of stitches along LET).

SIZES M (L) ONLY: *Tier 14* With E, work 9 (10) RR. Slide. Work WS CC row with D: [PUP5, p5] to end.

ALL SIZES: *Final Tier 1 Bind off RRs and LRs on Row 9.* **2** *When binding off and next shape is a RTT or LTT, leave remaining stitch on right needle and work RTT or LTT as directed. When next shape is anything else, slip remaining stitch onto left needle and begin with a p2tog or k2tog instead of first purl or knit.*

SIZES S (1X) ONLY *Tier 14* With E (B), work 2 (3) RR, 4 (5) RTT, 2 (3) RR.

SIZES M (L) ONLY *Tier 15* With D, work LST with bind-off, 2 LR, 4 (5) LTT, 2 LR, LET.

Front yoke Work as for back yoke through Tier 9 (10, 10, 11). Slide.

SIZES S (1X) ONLY *Shape center front neck* Work RS CC row with E (B): [k5, PUK5] to end (pick up last group of stitches along LET). *Tier 10 (12)* Work 3 (4) RR, binding off last RR, work 2 (3) Bo RTT, work 3 (4) RR. Slide.

Shape right neck and shoulder Work WS CC row with D (C): [PUP5, p5] 2 (3) times, PUP5 — 25 (35) stitches. *Tier 11 (13)* Work 2 (3) LR, LET. Slide. Work RS CC row with B (E): [k5, PUK5] 1 (2) times, k5, PUK5 along LET — 20 (30) stitches. Work 2 (3) RR. Slide.

Work WS CC row with C (D): [PUP5, p5] 2 (3) times. Binding off on last row of each unit, work LST, 1 (2) LR; work LET.

Shape left neck and shoulder Work WS CC row with D (C): beginning with live stitches at neck edge, [p5, PUP5] 2 (3) times, p5 — 25 (35) stitches. *Tier 11(13)* Work LST, 2 (3) LR, binding off last LR. Complete as for right neck.

SIZES M (L) ONLY *Shape center front neck* Work WS CC row with D: [PUP5, p5] to end. *Tier 11 (11)* Work LST, 3 LR, binding off last LR, 2 (3) Bo LTT, 3 LR, LET. Slide.

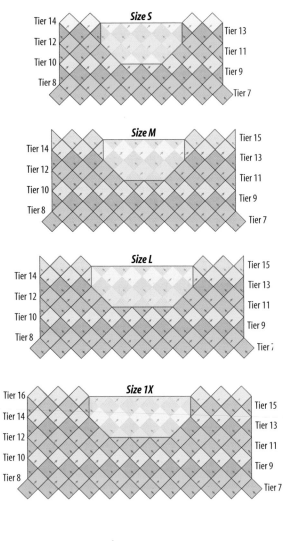

end of front yoke
bind-off
direction of work

Shape right neck and shoulder Work RS CC row with B: [k5, PUK5] 3 times — 30 stitches. *Tier 12 (12)* Work 3 RR, binding off last RR. Slide. Work WS CC row with C: [PUP5, p5] 2 times, PUP5 — 25 stitches. *Tier 13 (13)* Work 2 LR, LET. Slide. Work RS CC row with E: [PUK5, k5] 2 times, PUK5 along LET. *Tier 14 (14)* Work 2 RR with bind-off; work RET.

Shape left neck and shoulder Work RS CC row with B, [k5, PUK5] 3 times — 30 stitches. *Tier 12 (12)* Work 3 RR. Slide. Work WS CC row with C: [p5, PUP5] 2 times, p5 — 25 stitches. *Tier 13 (13)* Work LST, 2 LR. Slide. Work RS CC row with E: [k5, PUK5] 2 times, k5 — 25 stitches. *Tier 14 (14)* Binding off on last row of each unit, work RST, 2 RR.

Sleeves

Base number 5 stitches With dpns and C, cast on 60 (70, 80, 90) stitches. Join. Work 6 (7, 8, 9) LGR. Work WS CC row with B: [PUP5, p5] to end. Work 6 (7, 8, 9) RGR.

Chart B Work RS CC row with A: [k5, PUK5] to end, pm and work Chart B until piece measures 3" from beginning. End with Round 2, 5 stitches before marker. Bind off 10 stitches, removing marker.

Shape cap Each decrease of chart must be paired with a corresponding yo: If a decrease in chart pattern cannot be worked, omit the corresponding yo. Continue in pattern as established (stitch remaining on right needle after bind–off is 6th stitch of Row 1) and work back and forth in rows. Work 1 row even. Decrease 1 stitch each side every row 1 (1, 3, 5) times, every other row 3 (11, 18, 15) times, every 3rd row 9 (3, 0, 0) times, every other row 2 (5, 0, 0) times, every row 0 (0, 4, 10) times. Work 1 (1, 0, 0) row even. Bind off 5 stitches at beginning of next 2 rows. Bind off remaining stitches.

Finishing

Join shoulders by folding points from Back and sewing them into zig–zag formed by points from Front. Set in sleeves.

Neckband With RS facing, shorter needle and A, begin at left shoulder and PUK70 (70, 80, 80) evenly around neck edge. Pm, join and purl 1 round, increasing 14 (14, 18, 18) evenly around — 84 (84, 98, 98) stitches. Purl 3 (3, 4, 4) rounds. Bind off purlwise.

Small Shown in BERROCO Bonsai in colors #4152 Kaigun (**A**), #4125 Midori Green (**B**), #4153 Estuko Blue (**C**), #4155 Akane Red (**D**), and #4143 Kin Gold (**E**).

Circular yokes anyone? These three sweater options show the versatility of growing entrelac tiers and the power of great yarn combinations.

notes

◆ *See page 152 for any unfamiliar techniques.*

◆ *Sweater is worked in seamless entrelac from the top down and divided at the underarms for body and sleeves.*

◆ *When the previous tier has a larger base number, work 2 fewer rows in each unit on the subsequent tier by working an SSSK or p3tog at the first join incorporating 2 stitches from the previous tier.*

◆ *Vital information is color-coded as follows: Man's, Woman's, Child.*

Top downs for everyone

Yoke

Man's With smaller 16" circular needle, using waste yarn and temporary crochet cast-on, cast on 90 (90, 120, 120, 120) stitches, join and mark beginning of round. With B, work in k1, p1 rib for 2", changing to larger needle for last round. Remove temporary cast-on and place stitches onto smaller circular needle. *Work folded rib* With larger 16" circular needle, work in rib pattern, joining one stitch from the cast-on edge with one stitch from working edge.

Woman's With shorter circular or dpn, loosely cast on, 84 (84, 105, 105, 126, 126), join and mark beginning of round. Purl 8 rounds (reverse stockinette).

Child's With dpn and A, loosely cast on 72 (72, 90) stitches, join and mark beginning of round. Work k1, p1 rib: 5 rounds A, 1 round B, 5 rounds A.

Man's With longer circular needle, work 20 units each tier following Yoke diagram.
Woman's With longer circular needle, work 14 units each tier following Yoke diagram.
Child's With shorter circular needle, work 12 units each tier following Yoke diagram.

the
UNITS

Base number
Follow diagrams for yoke and sleeves; for body see page 66.

join LBT

LR

live LTT

RR

For woman's: Purl RS rows, knit WS rows and k2tog to join.

live RTT

For row-by-row instructions see page 158

Glow indicates a modified unit.

Intermediate

	Standard Fit	**Standard Fit**	**Standard Fit**	
	Man's **S (M, L, 1X, 2X)** **A** 36 (41, 46, 51, 56)" **B** 23 (24, 26, 30, 30)" **C** 28 (30, 31, 33, 34)"	Woman's **XS (S, M, L, 1X, 2X)** **A** 32 (36, 39, 42, 46, 49)" **B** 20 (22, 24, 26, 28, 30)" **C** 25 (26, 28, 28, 30, 31)"	Child's **2 (4, 6)** **A** 23 (26, 29)" **B** 11 (12, 13)" **C** 16 (17½, 19½)"	
10cm/4" 28/28/32 20/20/26 over stockinette stitch	1 2 3 **4** 5 6 **Medium weight** **A** 650 (775, 900, 1100, 1200) yds **B** 200 (250, 300, 350, 400) yds **C** 150 (175, 225, 275, 300) yds **D** 125 (150, 175, 225, 250) yds	1 2 3 **4** 5 6 **Medium weight** 1100 (1300, 1500, 1700, 2000, 2200) yds	1 2 **3** 4 5 6 **Light weight** **A** 125 (150, 200) yds **B** 60 (75, 90) **C** 125 (150, 200)	**&** safety pins waste yarn crochet hook
	4.5mm/US 7 60cm (24") or longer and 4mm/US 6, 40cm (16")	4.5mm/US 7 60cm (24") or longer and 40cm (16")	4mm/US 6 60cm (24"), 3.5mm/US 4 40cm (16")	3.5mm/US 4 or size to obtain gauge

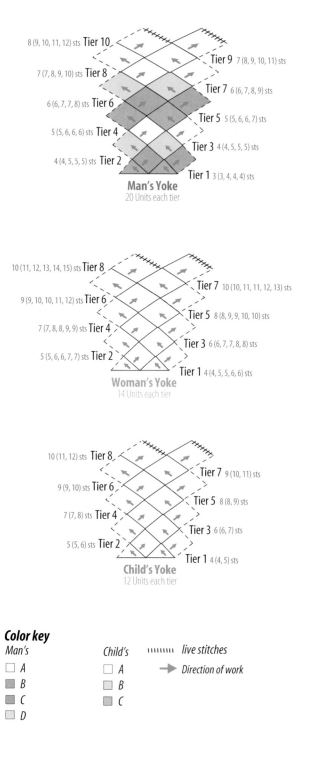

8 (9, 10, 11, 12) sts **Tier 10**

Tier 9 7 (8, 9, 10, 11) sts

7 (7, 8, 9, 10) sts **Tier 8**

Tier 7 6 (6, 7, 8, 9) sts

6 (6, 7, 7, 8) sts **Tier 6**

Tier 5 5 (5, 6, 6, 7) sts

5 (5, 6, 6, 6) sts **Tier 4**

Tier 3 4 (4, 5, 5, 5) sts

4 (4, 5, 5, 5) sts **Tier 2**

Tier 1 3 (3, 4, 4, 4) sts

Man's Yoke
20 Units each tier

10 (11, 12, 13, 14, 15) sts **Tier 8**

Tier 7 10 (10, 11, 11, 12, 13) sts

9 (9, 10, 10, 11, 12) sts **Tier 6**

Tier 5 8 (8, 9, 9, 10, 10) sts

7 (7, 8, 8, 9, 9) sts **Tier 4**

Tier 3 6 (6, 7, 7, 8, 8) sts

5 (5, 6, 6, 7, 7) sts **Tier 2**

Tier 1 4 (4, 5, 5, 6, 6) sts

Woman's Yoke
14 Units each tier

10 (11, 12) sts **Tier 8**

Tier 7 9 (10, 11) sts

9 (9, 10) sts **Tier 6**

Tier 5 8 (8, 9) sts

7 (7, 8) sts **Tier 4**

Tier 3 6 (6, 7) sts

5 (5, 6) sts **Tier 2**

Tier 1 4 (4, 5) sts

Child's Yoke
12 Units each tier

Color key

Man's

☐ *A*
☐ *B*
☐ *C*
☐ *D*

Child's

☐ *A*
☐ *B*
☐ *C*

⁀⁀⁀⁀⁀ *live stitches*

➡ *Direction of work*

Large shown in BROWN SHEEP
COMPANY Serendipity Tweed
in colors ST66 Steel Blue (A),
ST99 Midnight Forest (B), ST96
Oregano Leaves (C), ST87 Peat
Moss (D)

65

Sleeves

The underarm gusset worked separately then joined on Tier 1, creates the space between the sleeve and the body and technically is part of the last tier of the yoke.

Underarm gusset With shorter circular needle or dpn, waste yarn, and using temporary crochet cast-on, cast on base stitches. Work Unjoined RR. With main yarn, work Base rows (2 × Base stitches) in RR pattern stitch (stockinette for his or child's or reverse stockinette for hers), starting with a WS row and ending with a RS row, place unit on hold. *Work 5 (4, 3) units each tier following Sleeve diagram: Tier 1* Without breaking the yarn, work LR with base stitches, picking up stitches along edge of underarm gussett and joining with stitches from yoke; work 3 (2, 1) LR; work 1 LR, picking up along edge of next unit and joining to live stitches from gusset — 5 (4, 3) × Base stitches. Leave remaining yoke stitches on hold.

Sleeves are worked from the shoulder down so they can be tried on as you go. If necessary adjust shaping by changing the base number of stitches sooner to narrow the sleeve or later to widen the sleeve. Adjust length as needed; see bottom note on page 64.
Continue sleeve, following diagram for your size.

Cuff Increase 1 stitch for every 2 stitches and work in k1, p1 rib for 1½", (work 8 rounds reverse stockinette), (work in k1, p1 rib for 16 rounds). Bind off in pattern.

Begin second sleeve Slip 6 (4, 4) units of yoke from one needle to the other to reach the second underarm. Work underarm gusset and complete sleeve.

Small shown in JOJOLAND
Rhythm Superwash in
color RS72

*Entrée
to
Entrelac*

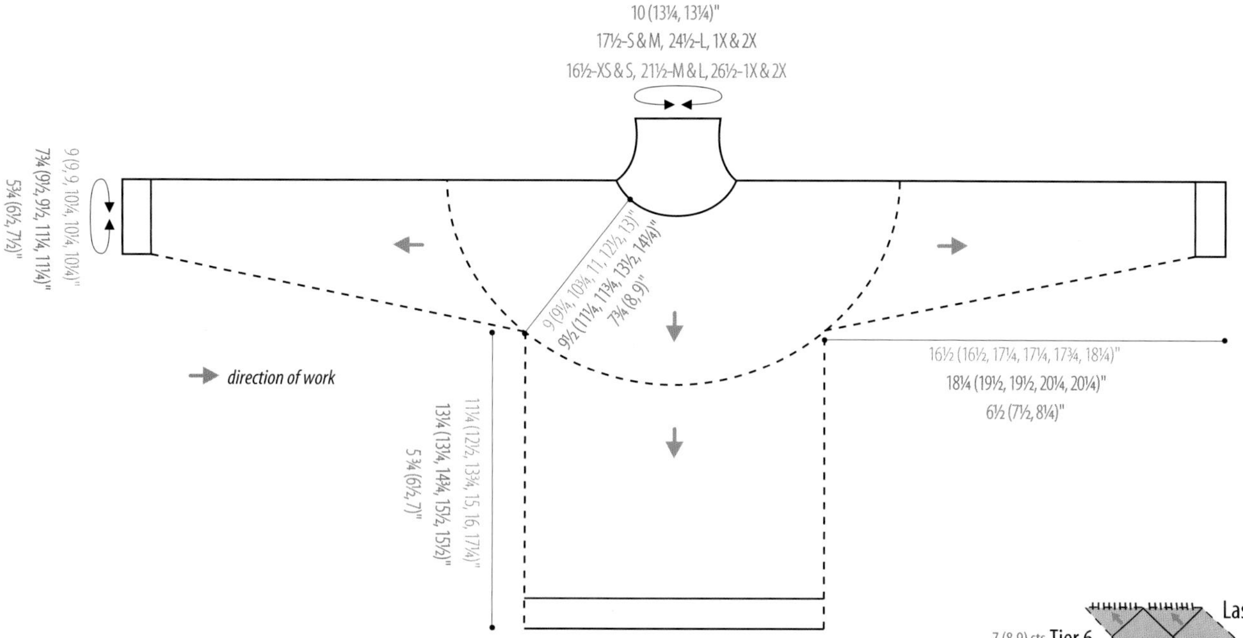
10 (13¼, 13¼)"
17½-S & M, 24½-L, 1X & 2X
16½-XS & S, 21½-M & L, 26½-1X & 2X
9 (9, 9, 10¼, 10¼, 10¼)"
7¾ (9½, 9½, 11¼, 11¼)"
5¾ (6½, 7½)"
9 (9¼, 10¾, 11, 12½, 13)"
9½ (11¼, 11¾, 13½, 14¼)"
7¾ (8, 9)"
direction of work
16½ (16½, 17¼, 17¼, 17¾, 18¼)"
18¼ (19½, 19½, 20¼, 20¼)"
6½ (7½, 8¼)"
11¼ (12½, 13¾, 15, 16, 17¼)"
13¼ (13¾, 14¾, 15½, 15½)"
5¾ (6½, 7)"
32½ (35¾, 39, 42½, 46, 49½)"
36½ (41½, 46½, 51¼, 56)"
23 (25¾, 28¾)"

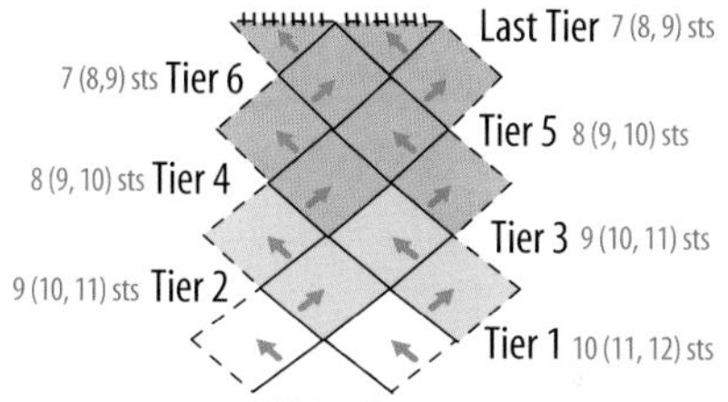
Last Tier 7 (8, 9) sts
7 (8, 9) sts Tier 6
Tier 5 8 (9, 10) sts
8 (9, 10) sts Tier 4
Tier 3 9 (10, 11) sts
9 (10, 11) sts Tier 2
Tier 1 10 (11, 12) sts

Child's Sleeve
3 Units each tier

Chart note *If sleeve ends on a RR tier, complete with LTTs; if sleeve ends on a LR tier, complete with RTTs.*

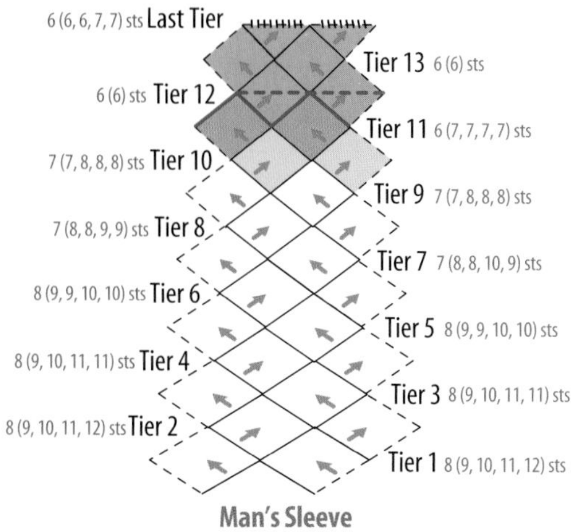
6 (6, 6, 7, 7) sts Last Tier
Tier 13 6 (6) sts
6 (6) sts Tier 12
Tier 11 6 (7, 7, 7, 7) sts
7 (7, 8, 8, 8) sts Tier 10
Tier 9 7 (7, 8, 8, 8) sts
7 (8, 8, 9, 9) sts Tier 8
Tier 7 7 (8, 8, 10, 9) sts
8 (9, 9, 10, 10) sts Tier 6
Tier 5 8 (9, 9, 10, 10) sts
8 (9, 10, 11, 11) sts Tier 4
Tier 3 8 (9, 10, 11, 11) sts
8 (9, 10, 11, 12) sts Tier 2
Tier 1 8 (9, 10, 11, 12) sts

Man's Sleeve
5 Units each tier

L (1X, 2X) Work Tiers 1-11, then Last Tier

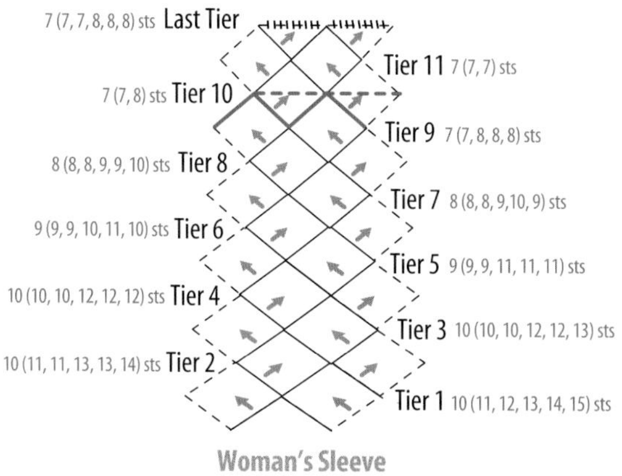
7 (7, 7, 8, 8, 8) sts Last Tier
Tier 11 7 (7, 7) sts
7 (7, 8) sts Tier 10
Tier 9 7 (7, 8, 8, 8) sts
8 (8, 8, 9, 9, 10) sts Tier 8
Tier 7 8 (8, 8, 9, 10, 9) sts
9 (9, 9, 10, 11, 10) sts Tier 6
Tier 5 9 (9, 9, 11, 11, 11) sts
10 (10, 10, 12, 12, 12) sts Tier 4
Tier 3 10 (10, 10, 12, 12, 13) sts
10 (11, 11, 13, 13, 14) sts Tier 2
Tier 1 10 (11, 12, 13, 14, 15) sts

Woman's Sleeve
4 Units each tier

L (1X, 2X) Work Tiers 1-9, then Last Tier

Child's size 4 shown in SKACEL-
SCHULANA Merino Cotton135 2
balls in color 21 (A), 1 ball in color
31 (B), 2 balls in color 15 (C)

Body

Man's Work 14 units each tier with 8 (9, 10, 11, 12) Base stitches.
Woman's Work 10 units each tier with 10 (11, 12, 13, 14, 15) Base stitches.
Child's Work 10 units each tier with 10 (11, 12) Base stitches.

Remove waste yarn from temporary cast-on of 1 underarm gusset and place base stitches onto needle holding body stitches. Slip next 6 (4, 4) units to reach second underarm. Remove waste yarn from second gusset and place Base Stitches onto needle holding body stitches — Base stitches × 14 (10, 10) units.

Body can be worked to any length desired. If body ends on a RR tier, complete with LTTs; if body ends on a LR tier, complete with RTTs.

Work 14 (10, 10) units in base stitches each tier as follows:

Man's

Tier 1 With A, work base stitches LR. **Tier 2** With A, work RR. Repeat last 2 tiers through Tier 6 (5, 5, 5, 4). Change colors for next 3 tiers: first tier D, second tier C, and third tier B. **Last Tier** With B, work Live LTT (RTT, RTT, RTT, LTT). **Next round** [K2, yo] around. Work in k1, p1 rib for 1½", working into back of yarn-overs on first round. Bind off in pattern.

Woman's

Tier 1 Work base stitches LR. **Tier 2** Work RR. Repeat last 2 tiers 2 times. Work Tier 1 once more. **Tier 8** Work Live RTT. **Next round** [K2, yo] around. Purl 6 rounds, working into back of yarn-overs on first round. Bind off in purl.

Child's

Tier 1 With A, work base stitches LR. **Tier 2** With B, work RR around. **Tier 3** Work LR around. **Tier 4** With C, work RR around. **Tier 5** Work LR around. Repeat last 2 tiers as necessary. **Last tier** Work Live RTT around. **Next round** [K2, yo] around. Work in k1, p1 rib for 10 rounds, working into back of yarn overs on first round. Bind off in pattern.

Diamond yoke jacket

While shopping, I noticed a Western-style jacket with a diamond-shaped yoke. Immediately the possibility of creating one in entrelac entered my mind. Although the original version presented many challenges, including not having enough of a long-since, discontinued yarn, the result was stellar! I have worn the jacket often receiving many compliments, from knitters, from friends, but most often and most refreshing, from an admiring stranger. Note: Once the yoke is complete, the remainder of the garment is constructed using mitered fabric.

stitches

INC 1 IN PATTERN If next stitch should be knit, increase by k&p into it; if next stitch should be purled, increase by p&k into it.

DEC 1 IN PATTERN
RS rows If next stitch should be knit, SSK; if next stitch should be purled, SSP.
WS rows If next stitch should be.knit, k2tog; if next stitch should be.purled, p2tog.

TINY TWILL
OVER A MULTIPLE OF 3 PLUS 2 STITCHES
Row 1 and all RS rows Purl.
Row 2 (WS) P1, [p1, sl2 wyib] to last stitch, p1.
Row 4 P1, [sl2 wyib, p1] to last stitch, p1.
Row 6 P1, [sl1 wyib, p1, sl1 wyib] to last stitch, p1.

notes

◆ *See page 152 for any unfamiliar techniques.*

◆ *Entrelac yoke is worked from center back up to neck and over shoulders; then down right and left fronts. Stitches are picked up around yoke and worked down for body and sleeves.*

◆ *For entrelac yoke use long-tail cast-on for first unit of tier. Cast-on at beginning of tier counts as Row 1, begin first unit with Row 2.*

◆ *Once the yoke is complete, the remainder of the garment is constructed using mitered fabric.*

Diamond yoke jacket

Yoke

Work all right-leaning tiers in A and left-leaning tiers in B.

1 **Tier 1** With size 4.5mm/US 7 needle, cast on 4. Beginning with a WS row, work 8 rows stockinette stitch. *For first unit of each tier through Tier 17 (17, 21, 21, 25, 25), cast on stitches and begin with Row 2.* **Tier 2** Work RR, Unjoined RR. **Tier 3** Work 2 LR, Unjoined LR. **Tier 4** Work 3 RR, Unjoined RR. **Tier 5** Work 4 LR, Unjoined LR. Repeat last 2 tiers, adding 1 unit each tier through Tier 15 (15, 20, 20, 23, 23).

XS AND S (1X AND 2X) *Divide for fronts* **Tier 16 (24)** Work 6 (9) RR, Unjoined RR for left shoulder, 4 (6) Bo RTT for back neck, 5 (8) RR, Unjoined RR for right shoulder. *Continue for Right Front* **Tier 17 (25)** Cast on 4, work 6 (9) LR; work LET. Follow schematic for your size through Tier 33 (49), then continue for Left Front.

M AND L ONLY **Tier 21** Work 8 LR for right shoulder, 5 Bo LTT for back neck; work 7 LR, Unjoined LR for left shoulder, binding off last unit. *Continue for Left Front* **Tier 22** Work 7 RR, RET. Follow schematic for your size through Tier 41, then continue for Right Front.

MOUNTAIN COLORS 4/8's Wool in color Blue/Green (A) and Mohair in Mountain Tango (B)

the
UNITS
Base number
4 stitches

LST

LR

LET

bo LTT

unjoined LR

unjoined RR

Entrée
to
Entrelac

Experienced

Loose Fit

XS (S, M, L, 1X, 2X)
A 34 (38, 42, 46, 50, 54)"
B 20½ (21, 21, 22, 23, 25½)"
C 25 (26, 26½, 27½, 28, 29)"

10cm/4"
54
24
over Tiny Twill using largest needle

 1 2 3 4 5 6
Medium weight
A 1225 (1400, 1500, 1650, 1775, 2100) yds
B 150 (150, 225, 225, 325, 325) yds

5mm/US 8, or size to obtain gauge
4.5mm/US 7
4mm/US 6
all 80cm (32") or longer

 markers
11 buttons

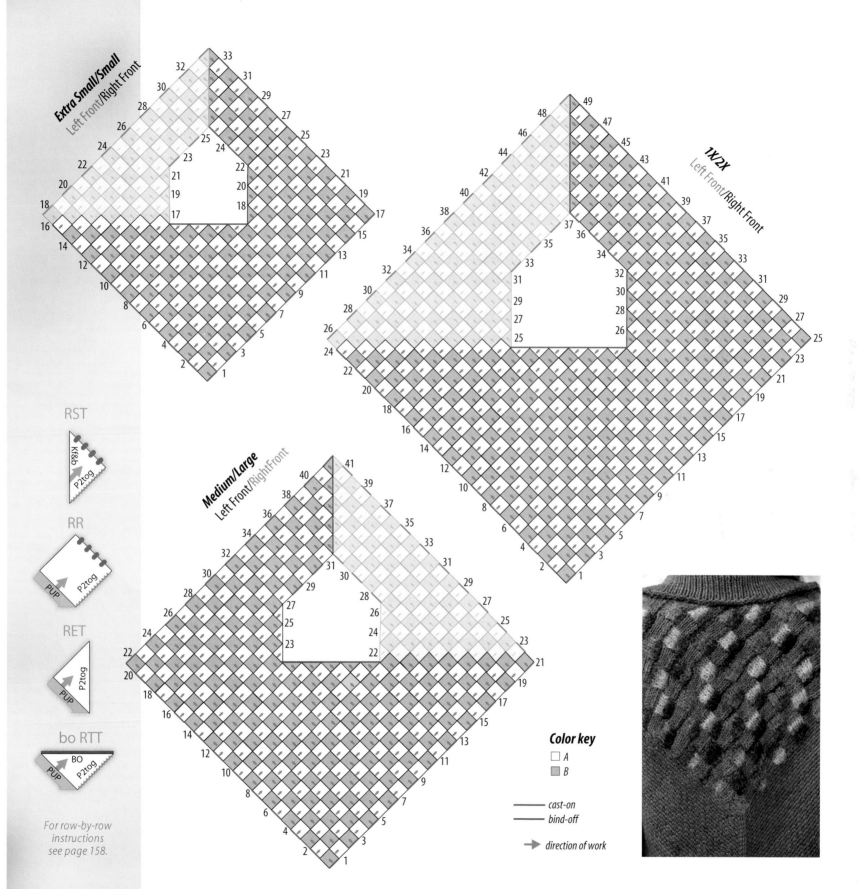

Extra Small/Small
Left Front/Right Front

1X/2X
Left Front/Right Front

Medium/Large
Left Front/RightFront

RST

Kf&b

P2tog

RR

PUP

P2tog

RET

PUP

P2tog

bo RTT

PUP

BO

P2tog

*For row-by-row
instructions
see page 158.*

Color key

☐ A
▨ B

──── cast-on
──── bind-off

➜ direction of work

71

Body

2 *Pick up stitches* With A, largest needle, and beginning at Yoke Left Front, PUK1, [pm, PUK90 (90, 111, 111, 132, 132) along side of diamond, pm, PUK1 in corner] 4 times — 365 (365, 449, 449, 533, 533) stitches.

3 *Begin Chart A* Work Tiny Twill pattern increasing every other row as shown in Chart A, until 142 (154, 165, 183, 198, 216) stitches between markers, end on RS row — 573 (621, 665, 737, 797, 869) stitches. *Every 6-row repeat begins and ends the same; the only difference is the number of 3-stitch repeats worked. Every 6 rows, 24 stitches are increased by adding 8 additional repeats.*

4 *Divide for Body and Sleeves* Work Tiny Twill pattern as established. **Next row** (WS) P1, sm, work 72 (81, 90, 96, 105, 111) stitches; place next 141 (147, 151, 175, 187, 211) stitches and markers on hold for Right Sleeve. Pm, cast on 1 for underarm, work 72 (81, 90, 96, 105, 111) stitches, sm, p1, remove marker, work 72 (81, 90, 96, 105, 111) stitches for back. Place next 141 (147, 151, 175, 187, 211) stitches & markers on hold for Left Sleeve, pm, cast on 1 for underarm, work 72 (81, 90, 96, 105, 111) stitches, sm, p1 — 293 (329, 365, 389, 425, 449) stitches for Body.

Begin Body Chart B Work 6 row repeat of Chart B — 11 (8, 5, 0, 0) times.

5 **Begin Body Chart C** With RS row, work pf&b in center back stitch — 294 (330, 366, 390, 426, 450) stitches. Place stitches for right half of Body on hold — 147 (165, 183, 195, 213, 225) stitches. Follow Chart C until 3 stitches remain. Bind off. Join yarn, repeat for other half of Body.

Sleeves

Place 141 (147, 151, 175, 187, 211) held Sleeve stitches on needle. **Next row** (WS) Cast on 1 stitch, pm, work 70, sm, work 1, remove marker, work 70, pm, cast on 1 stitch.

6 **Begin Sleeve Chart B** Work Chart B and dec 1 stitch after first and before last marker 5 (5, 5, 6, 6, 6) out of every 6 rows to 81 (91, 97, 101, 121, 159) stitches. **Next row** (WS) Work in pattern to center stitch, pf&b, work to end — 82 (92, 98, 102, 122, 160) stitches. Sleeve length is complete; place half of sleeve stitches on hold.

7 **Begin Sleeve Chart C** Continuing in established pattern; dec 1 at underarm 9 (10, 10, 10, 12, 12) out of every 12 rows AND dec 1 at cuff every other row until 3 stitches remain; bind off. Repeat for other half of sleeve cuff.

Front bands & collar

With smallest needle, RS facing, A, and beginning at bottom of Right Front, PUK1 for every 2 rows of pattern, 6 along each triangle, and 4 along each rectangle to bottom of Left Front. Cut yarn. **Left Front Band** Cast on 7. Begin at bottom edge of Left Front. **Row 1** (WS) [P1, k1] 3 times, p2tog to join (last stitch with picked-up stitch). **Row 2** (RS) [K1, p1] 3 times, k1. Repeat last 2 rows to V of entrelac

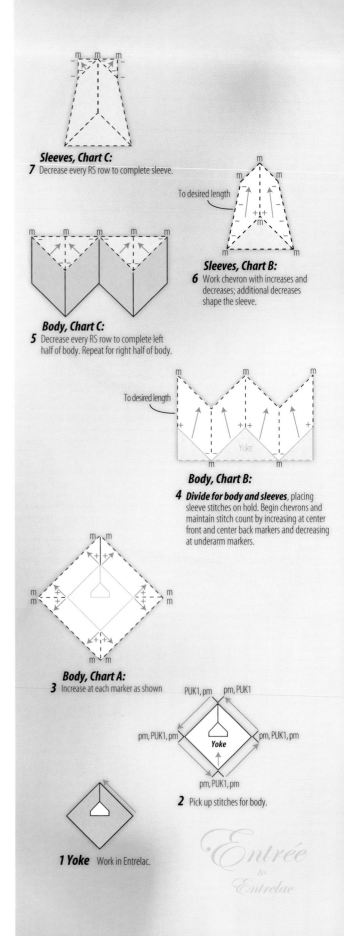

Sleeves, Chart C:
7 Decrease every RS row to complete sleeve.

To desired length

Sleeves, Chart B:
6 Work chevron with increases and decreases; additional decreases shape the sleeve.

Body, Chart C:
5 Decrease every RS row to complete left half of body. Repeat for right half of body.

To desired length

Yoke

Body, Chart B:
4 **Divide for body and sleeves**, placing sleeve stitches on hold. Begin chevrons and maintain stitch count by increasing at center front and center back markers and decreasing at underarm markers.

Body, Chart A:
3 Increase at each marker as shown

PUK1, pm   pm, PUK1

pm, PUK1, pm   Yoke   pm, PUK1, pm

pm, PUK1, pm

2 Pick up stitches for body.

1 Yoke Work in Entrelac.

Entrée to Entrelac

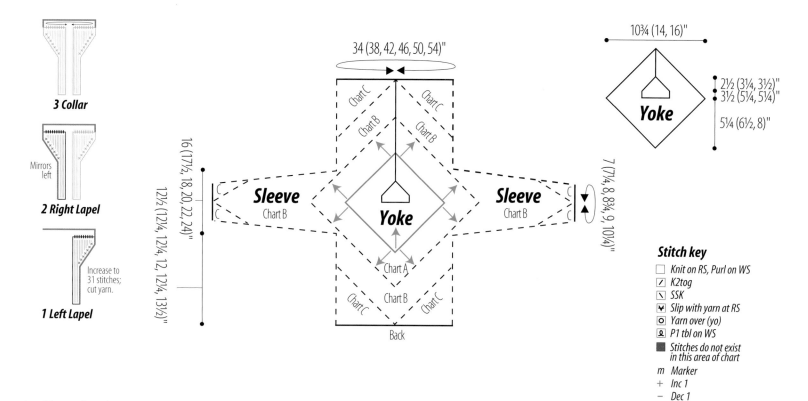

3 Collar

2 Right Lapel
Mirrors left

1 Left Lapel
Increase to 31 stitches; cut yarn.

34 (38, 42, 46, 50, 54)"

16 (17½, 18, 20, 22, 24)"

12½ (12¼, 12¼, 12, 12¼, 13½)"

Chart C   Chart C
Chart B   Chart B

Sleeve Chart B   **Sleeve** Chart B

Yoke

Chart A

Chart B   Chart B
Chart C   Chart C

Back

7 (7¼, 8, 8¾, 9, 10¼)"

10¾ (14, 16)"

2½ (3¼, 3½)"
3½ (5¼, 5¼)"
5¼ (6½, 8)"

Yoke

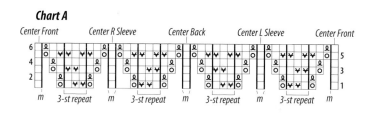

Stitch key
- ☐ Knit on RS, Purl on WS
- ☑ K2tog
- ☒ SSK
- ☒ Slip with yarn at RS
- ⊙ Yarn over (yo)
- Ⓠ P1 tbl on WS
- ▧ Stitches do not exist in this area of chart
- m Marker
- + Inc 1
- − Dec 1

yoke. *Shape lapel* Continue working rib and joining every other row, AT SAME TIME, inc 1 in first stitch every RS row and continue in established pattern to 23 (23, 27, 27, 31, 31) stitches. Cut yarn. *You are not yet at shoulder seam.* **Right Front Band** Cast on 7. Begin at bottom edge of Right Front. **Row 1** (RS) [K1, p1] 3 times, SSK to join. **Row 2** (WS) [P1, k1] 3 times, p1. Repeat last 2 rows, working eyelet buttonhole in 4th stitch on Row 5, and every 16th row to V of entrelac yoke. Working in established pattern and continuing to work buttonholes every 16 rows, inc 1 in first stitch of every WS row to 23 (23, 27, 27, 31, 31) stitches. On next RS row, work across Right Front Band, remaining picked-up stitches of right front, back neck, left front, and Left Front Band. Work in rib for 3½". Change to next largest needle, work 2" more. Change to largest needle, work 4 rows, bind off in pattern.

Seam underarms. Attach buttons to correspond to buttonholes.

Chart A

Center Front | Center R Sleeve | Center Back | Center L Sleeve | Center Front

m   3-st repeat   m   3-st repeat   m   3-st repeat   m   3-st repeat   m

Chart B

Body

Sleeve

R. Underarm (center sleeve)   L. Underarm (center sleeve)

m   3-st repeat   m   3-st repeat   m   3-st repeat   m   3-st repeat   m

Center Front   Center Back   Center Front

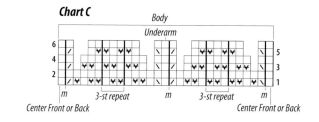

Chart C

Body

Underarm

m   3-st repeat   m   3-st repeat   m

Center Front or Back   Center Front or Back

Intriguing construction

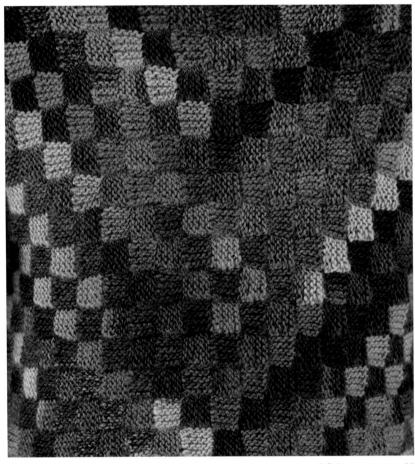

Sometimes creating a well-fitting garment isn't enough. Add the challenge to combine a garment shape with interesting patternwork in entrelac. One challenge leads me to a solution which takes me to another challenge and so on.

Arlis' sweater page 95

74

Quilted pocket bag
page 89

Building from any direction

Solving the 'ugly seam' problem, led to considering other options for attractive seams and joins. Temporary cast-ons (also known as provisional or invisible cast-ons) are a useful tool for knitters, allowing the knitting to continue in the opposite direction. In entrelac, the temporary cast-on allows the knitting to be worked in any number of directions. The waste yarn used for the cast-on can be removed, resulting in live stitches ready to be worked.

Consider the bottom of a purse or back pack. If a piece was started with waste yarn and rectangles in lieu of triangles, the rectangle could be folded in half to visually produce two triangles, front and back. The following tier would be worked circularly using the live stitches for half the units and the stitches from the temporary cast-on for the other half of the units.

If the yoke of a sweater is constructed with rectangles at the armhole edge, it is possible to continue the entrelac down the sleeve without any interruption in the fabric. All that is required are temporary cast-on rectangles along one edge and live stitches left on the other edge. An example of this construction is used in the Evening sweater (page 84). The result is a fitted garment that is truly seamless, a feat nearly impossible to accomplish in any technique.

Envelope clutch page 82

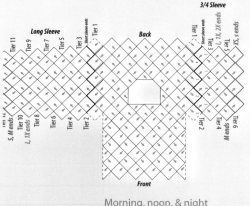

Morning, noon, & night
page 84

Entrée
to
Entrelac

Joining multiple layers

The next seaming challenge arose when I wanted to integrate a pocket into entrelac fabric. The zigzag method was always an option, but I wanted a more elegant solution. As is often the case when I have a construction problem to solve, I turned to paper diagrams. By laying the paper pocket over the garment diagram, the solution became obvious. At the points where stitches were picked up for the following tier, it was possible to pick up stitches through both layers of fabric. A similar solution also worked for the point of joining live stitches. Instead of using a 2-stitch decrease, use a 3-stitch decrease — 1 stitch from the current unit, 1 stitch from the pocket joining unit, and 1 stitch from the garment joining unit. The Quilted pocket bag (page 89) uses a temporary cast-on and multiple layer joins to attach the pocket.

Creating gussets and other shapes

Gussets are created when fabric is added or subtracted to form a particular shape. A simple example is at the point a mitten or glove becomes wider for the thumb. Doing this in entrelac requires adding or removing units mid-tier.

For an increasing gusset, add a unit within a tier. To do this, first work an unjoined rectangle. For the next unit, pick up stitches along the unjoined unit's selvedge and work in the traditional fashion, joining with the next unit from the previous tier.

For a decreasing gusset, work 2 units together; this eliminates a unit for the next tier. A decreasing gusset is created with a double-join rectangle with joins on every row. Odd-numbered rows join 1 stitch of the current unit and 1 stitch from the unit just completed in the same tier. This eliminates one set of live stitches and a pick-up selvedge that normally would be available on the following tier.

Practical application of both adding and subtracting units can be seen in the Felted entrelac mittens (page 80), worked from finger tip to wrist. Adding units within the tier shapes the mitten tip. Subtracting a unit within the tier joins the thumb and shapes the gusset.

3-D objects

By using the above techniques, it is possible to create all sorts of interesting 3-dimensional objects. For example, a cube is just 6 squares joined together. A pyramid is four joined triangles atop a square base. The trick to creating these shapes is determining where to start and in which order to build the shapes.

Other applications

The double-join rectangle can also be used to join pieces of entrelac together. In Arlis' sweater the fronts are constructed outward from the side corner toward the band. With the long-repeat yarn that is used, this creates distinctive chevron lines. To replicate the pattern on the back, it was necessary to join 2 corners at the center back. The double-join rectangles creates a continuous chevron shape without having to break the yarn or seam 2 pieces together.

By combining many of the techniques in this section, it is possible to create a wide range of projects in all shapes. Here are a few to get your creative juices flowing.

Arlis' sweater and vest page 95

Base number
6 stitches

The chevron shape is created by building the bottom corners of entrelac, then joining them at the center with a Double-join rectangle. The yarn color changes mid-tier to emphasize the chevron shape..

Icon key

live stitches

| PUP |

pick up and purl stitches in direction of arrow

| PUK |

pick up and knit stitches in direction of arrow

joined edge

direction of work

LR Left-leaning Rectangle

With RS facing, pick up and knit 6 stitches along edge of unit in previous tier (PUK6).
Row 1 (WS) P6.
Row 2 (RS) K5, SSK to join (last stitch of unit with stitch from previous tier).
Repeat last 2 rows until all 6 stitches from previous tier have been joined — 6 stitches.

RR Right-leaning Rectangle

With WS facing, pick up and purl 6 stitches along edge of unit in previous tier (PUP6).
Row 1 (RS) K6.
Row 2 (WS) P5, p2tog to join (last stitch of unit with stitch from previous tier).
Repeat last 2 rows until all 6 stitches from previous tier have been joined — 6 stitches.

LR Double-join Rectangle

PUK6 along edge of unit in previous tier.
Row 1 (WS) P5, p2tog to join (last stitch with stitch from right corner).
Row 2 (RS) K5, SSK to join (last stitch with stitch from left corner).
Repeat last 2 rows until all 6 stitches from each corner unit have been joined—6 stitches.

RR Double-join Rectangle

PUP6 along edge of unit in previous tier.
Row 1 (RS) K5, SSK to join (last stitch with stitch from left corner).
Row 2 (WS) P5, p2tog (last stitch with stitch from right corner).
Repeat last 2 rows until all 6 stitches from each corner unit have been joined—6 stitches.

LR Unjoined Rectangle

Work same as LR EXCEPT Row 2 (RS). K6. Repeat last 2 rows until unit has twice as many rows as base stitches.

RR Unjoined Rectangle

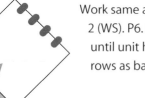

Work same as RR EXCEPT Row 2 (WS). P6. Repeat last 2 rows until unit has twice as many rows as base stitches.

notes

◆ *See page 16 for vitals for practice blocks; see page 152 for any unfamiliar techniques.*

◆ *Cut yarn at end of each tier.*

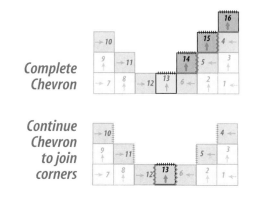

Complete Chevron

Continue Chevron to join corners

Tier 7

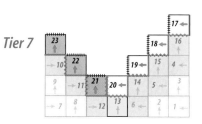

Chevron

Right corner

Begin Chevron Tier 6

Complete Tier 5

Begin Tier 5

Tier 4

Begin Left Corner

Tier 3

Continue Tier 2

Begin Tier 2

Tier 1

Begin Right Corner

Tier 1, Unit 1 With A, cast on 6. Beginning and ending with a RS row, work 11 rows of stockinette stitch (St st).

For Tiers 2–10, for first unit, cast stitches onto needle, holding stitches from previous tier and begin with Row 2.

For last unit, PUP6 on even-numbered tiers or PUK6 on odd-numbered tiers, then work 12 rows St st.

Tier 2, Units 2 & 3 With A, work RR. PUP6 along Unit 1. Work Unjoined RR. *Tier 3, Units 4-6* With B, work 2 LR, work Unjoined LR. Place stitches on hold.

Left corner

Tier 4, Unit 7 With A, cast on 6. Beginning and ending with a WS row, work 11 rows of St st.

Tier 5, Units 8 & 9 With A, work LR, work Unjoined LR.

Begin chevron Tier 6, Units 10-16 With B, work 2 RR, work Unjoined RR, work Double RR joining to Unit 6 on WS rows and Unit 12 on RS rows, work 2 RR, work Unjoined RR. *Tier 7* With A, work 4 LR. With B, work Double LR joining Unit 17 to Unit 20, as before; work LR, work Unjoined LR. *Tier 8* With A, repeat Tier 6 joining Unit 26 to Unit 19, as before. *Tier 9* With B, repeat Tier 7 joining units, as before.

For Tiers 10–12, bind off all stitches on last row of last unit.

Tier 10 Repeat Tier 6 joining units, as before, but eliminating last Unjoined RR. *Tier 11* With A, work 2 LR. With B, work Double LR, work LR. *Tier 12* With A, work RR, work Double RR.

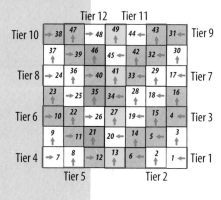

Color key

☐	☐	A
☐	☐	B
☐	☐	Double-join RR
☐	☐	Double-join LR
existing	active	

79

A family of mittens

The evolution from the cell phone case, on page 51, to a mitten with gusset thumb proves that big things come from small packages.

Note that the pre-felting and post-felting sizes are relatively close. The fabric is worked close to standard gauge and felting is meant to add density. For a finished mitten a bit larger, felt less vigorously or eliminate the felting all together.

notes

◆ *See page 152 for any unfamiliar techniques.*

◆ *Mittens are worked in seamless entrelac from tips down. Cut yarn after each tier.*

Thumb

TOP RECTANGLE **a** With waste yarn, dpn, and using temporary crochet cast-on, cast on base number of stitches (Base Stitches). With B and beginning with a WS row, work 1 Unjoined RR (Unit 1).

Tier 1 **b** Working each unit with a new dpn and A: PUK along right side of Unit 1, work LR joining to live stitches from Unit 1. Remove waste yarn from unit 1 and place Base Stitches on new dpn; PUK along left side of Unit 1; work LR, joining to cast-on stitches from Unit 1.

Tier 2 **c** With B, work 2 RR. Place stitches on hold.

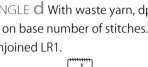

Mitten

TOP RECTANGLE **d** With waste yarn, dpn, and using temporary crochet cast-on, cast on base number of stitches. With A and beginning with a RS row, work Unjoined LR1.

Tier 1 **e** Working each unit with a new dpn, and B: PUP along left side of LR1, work Unjoined RR2. PUP along right side of RR2, work RR3 joinig to live stitches from LR1. PUP base stitches along right side of LR1, work Unjoined RR4. PUP along right side of RR4; remove waste yarn from LR1 and place base stitches on new dpn; work RR5 joining tocast-on stitches from LR1.

the UNITS

Base number
5 (6, 7, 8, 9) stitches

LR
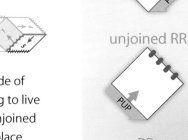

bo LTT

dbl join LR

unjoined LR

unjoined RR

RR

For row-by-row instructions, see page 158.

Entrée à Entrelac

Experienced	10cm/4"			&
S (M, L, XL, XXL)	34	1 **2** 3 4 5 6	3.75mm/US 5, or size to obtain gauge, 40cm (16") (optional)	waste yarn & crochet hook
7 (9, 11, 12¼, 14)" around hand before felting 6½ (8¼, 9, 9¾, 11)" around hand after felting	**24** over stockinette stitch before felting	**Fine weight** A 90 (135, 200, 235, 250) yds B 75 (100, 145, 165, 195) yds	3.75mm/US 5	steel crochet hook (for cuff pick-up)

BROWN SHEEP COMPANY Lanaloft Sport: Small in colors LL92 (A) and LL33 (B); Medium LL93S (A & B); 2X LL100 (A) and LL36 (B)

LR along edge of unit in previous tier, work LR] twice. Change to circular needle if desired. *Tier 3* With B, work 6 RR.

Tier 4 With A, work 6 LR.

Tier 5 With B, work 6 RR.

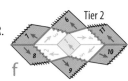

Tier 2

Join Thumb g *Tier 6* With A, work 2 LR on Mitten. *Join Thumb with attached yarn* PUK base stitches along Thumb RR. Place held stitches of adjoining RR on dpn. Work Dbl-join LR.

h Continuing on Thumb, place remaining held stitches on dpn and work LR. *Join mitten with attached yarn* PUK base stitches along Mitten RR. Work Dbl-join LR. Work 3 LR — 6 units on needles *Tier 7* With B, work 6 RR. *Tier 8* (Gusset) With A, work LR. Work Dbl-join LR. Work 4 LR — 25 (30, 35, 40, 45) stitches total. *Tier 9* With B, work 5 RR.

Short Wrist *Tier 10* With A, work 5 BO LTT.

Long Wrist *Tier 10* With A, work 5 LR. *Tier 11* With B, work 5 RR. *Tier 12* With A, work 5 BO LTT.

Finishing

Felt mittens and then add cuffs.

Cuff With A, PUK34 (40, 46, 54, 60) around cuff of mitten. Work in k1, p1 rib for 12 (15, 15, 17, 17) rows or to desired length; bind off in pattern.

Color key
☐ A
▨ B

→ direction of work
᠁᠁᠁ live stitches
——— picked-up stitches
∿∿∿ joined edge
——— temporary cast-on

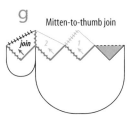

g Mitten-to-thumb join

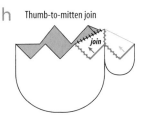

h Thumb-to-mitten join

81

Envelope clutch

This seamless design starts with a row of temporarily cast-on rectangles that are then folded and the waste yarn removed to create the base for Tier 2. A bank bag provides a simple lining. Completely elegant, but totally secure.

stitches

WORK UNIT WITH BIND-OFF
Bind off stitches on last row of unit.

notes

◆ *See page 152 for any unfamiliar techniques.*

◆ *Bag is started at the bottom, worked seamlessly to the flap, then worked flat.*

◆ *Green lines indicate rectangle is started by casting on 8 stitches. Blue lines indicate all stitches are bound off in pattern.*

Bag body

Tier 1, base rectangles [With waste yarn and temporary crochet cast-on, cast on 8. With A, work Unjoined LR] 5 times — 40 stitches, 5 rectangles.

Main bag Tier 2 With WS facing and B, slip live stitches from last rectangle to right needle and PUP8 along its selvedge. Work 4 RR. PUP8 and remove waste yarn from Rectangle 1, placing stitches on left needle. Work RR, joining to stitches from temporary cast-on. Removing waste yarn and joining to stitches from temporary cast-ons, work 4 RR along bottom of Tier 1 rectangles, PUP8 along remaining selvedge of rectangle 1. Work RR, joining to live stitches from rectangle — 80 stitches, 10 RR. **Tier 3** With C, work 10 LR. **Tier 4** With A, work 10 RR. **Tier 5** With B, work 10 LR. **Tier 6** With C, work 10 RR. **Tier 7** With A, work 5 BO LTT, 5 LR — 40 stitches.

Envelope flap Tier 8 With B, work RST, 4 RR, RET. **Tier 9** With C, work 5 LR, binding off last LR — 32 stitches. **Tier 10** With A, work 4 RR, binding off last RR — 24 stitches. **Tier 11** With B, work 3 LR, binding off last LR — 16 stitches. **Tier 12** With C, work 2 BO RTT.

Finishing

String approximately 100 beads onto yarn A. Work a row of half double crochet around edge of flap and bag opening, sliding 1 bead next to every stitch along flap edge. Slip bank bag inside of entrelac envelope. With matching carpet thread side, hand stitch bound-off edge to edge of zipper tape, and tack side corners of each Tier 7 LR along opposite zipper tape.

Wrist loop If desired, work a twisted cord with all 3 yarns used in the project. Knot to desired length and sew to inside of bank bag, just below the zipper.

For row-by-row instructions see page 158

Glow indicates a modified unit.

Intermediate
11" x 6"

40
20
over stockinette stitch

1 2 3 **4** 5 6
Medium weight
A 125 yds
B 100 yds
C 75 yds

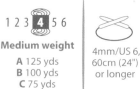
4mm/US 6, 60cm (24") or longer

4mm/US G, or same size as the needle size used to obtain gauge

100 #6 seed beads
needle
carpet thread
zippered bank bag
waste yarn

82

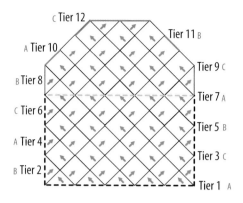

3D view of Tiers 1 and 2.

Rotate work and complete Tier 2: Work LR 11–14, then work LR15, joining to live stitches from RR5.

Begin Tier 2 Work RR 6–9, then work RR 10, joining to stitches from temporary cast-on.

Tier 1 Work 5 base rectangles with temporary cast-ons.

BERROCO Ultra Alpaca Light in color 4201 (A), Bonsai in color 4134 (B), and Pure Pima in color 2201 (C).

〰〰〰 *live stitches*
———— *temporary cast-on*
———— *bind-off*
———— *picked-up stitches*
〰〰〰 *joined edge*

➡ *direction of work*

83

Morning, noon, & night

Simplicity times three! The yoke of this trio begins with provisionally cast-on rectangles and angled edges to form the neckline. Then work seamless entrelac as you add the sleeves and lower body.

INC 1 Yarn over and work through back of stitch on next row.

notes

◆ *See page 152 for any unfamiliar techniques.*

◆ *If using one yarn, ignore references to B; work A throughout.*

◆ *Work all cast-ons with waste yarn and using temporary crochet cast-on.*

◆ *Leave knots of Neat Stuff on the wrong side, or trim and weave in ends as you go. Occasionally add some of Frost, using 1–1½ skeins.*

◆ *Vital information is color-coded as follows:* **Long sleeve,** *Three-quarter length sleeve,* **Short sleeve,** *All versions*

Yoke

Tier 1 [Cast on Base number of stitches. With A, work 1 Unjoined LR] 5 times. ***Tier 2*** Cast on Base stitches. With A, work 2 RR, 2 Bo RTT, RR; work 1 Unjoined RR, placing last row on hold; cut yarn. *Continue Left Shoulder* ***Tier 3*** With A, work 1 LR, LET. ***Tier 4*** Work RR; work 1 Unjoined RR, placing last row on hold; cut yarn. *Continue Right Shoulder* ***Tier 3*** With A, work LST, 1 LR.

Tier 4 Cast on Base stitches. With A, work 2 RR. *Re-join Yoke* ***Tier 5*** With A, work 1 LR, 1 Unjoined LR, 1 Inc LBT; cast on Base stitches; work 2 LR, each joining with Tier 4 of right shoulder. ***Tier 6*** Cast on Base stitches. With A, work 5 RR, 1 Unjoined RR; cut yarn. ***Tier 7*** With A, work 5 LR. ***Tier 8*** Repeat Tier 6. ***Tier 9*** With A, work 5 LR and place stitches on hold —Base stitches × 5.

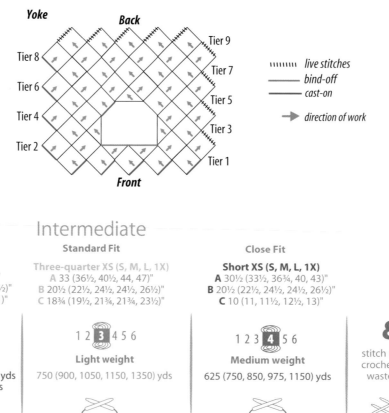

Legend:
- ⁝⁝⁝⁝⁝⁝ *live stitches*
- ——— *bind-off*
- ——— *cast-on*
- → *direction of work*

the
UNITS

Base number
9 (10, 11, 12, 13) stitches
10 (11, 12, 13, 14) stitches
10 (11, 12, 13, 14) stitches

inc LBT

Kf&b

LST

Pf&b
SSK

LET

SSK
PUK

LR

SSK
PUK

unjoined LR

PUK

Intermediate

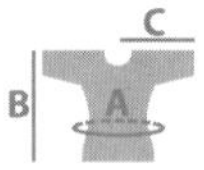

	Standard Fit **Long S (M, L, 1X, 2X)**	**Standard Fit** **Three-quarter XS (S, M, L, 1X)**	**Close Fit** **Short XS (S, M, L, 1X)**	
	**A** 33 (36½, 40½, 44, 47)" **B** 20½ (22½, 24½, 24½, 26½)" **C** 27½ (28½, 28½, 29½, 31)"	**A** 33 (36½, 40½, 44, 47)" **B** 20½ (22½, 24½, 24½, 26½)" **C** 18¾ (19½, 21¾, 21¾, 23½)"	**A** 30½ (33½, 36¾, 40, 43)" **B** 20½ (22½, 24½, 24½, 26½)" **C** 10 (11, 11½, 12½, 13)"	

10cm/4"

26, 28, 34

18, 21, 19
over stockinette stitch

1 2 3 **4** 5 6

Medium weight
A 750 (900, 1050, 1150, 1350) yds
B 150 (175, 200, 225, 250) yds

5mm/US 8

1 2 **3** 4 5 6

Light weight
750 (900, 1050, 1150, 1350) yds

4.5mm/US 7
or size to obtain gauge, 60cm (24") or longer

1 2 3 **4** 5 6

Medium weight
625 (750, 850, 975, 1150) yds

3.75mm/US 5

&
stitch marker
crochet hook
waste yarn

set of 5 (same
size as circulars)

Entrée to Entrelac

84

RR

unjoined RR

bo RTT

For row-by-row instructions see page 158.

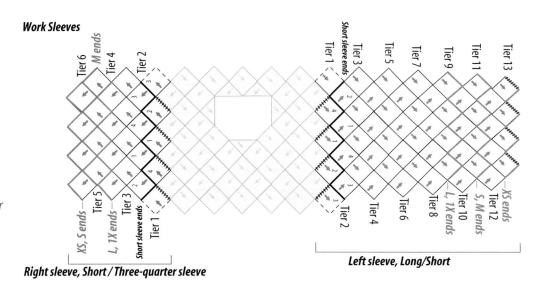

Work Sleeves

Tier 6 · M ends · Tier 4 · Tier 2

Tier 5 · Tier 4 · Tier 3 · Short sleeve ends · Tier 1

XS, S ends · L, 1X ends

Right sleeve, Short / Three-quarter sleeve

Short sleeve ends

Tier 1 · Tier 3 · Tier 5 · Tier 7 · Tier 9 · Tier 11 · Tier 13

Tier 2 · Tier 4 · Tier 6 · Tier 8 · Tier 10 · Tier 12 · L, 1X ends · S, M ends · XS ends

Left sleeve, Long/Short

Begin seamless entrelac

Work 4 units each tier for Long, Three-quarter, or Short sleeve as follows, reducing base numbers when indicated:

Long sleeve

Left sleeve Place held stitches from side of yoke onto dpns, one unit per needle — Base stitches × 4. **Tiers 1–13** With A, work 4 units each tier as follows: **Tier 1** Starting at shoulder, work RR. **Tier 2** Work LR. **Tier 3** Work 9 (9, 10, 11, 12)-stitch RR. **Tier 4** Work 8 (9, 10, 11, 11)-stitch LR. **Tier 5** Work 8 (9, 9, 10, 10)-stitch RR. **Tier 6** Work 7 (9, 9, 10, 10)-stitch LR. **Tier 7** Work 7 (8, 8, 9, 9)-stitch RR. **Tier 8** Work 6 (8, 8, 8, 8)-stitch LR. **Tier 9** Work 6 (7, 7, 7, 7)-stitch RR. LARGE & 1X ONLY With B, work border. XS (S, M) ONLY **Tier 10** Work 6 (7, 7)-stitch LR. **Tier 11** Work 5 (6, 6)-stitch RR. SMALL & MEDIUM ONLY With B, work border. XS ONLY **Tier 12** Work 5-stitch LR. **Tier 13** Work 5-stitch RR. With B, work border.

Right Sleeve Remove waste yarn from first rectangle of Tiers 2, 4, 6, and 8 and place stitches for each rectangle on a dpn — Base stitches × 4. Work same as Left Sleeve.

Short sleeve

Left and Right sleeves Work same as Long sleeve through Tier 1. Work border.

Three-quarter length sleeve

Left sleeve Place held stitches from side of yoke onto dpns, one unit per needle — Base stitches × 4. **Tier 1** Starting at the shoulder, work 10 (11, 12, 13, 14)-stitch RR. **Tier 2** Work 10 (11, 12, 13, 14)-stitch LR. **Tier 3** Repeat Tier 1. **Tier 4** Work 9 (10, 11, 12, 13)-stitch LR. LARGE, 1X ONLY Work border. XS (S, M) ONLY **Tier 5** Work 9 (10, 11)-stitch RR. MEDIUM SIZE ONLY Work border. XS, S ONLY **Tier 6** Repeat Tier 4. Work border. Bind off.

Right Sleeve Remove waste yarn from first rectangle of Tiers 2, 4, 6, and 8 and place stitches for each rectangle on a dpn — Base stitches × 4. Work same as Left sleeve.

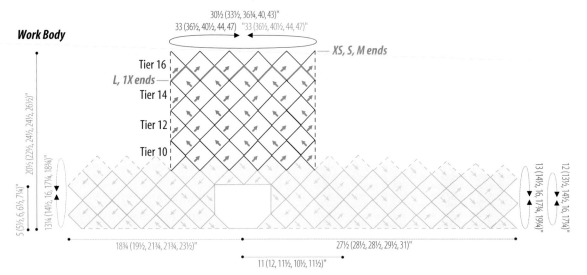

Work Body

30½ (33½, 36¾, 40, 43)"

33 (36½, 40½, 44, 47)" "33 (36½, 40½, 44, 47)"

XS, S, M ends

Tier 16

L, 1X ends

Tier 14

Tier 12

Tier 10

5 (5½, 6, 6½, 7¼)"

20½ (22½, 24½, 24½, 26½)"

13¾ (14½, 16, 17¾, 18¾)"

18¾ (19½, 21¾, 21¾, 23½)"

11 (12, 11½, 10½, 11½)"

27½ (28½, 28½, 29½, 31)"

12 (13½, 14½, 16, 17¾)"

13 (14½, 16, 17¾, 19¾)"

Entrée to Entrelac

Border

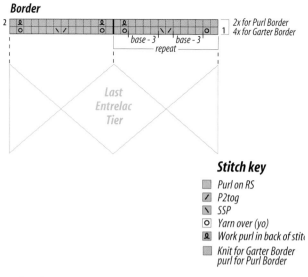

2x for Purl Border
4x for Garter Border

base - 3   base - 3

repeat

Last
Entrelac
Tier

Stitch key

- Purl on RS
- ⁄ P2tog
- ＼ SSP
- ○ Yarn over (yo)
- Work purl in back of stitch
- Knit for Garter Border
  purl for Purl Border

Body

Place held stitches from Tier 9 of Yoke onto circular needle (Back). Remove waste yarn from Tier 1 of yoke and place stitches on same needle (Front) — Base stitches × 10.

Begin seamless entrelac: **Tier 10** With A, work 10 RR. **Tier 11** Work 10 LR. Repeat Tiers 10 and 11 through Tier 16 (16, 16, 15, 15).

Borders

Base number used on last tier is Base number for border. Starting at point of unit, if last tier was RR [PUK Base stitches, knit Base stitches] around tier; if last tier was LR [knit Base stitches, PUK Base stitches] around tier, placing marker at end of round. Work either Purl or Garter border.

Purl border * P1, Inc 1, purl Base number minus 3 (Base-3), p2tog, SSP, purl Base-3, Inc 1, p1; repeat from * to end. **Next round** Purl. Repeat last 2 rounds once more. Bind off in purl.

Garter border * P1, Inc 1, purl Base number minus 3 (Base-3), p2tog, SSP, purl Base-3, Inc 1, p1; repeat from * to end. **Next round** Knit. Repeat last 2 rounds 4 times. Bind off in purl.

Finishing

Neck edging With B, starting at back right shoulder, PUK1 for each stitch or every 2 rows along rectangles and 2 stitches for every 3 rows along triangles. Mark beginning of round. Purl 4 rounds. Bind off in pattern. Block.

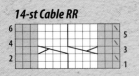

Work same as BO
RTT EXCEPT in reverse
stockinette stitch (purl RS
rows and knit WS rows)
AND k2tog to join.

This version adds a cable in each right-leaning rectangle and reverse stockinette in the triangles. Because the bias fabric has both give and recovery, there's no need to adjust gauge for the added cables. Just follow instructions for working the Three-quarter version top following charts for the cable rectangles.

It is interesting to note in each version of the sweater, a 10 stitch rectangle has a different diagonal measurement: 3.7" for the Long Sleeve, 3.3" for the Three-quarter Sleeve, and 3" for the Short Sleeve. Although the Long Sleeve and Short Sleeve have similar stitch gauges, the difference in row gauge significantly changes the size of each unit. A more in-depth discussion of entrelac gauge, including how to calculate the diagonal measurement of a unit, can be found in the Designing with entrelac section of the book starting on page 144.

14-st Cable RR

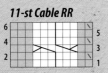

13-st Cable RR

12-st Cable RR

11-st Cable RR

10-st Cable RR

9-st Cable RR

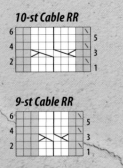

Repeat Rows 1–6 until all stitches
from unit in previous tier have been joined.

Cable RR for Base stitches
9 (10, 11, 12, 13, 14) PUP9 (10, 11, 12, 13, 14). *Rows 1, 5* (RS) P2 (2, 2, 3, 2, 3), k4 (6, 6, 6, 8, 8), purl to end. *Rows 2, 4, 6* (WS) Work in pattern to last stitch, k2tog (1 stitch from Cable CR with 1 stitch from joining unit). *Row 3* P2 (2, 2, 3, 2, 3); place half of knit stitches on cable needle (cn), hold to front, knit remaining half of stitches; knit stitches from cn, purl to end. Repeat Rows 1–6 until all stitches from previous unit have been joined.

Stitch key
- ☐ Knit on RS, purl on WS
- ☐ Purl on RS, knit on WS
- ◹ K2tog to join on WS

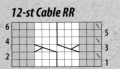

2/2 LC Place 2 stitches on cn to front, k2; k2 from cn

3/3 LC Place 3 stitches on cn to front, k3; k3 from cn

4/4 LC Place 4 stitches on cn to front, k4; k4 from cn

Small shown in PLYMOUTH YARNS Grass in color 9063

Quilted pocket bag

The pocket on this purse has both increasing and decreasing numbers of units within a tier. Start the bag body with a temporary cast-on at a non-traditional location at the widest point of the pocket and worked toward the top of the pocket. When the top is complete, work in the opposite direction.

Shown in LOUET Merlin in color 11
cherry red and 22 black

89

Quilted pocket bag

Pocket *Tier 1* Work 2 Inc LBT. *Tier 2* With waste yarn and using temporary crochet cast-on, cast on base number. Work 2 RR and 1 Unjoined RR. **Note Tiers 3–6** *At end, place stitches from last unit on hold and cut yarn.* *Tier 3* With waste yarn and temporary crochet cast-on, cast on 6. With main yarn, work 3 LR and 1 Unjoined LR. *Tier 4* Work 3 RR. *Tier 5* Work 2 LR. *Tier 6* Work 1 RR.

Body panel *Tier 1* [With waste yarn and temporary crochet cast-on, cast on 6, work Unjoined LR] 4 times.

Join upper pocket Remove waste yarn from Tier 3 of pocket, placing 6 stitches on spare needle. Hold pocket in front of RS of bag body as shown on diagram with RS out. *Tier 2* Work RST, working p3tog instead of p2tog to join stitch from RST, stitch from pocket, and stitch from previous tier. Holding pocket to front, work 3 RR. Work RET, picking up stitches through pocket and Tier 1 unit. Remove waste yarn from Tier 2 of pocket, placing 6 stitches on spare needle. *Tier 3* Work LR, working SSSK instead of SSK to join stitch from LR, stitch from pocket, and stitch from previous tier. Holding pocket to front, work 2 LR. Work last LR, picking up stitches through pocket and Tier 2 unit, and binding off on last row. Cut yarn. *Tier 4* Work 3 RR as shown on chart, binding off on last row of each unit and pulling last stitch over first picked-up stitch of next unit. Fasten off. *Join lower pocket* Remove waste yarn from Tier 1 rectangles of Body Panel, placing 6 stitches from each unit on right needle — 24 stitches. Place held stitches from Tier 3 of pocket on spare needle. *Tier 5* Work RST, working p3tog to join pocket. Work 3 RR. Work RET, picking up stitches through pocket and previous tier. Place stitches on hold from Tier 4 of pocket on spare needle. *Tier 6* Work LR, working SSSK to join pocket. Work 3 LR, picking up stitches through pocket and previous tier for last LR. Place stitches on hold from Tier 5 of pocket on spare needle. *Tier 7* Work RST.

stitches

HALF LINEN STITCH
OVER AN ODD NUMBER OF STITCHES
Row 1 (RS) [K1, sl 1 wyif] to last stitch, k1. **Rows 2, 4** (WS) Purl. **Row 3** K1, [k1, sl 1 wyif] to last 2 stitches, k2.

notes

◆ *See page 152 for any unfamiliar techniques.*

◆ *Pocket is worked from opening to bottom. Entrelac panel is worked from temporary cast-on in 2 directions, with pocket attached at the same time.*

the
UNITS
Base number
6 stitches decreased to 5

inc LBT
Kf&b

LR
SSK / PUK

unjoined LR
PUK

RR
PUP / P2tog

RST
Kf&b / P2tog

unjoined RR
PUP

RET
PUP / P2tog

For row-by-row instructions see page158.

Entrée to Entrelac

Experienced
8" x 7½" x 3½"

10cm/4"
34
20
over Half Linen Stitch

1 2 3 **4** 5 6
Medium weight
300 yds

4.5mm US 7, or size to obtain gauge, 60cm (24") or longer
Second needle for 3-needle bind-off

purse handles and feet
plastic canvas
crochet hook
waste yarn
spare needle (dpn)

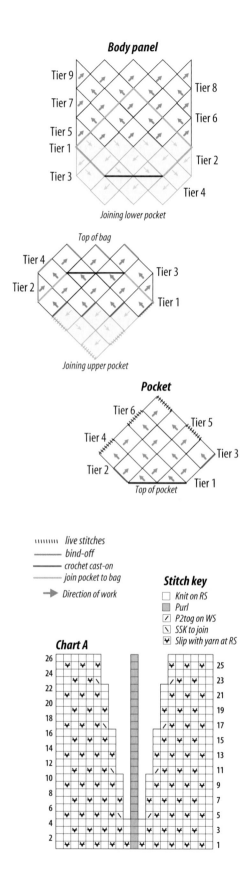

Body panel

Tier 9
Tier 8
Tier 7
Tier 6
Tier 5
Tier 1
Tier 2
Tier 3
Tier 4

Joining lower pocket

Top of bag

Tier 4
Tier 3
Tier 2
Tier 1

Joining upper pocket

Pocket

Tier 6
Tier 5
Tier 4
Tier 3
Tier 2
Tier 1

Top of pocket

〰️〰️〰️ *live stitches*
———— *bind-off*
———— *crochet cast-on*
———— *join pocket to bag*
➔ *Direction of work*

Stitch key
☐ Knit on RS
▨ Purl
☑ P2tog on WS
◺ SSK to join
☒ Slip with yarn at RS

Chart A

Work 1 RR, working p3tog to join pocket. Work 2 RR, picking up stitches through pocket and previous tier for second RR. Work RET. Place stitches on hold from Tier 6 of pocket on spare needle.

Tier 8 Work 4 LR, working SSSK to join pocket on 2nd, and picking up stitches through pocket and previous tier on 3rd. The pocket is now joined. *Tier 9* Work RST, 3 RR, RET. *Tier 10* Work 4 LR. *Tiers 11–22* Repeat last 2 tiers 6 times, binding off on last row of last unit of tier 22. *Tier 23* Work 3 center RR, binding off on Row 12 of each unit, pulling last stitch of unit over first picked-up stitch of next unit. Fasten off last stitch.

Bottom panel PUK on RS and immediately bind off 36 across middle of Tiers 10 and 14 to define bottom panel.

Side/Bottom/Side Panel With waste yarn and temporary crochet cast-on, cast on 21. Work 52 rows of Half Linen Stitch (bottom panel), * 2 rows of reverse stockinette stitch; beginning on Row 3, 26 rows of Half Linen Stitch. Work Chart A, binding off in pattern on Row 26 (first side panel). Remove waste yarn, placing 21 stitches on needle. Repeat from * for second side panel.

Finishing

Seams * On Body Panel, with RS facing, A, and circular needle, PUK36 between A and B, 21 between B and C, 36 between C and D. On Side Panel, with RS facing, attached yarn, and second circular needle, PUK36 between D and C, 21 between C and B, 36 between B and A. Slide Body Panel to other end of needle. Holding WS together, with Body in front and Side behind, work 3-needle bind-off to join 93 stitches of each panel. Do not cut yarn. Following diagram, PUK and immediately bind off 6 stitches along edge of LR, 9 stitches diagonally across each RR, 6 stitches along edge of LR. Do not cut yarn. Repeat from * for other side of bag, placing center of Side Panel inside bag parallel to Body bottom. Fasten off. Attach handles by folding rectangle points over handle, along gold dashed line, and stitching to inside of bag. Cut plastic canvas to fit inside bag bottom. Insert between bottom of Side and Body Panels. Attach purse feet to bottom of bag by pushing brads through Body Panel and plastic canvas. Stitch bottom of Side Panel to Body Panel.

Crochet piping With CC, work single crochet along all bound-off edges.

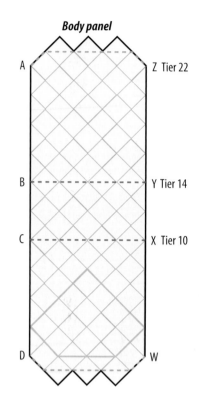

Body panel

A — Z Tier 22
B — Y Tier 14
C — X Tier 10
D — W

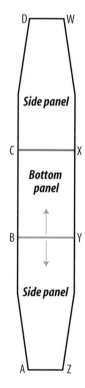

D — W
Side panel
C — X
Bottom panel
B — Y
Side panel
A — Z

Child's hoodie with kangaroo pocket

This sweater features a variety of shaping and seaming techniques. Increasing entrelac is used in the sleeves and decreasing entrelac in the yoke. The pocket and neckline are shaped by eliminating entrelac units. The pocket attaches via a multiple layer join and the underarms and hood join at a zigzag seam.

stitches

WORK UNIT WITH BIND-OFF
Bind off stitches on last row of unit.

notes

◆ *See page 152 for any unfamiliar techniques.*

◆ *Project is knit in seamless entrelac; cut yarn after each tier.*

◆ *Work left-leaning tiers in A, right-leaning tiers in B.*

◆ *When subsequent tier has a smaller base number, work 1 p3tog or SSSK (1 stitch from current unit and 2 from joining unit) for each unit to maintain 2:1 row-to-stitch ratio.*

Sleeves

With A and dpn, cast on 21 (21, 27, 27) stitches, divide evenly between 3 needles. Join, mark beginning of round and work k2, p1 rib for 1". **Tier 1** Continue with A, working 3 Join LBT with base stitches indicated on sleeve diagram. **Tiers 2–9** Continue following sleeve diagram. **Tier 10** With B, work 1 RR, binding off on last row. *Tip: This 'extra' rectangle is used at the underarm join prior to beginning the yoke.* Place remaining 12 (14, 16, 18) stitches on hold. Work second sleeve.

Body

With A and circular needle, cast on 72 (81, 96, 105) stitches. Join, mark beginning of round and work k2, p1 rib for 1 (1, 1¼, 1½)".

Increase for Pocket Continue with A, knit into front and back (kf&b) of next 36 (40, 48, 52) stitches; work to end, decrease 0 (1, 0, 1) — 108 (120, 144, 156) stitches.

Separate Pocket and Body With spare dpn in front and stitch holder in back, alternately slip 1 stitch to dpn and slip 1 stitch to holder until 72 (80, 96, 104) stitches have been slipped — 36 (40, 48, 52) stitches on each.

Base number for Pocket and Body to underarm 6 (7, 8, 9) stitches.

Pocket Tier 1 Continue with A and working from dpn, work 4 Join LBT, binding off last LBT. **Pocket Tier 2** Work 3 RR, binding off last unit. **Pocket Tier 3** Work 2 LR. Place remaining 12 (14, 16, 18) stitches on hold; cut yarn. Let pocket fall to the front until needed for the pocket join.

Body Through Pocket Join Slip 36 (40, 48, 52) sts from hold back to circular needle ready to start at marker. **Body Tier 1** Work 8 Join LBT. **Body Tier 2** Work 8 RR. **Body Tier 3** Work 8 LR. **Body Tier 4** Work 5 RR. Place pocket stitches on spare dpn. Hold pocket in front of RS of body with RS out, as indicated by pink and purple lines. Work 1 RR, replacing all p2tog

the
UNITS
Base number
6 (7, 8, 9) stitches

join LBT

LR

RR

For row-by-row instructions see page 158.

Intermediate

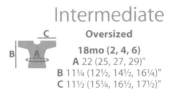

Oversized

18mo (2, 4, 6)
A 22 (25, 27, 29)"
B 11¼ (12½, 14½, 16¼)"
C 11½ (15¼, 16½, 17½)"

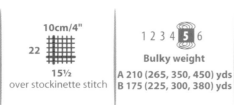

10cm/4"

22

15½

over stockinette stitch

1 2 3 4 **5** 6
Bulky weight
A 210 (265, 350, 450) yds
B 175 (225, 300, 380) yds

6mm/US 10, or size to obtain gauge, 60cm (24")

6mm/US 10, or size to obtain gauge, set of 4

& markers

Entrée to Entrelac

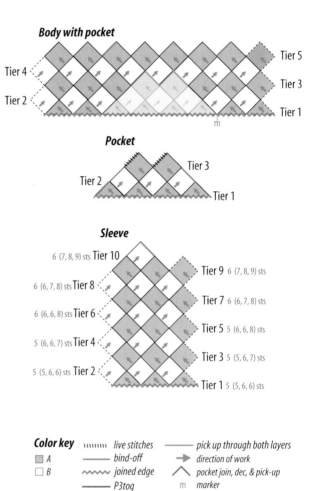

Body with pocket

Tier 4
Tier 2
Tier 5
Tier 3
Tier 1
m

Pocket

Tier 2
Tier 3
Tier 1

Sleeve

6 (7, 8, 9) sts Tier 10
6 (6, 7, 8) sts Tier 8   Tier 9 6 (7, 8, 9) sts
6 (6, 6, 8) sts Tier 6   Tier 7 6 (6, 7, 8) sts
5 (6, 6, 7) sts Tier 4   Tier 5 5 (6, 6, 8) sts
5 (5, 6, 6) sts Tier 2   Tier 3 5 (5, 6, 7) sts
                             Tier 1 5 (5, 6, 6) sts

Color key

⊹⊹⊹⊹ live stitches	——— pick up through both layers
▨ A	——— bind-off	➡ direction of work
☐ B	∿∿∿ joined edge	⤝ pocket join, dec, & pick-up
	——— P3tog	m marker

Child's size 6 shown in KNIT ONE CROCHET TOO PJ's in colors 566 (A) and 518 (B)

with p3tog (1 stitch from RR, 1 from pocket, and 1 from previous tier of body); work 1 RR, picking up through both pocket and body and replacing p2tog with p3tog; work 1 RR, picking up through both pocket and body.

Body to Armholes Tier 5 Work 8 LR, binding off 4th and 8th units. *Bind off last stitch of unit over first picked-up stitch of following unit.*

Join sleeves to body Seam Tier 10 rectangle from one sleeve to a bound-off LR of body, rows seamed to stitches and stitches to rows. Slip 12 (14, 16, 18) stitches (2 rectangles) remaining from sleeve onto right needle holding body stitches. Slip 3 rectangles from left to right

needle. Seam second sleeve to body. Slip 2 rectangles from remaining sleeve onto left needle holding body stitches. Slip 1 rectangle from right to left needle to begin yoke at center front — 60 (70, 80, 90) stitches on needle.

Yoke *Tier 6–10* *Using base stitches indicated in diagram.* Work 10 units each tier. *Tier 11* Work 9 LR, binding off last unit.

Hood *Base number 3 stitches Tier 12* Work 8 RR. *Tier 13* Work LST, work 7 LR, work LET. *Tier 14–21* Repeat last 2 tiers 4 more times. *Tier 22* Repeat Tier 12. *Tier 23* Repeat Tier 13 binding off first 4 units. *Tier 24* Work 4 RR with bind-off.

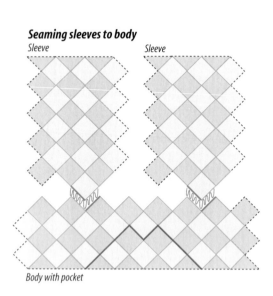

Seaming sleeves to body

Sleeve   Sleeve

Body with pocket

Color key

⑄⑄⑄	live stitches	
▨ A	—— bind-off	
▢ B	⋀⋁⋀ joined edge	
	→ direction of work	

◇ F first rectangle of tier

◇ L last rectangle of tier

Hood

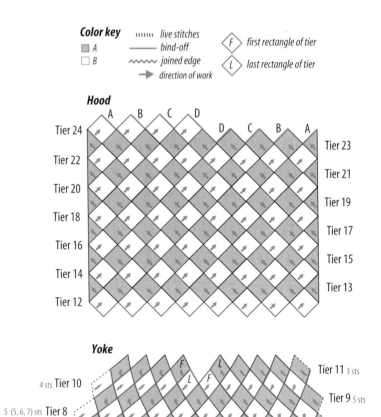

Tier 24   A   B   C   D
               D   C   B   A   Tier 23

Tier 22   Tier 21

Tier 20   Tier 19

Tier 18   Tier 17

Tier 16   Tier 15

Tier 14   Tier 13

Tier 12

Yoke

4 sts Tier 10   F   L   Tier 11 3 sts
                   L   F

5 (5, 6, 7) sts Tier 8   Tier 9 5 sts

6 (7, 8, 9) sts Tier 6   Tier 7 6 (6, 7, 8) sts

Finishing

Seaming Hood Fold hood in half and seam point A to dent A, B to B, C to C, and D to D, seaming stitches to rows and rows to stitches.

Edgings With RS facing, B, and dpns, PUK68 around head opening. Join, purl 3 rounds. Bind off loosely.

With RS facing B, and dpn, PUK12 (14, 16, 18) along pocket opening. Knit 1 row, purl 1 row, knit 1 row. Bind off. Repeat for other pocket opening. Block.

To help the reverse stockinette stitch roll along pocket edges, stitch each top corner inside pocket.

Arlis' sweater

The handsome V-shaping of mini garter blocks and V-garter sleeves, create an interesting cardigan for your favorite guy!

Large Shown in TRENDSETTER YARNS Tonalita in color 2355

Arlis' sweater

I have never knit my husband a sweater, but felt with the writing of this book, that omission should be rectified. Arlis was asked to assist in the design process, along with the selection of the yarn. The mitered fabric on the sleeves mimics the chevrons formed by the unique construction of the entrelac body. The final result was so pleasing, a vest version was developed as well.

notes

◆ *See page 152 for any unfamiliar techniques.*

◆ *Fronts begin at bottom side edge with a single unit and are worked in diagonal tiers. Back begins with 2 diagonal halves as for fronts, joined at center and worked to shoulders. Sleeves are worked separately from top down. All entrelac units are worked in garter stitch.*

◆ *Cast-on at beginning of tier counts as Row 1; begin first unit with Row 2.*

Sweater

Right Front

Tier 1 Cast on 5. Knit 10 rows.

For first unit of each tier, cast on stitches and begin with Row 2. All units are worked in garter stitch.

Tiers 2–5, All sizes, *Begin Diagram A*

S (L, 2X) *Tier 2* Work 1 RR, 1 Unjoined RR. *Tier 3* Work 2 LR, 1 Unjoined LR. *Tier 4* Work 3 RR, 1 Unjoined RR. *Tier 5* Work 4 LR, 1 Unjoined LR. Repeat last 2 tiers, adding 1 unit each tier, through Tier 9 (11, 13).

M (1X, 3X) *Tier 2* Work 1 LR, 1 Unjoined LR. *Tier 3* Work 2 RR, 1 Unjoined RR. *Tier 4* Work 3 LR, 1 Unjoined LR. Repeat last 2 tiers adding 1 unit each tier through Tiers 10 (12, 14).

ALL SIZES The front width has now been reached. *Tier 10 (11, 12, 13, 14, 15)* Cast on 5; work RR to end, binding off last unit. *Next tier* Work LR to last unit, work Unjoined LR. Repeat last 2 tiers until center edge is 14 (14, 16, 16, 18, 18) units high, end with RR tier.

This tier is marked in blue on diagram.

2X AND 3X SIZES ONLY *Next tier* Work LR tier, omitting Unjoined LR, binding off last unit. *Next tier* Work RR to end, binding off last unit.

Neck and shoulder shaping

ALL SIZES *Begin Diagram B: Next tier* With RS facing, work 3 (3, 3, 3, 4, 4) Bo LTT and 5 (6, 7, 8, 6, 7) LR —8 (9, 10, 11, 10, 11) units. Follow Right Front Sweater diagram to complete shoulder shaping.

Sweater, Left Front

Work as for Right Front, reversing units (LR for RR, RR for LR, Bo RTT for Bo LTT, etc.), through neck shaping and following Diagrams C and D.

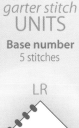

Sweater Right Front

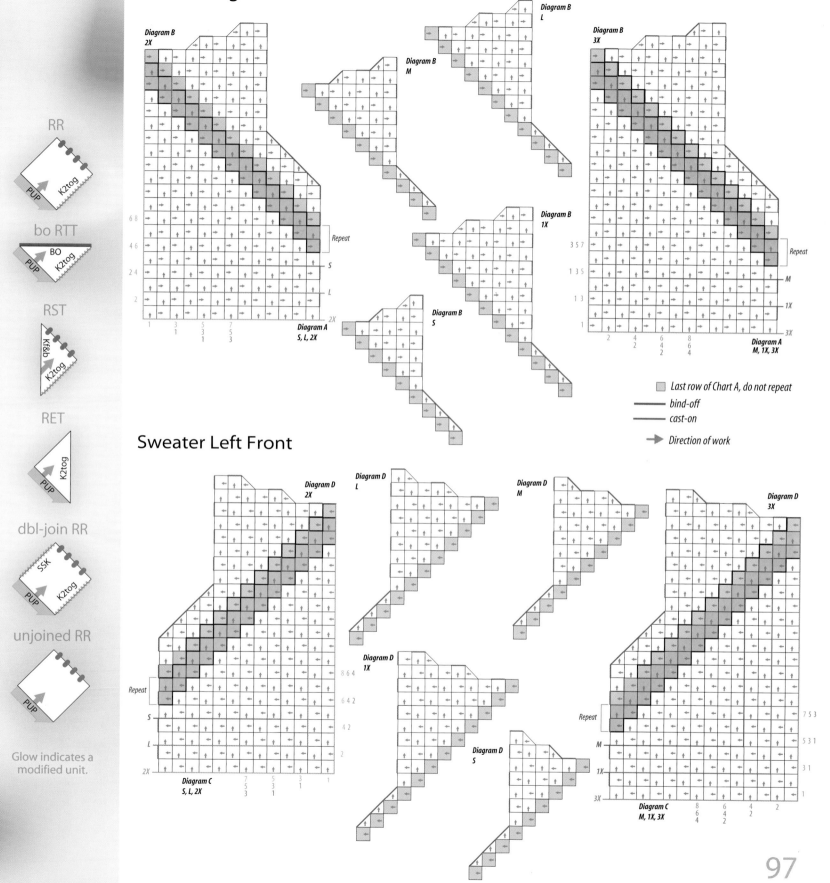

Sweater Left Front

Legend (left column):

RR

bo RTT

RST

RET

dbl-join RR

unjoined RR

Glow indicates a modified unit.

Legend (right):

Last row of Chart A, do not repeat

bind-off

cast-on

Direction of work

Vest Fronts

Work as for Sweater until center edge is 4 (3, 5, 5, 6, 5) units high (or to desired length along side seam); end on RR tier for Right Front and LR tier for Left Front.

This tier is marked in blue on diagram.
Follow Diagrams E and F for underarm and neck shaping.

Sweater and Vest Back

Left Back, corner Work as for Left Front through Tier 8 (9, 10, 11, 12, 13), cut yarn.

Right Back, corner Work as for Right Front, through Tier 9 (10, 11, 12, 13, 14). Do not cut yarn.

Left Front rotates 90º clockwise to become Left Back and Right Front rotates 90º counter-clockwise to become Right Back.

Begin Diagram G: Join Backs With RS facing, slip Left Back onto needle as shown. With attached yarn, cast 5 stitches onto Right Back, work Double-join LR; work 8 (9, 10, 11, 12, 13) LR along left back, 1 Unjoined LR.

Begin Diagram H: RR chevron tier Casting on 5 stitches for first unit, work 10 (11, 12, 13, 14, 15) RR, 1 Double-join RR, 7 (8, 9, 10, 11, 12) RR, 1 Unjoined RR. **LR chevron tier** Casting on 5 stitches for first unit, work 9 (10, 11, 12, 13, 14) LR, 1 Double-join LR, 8 (9, 10, 11, 12, 13) LR, 1 Unjoined LR.

SWEATER ONLY Repeat last 2 tiers until length at Right Back is one unit shorter then length of Right Front at shoulder edge.

Continue Back as shown in diagram H working shorter chevron tiers as follows: **LR chevron tier** Work LR to center, 1 Double-join LR; work LR to end, binding off last LR. **RR chevron tier** Work RR to center, 1 Double-join RR; RR to end, binding off RR. Repeat last 2 tiers, decreasing 1 unit at beginning of each tier until only center units remain; work 1 RR, 1 Double join RR. Work center unit, bind off.

Diagram G, Join Backs

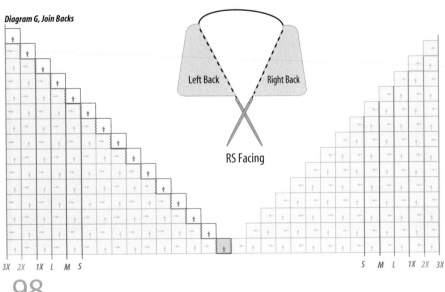

Vest Right Front   Diagram E

Vest Left Front   Diagram F

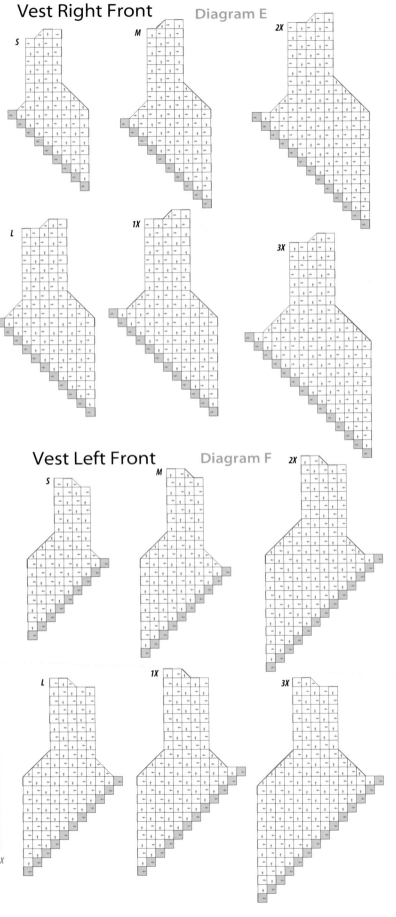

98

VEST ONLY Repeat last 2 tiers until side seam edge matches start of armhole shaping on Front. Continue chevron tiers, AND AT SAME TIME work armhole shaping as for Fronts to shoulder.

Sleeves

Cast on 3 stitches. K1, place marker (pm), k1 (center stitch), pm, k1. Work garter stitch, increasing 1 stitch each edge and each side of center stitch every other row to 103 (103, 115, 131, 143, 159) stitches.

Continuing to increase 1 stitch each side of center stitch, begin decreasing 1 stitch each edge every other row. AT THE SAME TIME decrease 1 additional stitch each edge every 6 (8, 6, 5, 4, 3) rows 16 (14, 18, 22, 26, 32) times — 71 (75, 79, 87, 91, 95) stitches.

Next row Work to first marker, bind off center stitch, removing 2nd marker; knit to end of row.

Continue, working half of Sleeve stitches, decreasing 1 stitch each edge (underarm and center) every other row to 3 stitches; SK2P. Fasten off.

Join yarn and repeat for stitches on other half of Sleeve.

Finishing

Seam shoulders, matching 1 unit on Front to 1 unit on Back.

Buttonhole Place markers on Left Front placing first 1" from hem and last at beginning of V-neck, then evenly space the other 7. For her, place marker at V-neck on Right Front.

Front Band With RS facing and beginning at bottom of Right Front, PUK5 for each rectangle and 8 for each triangle around front to bottom of Left Front.

Knit 10 rows, working eyelet buttonholes (2-stitch buttonhole for hers) on 4th row to correspond with marker placement. Bind off.

Cardigan Seam top of sleeves to body, placing center stitch at shoulder seam. Sew sleeve and side seams.

Vest Armhole bands Pick up as for Front bands. Knit 10 rows. Bind off. Seam sides.

TRENDSETTER YARNS, Tonalita; sweater (shown in color 2355), vest (shown in color 2398).

Color key
- ☐ *dbl LR*
- ▨ *dbl RR*

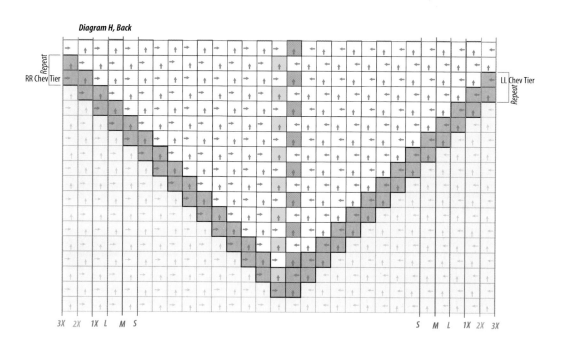

Diagram H, Back

RR Chev Tier — Repeat

LL Chev Tier — Repeat

3X 2X 1X L M S   S M L 1X 2X 3X

Color, texture
& other creative units

Lightning bolt rucksack page 110

Traditionally, when people think about entrelac, a stockinette, garter stitch, or other simple fabric comes to mind. But, there is no reason entrelac cannot be exciting — add color and additional techniques.

Color in entrelac

When people think of entrelac in color, they imagine tiers of diamond shapes in alternating colors (a harlequin pattern) or a self-striping yarn. There are many more color options.

One of the unique characteristics of entrelac is that each rectangle is worked as a stand-alone unit. As such, each unit is a mini canvas and can be as plain or as intricate as the knitter chooses.

My early entrelac projects were monochromatic. The first was done in shades of gray with each tier in a different yarn. The second used only 2 yarns, alternating every tier, but they were nearly the same color; the depth was created by the difference in the fibers. Monochromatic entrelac can run the gamut from playful to elegant.

Self-striping yarns have long been associated with entrelac. For short-repeat yarns, the small number of stitches in an entrelac unit results in one or two stripes. For long-repeat yarns, each unit (or 2) is a single color. The directional nature of entrelac, combined with the stripes formed by the yarns, is a simple way to create a complex blend of color.

But, what happens if we control the striping and place stripes purposefully and consistently throughout a project? I played with the idea and the result was interesting, but the felted version was truly remarkable. Just like magic, vertical zigzag lines form lightning bolts of color on what appears to be a solid fabric. At first it looks like intarsia, but the diagonal lines are smooth, not jagged, regardless of the direction.

In knitting, color techniques include slip stitch color work, mosaic patterns, stranded knitting, and intarsia. When you begin thinking of each entrelac unit as a mini canvas, playing with these techniques is the next step. Slip stitch color work is often mistaken for stranded or fair isle knitting. Slipping the stitch with the yarn on the right side of the work adds texture to the color story.

Intarsia (also known as color block or picture knitting) is typically used in the creation of large graphics. Since it can also be used for smaller graphics, it is well suited to our mini canvas.

Messenger bag page 112

101

Texture in entrelac

Even when worked in stockinette, entrelac has a very distinctive texture that is quilted in appearance. But just as each unit can be considered a canvas of color, it can also be a canvas of texture. The only real consideration is the relationship between the stitches and rows in 1 repeat (or several) of a stitch pattern. A repeat with 10 stitches and 30 rows cannot be shown to its fullest in a 10-stitch rectangle, since only 20 rows are worked.

As is true with many things in life, simpler is often better. When adding texture within entrelac units this is particularly true. Simple texture patterns, because their repeat is small, are easy to adjust to varying size rectangles. It is also relatively easy to work the join, in pattern, as texture patterns primarily use knits and purls. Assuming that the gauge of your texture pattern is appropriately close to the gauge specified, a replacement texture pattern is feasible. But, be aware that the elasticity in the bias direction of different knitted fabrics can vary greatly, producing differing results.

Cables & lace page119

Lace patterns are a type of texture and pattern where the interest is created in the negative spaces. If the pattern distorts when pulled on the bias, it is not an appealing choice for entrelac. When combining lace with other patterns within the entrelac fabric, it is important to remember lace often has a much larger gauge than its stockinette counterpart. In the Flounce duo, this tendency is used as a design element; each tier grows in circumference by changing lace pattern, not stitch count. In Cables & lace, the lace tiers have half the number of stitches as the cabled tiers.

Flounce duo page 122

Creative Units

When I began to consider how to use common stitch patterns and techniques in entrelac and how to combine entrelac with other types of knitting, my creative juices really began to flow.

Although modular knitting and entrelac are not the same, they are cousins and it is easy to think about them together. Both techniques work only one unit at a time and join units as they are created. Then, the techniques diverge. Modular knitting works with a variety of shapes, generally has only one 'active' unit at a time, and, in almost all cases, joins units by picking up stitches.

But, what would happen if we added another shape to the entrelac library? In most cases, additional entrelac 'rules' would need to be modified.

With each exploration came thoughts of a new shape. I am sure that there are many more variations that are waiting to be discovered. Although these new variations may not be technically entrelac, they are not truly modular, either.

Reversibility

The only real disappointment I have long held with entrelac is the one-sided nature of the fabric. Although it is possible to minimize the elements on the wrong side, there is always a side where stitches are picked up. For a person who likes to have blankets, scarves, or throws be reversible, this means entrelac would not be considered. However, as I thought about an afghan for this book, I found not 1, but 2 solutions.

Double knitting is a reversible fabric. Where other fabrics have only 1 layer, double knitting has 2 layers. The area between them provides a place to hide the wrong-side elements of entrelac.

To further reduce the wrong-side effects, work the pick-up with yarnovers: For the double layers, * pick up and knit 1 (to provide a 1 stitch layer) and yo (to provide a stitch for the other layer); repeat from * until you have 2 times the base number of stitches.

And then I realized, for any single-layer fabric, I could pick up and knit half the base number of stitches with a yarn-over after each.

Combine this single-layer pick-up method with any reversible fabric and you will magically create reversible entrelac.

Double knit blanket page 137

By placing a stripe of contrasting color at the end of each unit, it is possible to create a lightning bolt of color.

Because the typical gauge for Linen Stitch is nearly 2 rows per stitch, this block comes off the needles flat and square with minimal blocking required.

Icon key

live stitches

PUP

pick up and purl stitches in direction of arrow

PUK

pick up and knit stitches in direction of arrow

joined edge

direction of work

Glow indicates a modified unit.

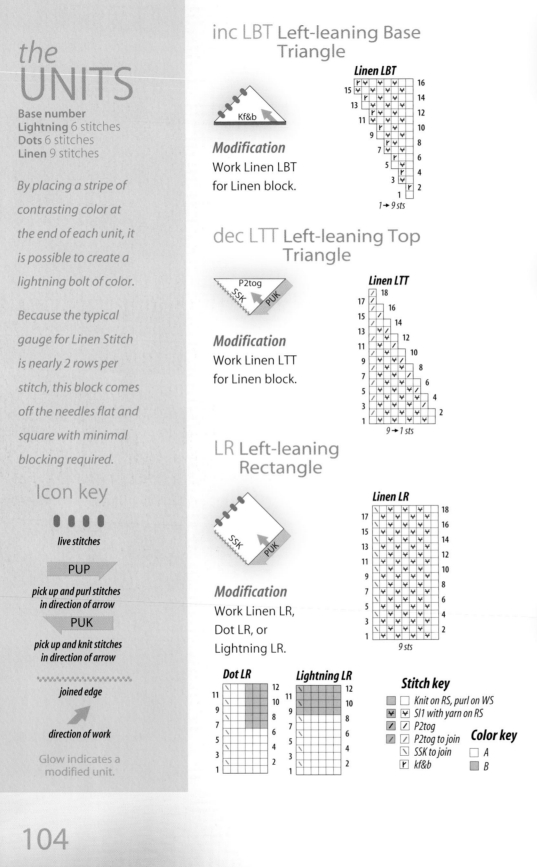

inc LBT Left-leaning Base Triangle

Linen LBT

Kf&b

Modification

Work Linen LBT for Linen block.

1 → 9 sts

dec LTT Left-leaning Top Triangle

Linen LTT

P2tog / SSK / PUK

Modification

Work Linen LTT for Linen block.

9 → 1 sts

LR Left-leaning Rectangle

Linen LR

SSK / PUK

Modification

Work Linen LR, Dot LR, or Lightning LR.

9 sts

Dot LR   *Lightning LR*

Stitch key

☐	☐	Knit on RS, purl on WS
↧	↧	Sl1 with yarn on RS
⧄	⧄	P2tog
⧄	⧄	P2tog to join
⧅		SSK to join
⌄		kf&b

Color key
☐ A
▨ B

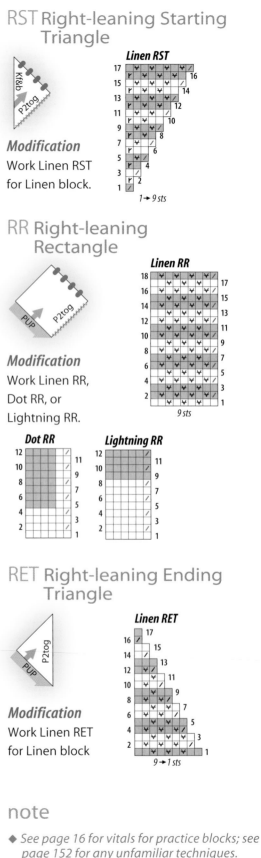

RST Right-leaning Starting Triangle

Linen RST

Kf&b / P2tog

Modification

Work Linen RST for Linen block.

1 → 9 sts

RR Right-leaning Rectangle

Linen RR

PUP / P2tog

Modification

Work Linen RR, Dot RR, or Lightning RR.

9 sts

Dot RR   *Lightning RR*

RET Right-leaning Ending Triangle

Linen RET

PUP / P2tog

Modification

Work Linen RET for Linen block

9 → 1 sts

note

◆ *See page 16 for vitals for practice blocks; see page 152 for any unfamiliar techniques.*

Lightning bolt

Tier 1 With B, work 4 Inc LBT.

Tier 2, 4, 6 With B, work RST, work 3 Lightning RR; with B, work RET.

Tier 3, 5, 7 With B, work 3 Lightning LR; with B, work 1 LR fastening off each strand of B on Tier 7.

Tier 8 With B, work RST, 3 RR, RET.

Tier 9 With B, work 4 Dec LTT.

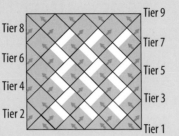

Diamond dots

Tier 1 With A, work 4 Inc LBT.

Tier 2 With A, work RST; work 3 Dot RR; with A, work RET.

Tier 3 Work 4 Dot LR.

Tiers 4–7 Repeat Tiers 2 and 3 twice.

Tier 8 Repeat Tier 2.

Tier 9 With A, work 4 Dec LTT.

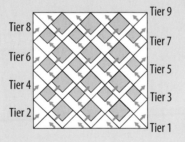

notes

◆ *For Lightning Bolt: Use three 5-yd lengths of B. In Tier 2, join 1 length for each lightning bolt; carry B along join from tier to tier, catching every 2 rows, until needed.*

◆ *For Diamond Dots: For each dot (RR), cut a 3-ft strand of B; for dot (LR), a 2-ft strand.*

Linen stitch

Tier 1 With A, work 3 Inc LBT.

Tier 2 Work RST, 2 RR, RET.

Tier 3 With A, work 3 LR.

Tiers 4 & 5 Repeat Tiers 2 & 3 once.

Tier 6 Repeat Tier 2.

Tier 7 With A, work 3 Dec LTT.

the UNITS

Base number
Mosaic 8 stitches
Reversible 6 stitches

Mosaic patterns, if worked over a small enough repeat, are a perfect example of how a small change in entrelac results in a big impact.

This reversible pattern uses garter stitch as the fabric for each unit, but other reversible fabrics create wonderful variations.

Icon key

live stitches

PUP

pick up and purl stitches in direction of arrow

PUK

pick up and knit stitches in direction of arrow

joined edge

direction of work

Glow indicates a modified unit.

Inc LBT Left-leaning Base Triangle

Modification
Work in garter stitch (knit WS rows).

Dec LTT Left-leaning Top Triangle

Modification
Work in garter stitch (knit WS rows AND k2tog decrease on WS rows).

LR Left-leaning Rectangle

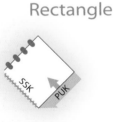

Mosaic LR

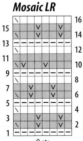

8 sts

Modification
Work Mosaic LR or Garter LR (knit WS rows).

RST Right-leaning Starting Triangle

Modification
Work in garter stitch (knit WS rows AND k2tog to join on WS rows).

RR Right-leaning Rectangle

Mosaic RR

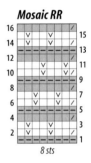

8 sts

Modification
Work in Mosaic RR or Garter RR (knit WS rows AND k2tog to join on WS rows).

RET Right-leaning Ending Triangle

Modification
Work in garter stitch (knit WS rows).

Stitch key
- ☐ *Knit on RS, purl on WS*
- ⊟ *Purl on RS, knit on WS*
- ⋁ *Sl 1 with yarn on WS*
- ⟋ *P2tog to join*
- ⟍ *SSK to join*

Color key
- ☐ *A*
- ▨ *2 rows A, 2 rows B*
- ▪ *B*

note

◆ *See page 16 for vitals for practice blocks; see page 152 for any unfamiliar techniques.*

Mosaic

Tier 1 Work 3 Inc LBT.

Tier 2 Work RST, 2 Mosaic RR, RET.

Tier 3 Work 3 Mosaic LR.

Tiers 4 & 5 Repeat Tiers 2 & 3 once.

Tier 6 Repeat Tier 2.

Tier 7 Work 3 Dec LTT.

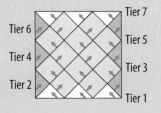

note

◆ *Change color at beginning of every WS row of Mosaic RR and every RS row of Mosaic LR.*

Reversible entrelac

Tier 1 With A, work 4 Inc LBT.

Tier 2 With B, work RST, 3 RR, RET.

Tier 3 With A, work 4 LR.

Tiers 4–7 Repeat last 2 tiers 2 times.

Tier 8 Repeat Tier 2.

Tier 9 With A, work 4 Dec LTT.

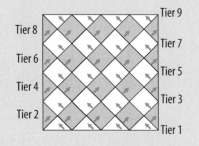

note

◆ *For pick-up row, [PUP1, yo] 5 times, end PUP1; OR [PUK1, yo] 5 times, end PUK1 — 11 stitches. Next row, k1,[k2tog] 5 times — 6 sttiches.*

the UNITS

Base number
8 stitches

Two texture patterns,
a cable and a welt,
enhance the natural
woven effect of entrelac.

In the gingham block,
careful placement of
color combined with
texture produces a
complex fabric, but in a
relatively easy manner.

Icon key

live stitches

*pick up and purl stitches
in direction of arrow*

*pick up and knit stitches
in direction of arrow*

joined edge

direction of work

Glow indicates a
modified unit.

inc LBT Left-leaning Base Triangle

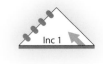

dec LTT Left-leaning Top Triangle

LR Left-leaning Rectangle

Texture sample block

2/2 Left Cross (2/2 LC) Slip 2 stitches to cable needle, hold to front; k2; k2 from cable needle.

Work all triangles in reverse stockinette (knit on WS, purl on RS)

Tier 1 With A, work 3 Inc LBT.

Tier 2 With B, work 1 RST, 2 RR, 1 RET.

Tier 3 With A, work 3 LR.

Tiers 4 & 5 Repeat Tier 2 & 3 once.

Tier 6 Repeat Tier 2.

Tier 7 With A, work 3 Dec LTT.

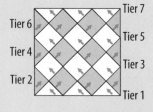

→ direction of work

Color key
☐ A
☐ B

note

◆ *See page152 for any unfamiliar techniques.*

Stitch key

☐ Knit on RS, purl on WS
☐ Purl on RS, knit on WS
☑ P2tog to join
☑ K2tog on WS
☐ SSP to join
▨ **2/2 LC** Sl 2 to cn, k2; k2 from cn

LR Chart

8 sts

RR Chart

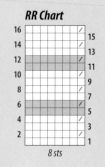

8 sts

RST Right-leaning Starting Triangle

RR Right-leaning Rectangle

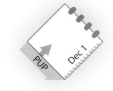

RET Right-leaning Ending Triangle

Gingham block

Tier 1 Work 4 Inc LBT.

Tier 2 Beginning with B and alternating the color of each unit across the tier, work 1 RST, 3 RR, 1 RET.

Tier 3 Work 4 LR.

Tier 4 Beginning with A and alternating colors across the tier, work 1 RST, 3 RR, 1 RET.

Tier 5 Repeat Tier 3.

Tiers 6–8 Repeat Tiers 2–4.

Tier 9 With A, work 4 Dec LTT.

notes

◆ *See page 16 for vitals for practice blocks; see page 152 for any unfamiliar techniques.*

◆ *Units on even, right-leaning tiers are worked in solid colors, changing color every unit. Units on odd, left-leaning tiers are worked with both colors, changing color every 2 rows.*

◆ *Maintain Seed Stitch pattern as you increase or decrease for triangles.*

SEED STITCH (2-STITCH REPEAT)

RS rows [P1, k1] to end.
WS rows [K1, p1] to end.

To maintain the pattern as stitch number changes, knit the purls and purl the knits.

INC 1 IN PATTERN

If next stitch should be knit, increase by k&p into it; if next stitch should be purled, increase by p&k into it.

DEC 1 IN PATTERN

RS rows If next stitch should be knit, decrease by SSK; if next stitch should be purled, decrease by SSP.

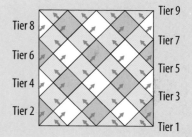

Tier 8 · Tier 6 · Tier 4 · Tier 2 · Tier 9 · Tier 7 · Tier 5 · Tier 3 · Tier 1

Color key

☐ A
☐ 2 rows A, 2 rows B
▨ B

→ *direction of work*

Seed stitch

2 ▨☐ 1
2-st repeat

Stitch key

☐ Knit on RS, purl on WS
▨ Purl on RS knit on WS

Lightning bolt rucksack

The rucksack demonstrates what will happen when stripes are added to felted entrelac fabric. The lightning bolt is created by strategically placing stripes of color within each entrelac unit. Since the contrasting color (B) is only used for a few rows, the main color (A) can be carried from unit to unit. Color B can be carried up along the joining selvedge, minimizing the number of ends.

notes

◆ See page 152 for any unfamiliar techniques.

◆ Project is worked in seamless entrelac.

◆ Join new length of B in each unit of first tier; carry B along join from tier to tier. Cut A at end of each tier when changing direction.

◆ When binding off stitches on final tier, lift last stitch bound-off for unit over the first stitch picked up for the next unit.

Bottom

Tier 1, base rectangles [With waste yarn and crochet cast-on, cast on 11. With A, work Unjoined LR] 4 times — 44 stitches, 4 rectangles. Cut A. *Tier 2,* b With WS facing, slip live stitches from last rectangle to right needle and PUP11 along its selvedge. Work 3 RR. PUP11 and remove waste yarn from Rectangle 1, placing stitches on left needle. Work RR, joining to stitches from temporary cast-on. c Removing waste yarn and joining to stitches from temporary cast-on, work 3 RR along bottom of Tier 1 rectangles — d 88 stitches, 8 RR.

Main Bag

e Continue working entrelac in the round, carrying color B along the join. *Tier 3* Work 8 LR. *Tier 4* Work 8 RR. *Tiers 5–10* Repeat last 2 tiers 3 more times. *Tier 11* Cut B. With A only, work 8 LR, binding off all stitches on Row 22.

Finishing

f Fold points of last 8 units to outside of bag and stitch where indicated by red dots to form casing for strap.

Straps *Each strap should measure approximately 1 yard after felting. Felting will reduce length by one-quarter to one-third.*

Twisted cord g Cut one 8-yard length of A and two of B; hold A and B together for each cord. Make 4.

h Carefully remove knots from 2 cords and knot them together; repeat for other pair of cords. Insert cords from inside to outside of bag between stitches at points shown, pulling knot snug against inside of bag and secure.

Felt bag to desired size. Shape as necessary and air dry.

i, j Insert cords in casing, beginning above attachment point and taking cords from each pair in opposite directions around to other side of bag top. Adjust to desired length; knot ends together; trim excess cord.

the
UNITS
Base number
11 stitches

For LR and RR Pick up stitches and work first 9 joins (18 rows) with A then change to B and complete unit.

LR

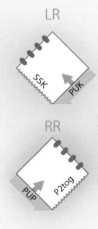

RR

Glow indicates a modified unit.

unjoined LR

For row-by-row instructions, see page 158

Intermediate				
20" high x 17" wide before felting	**10cm/4"** 28 18 over stockinette stitch before felting	 1 2 3 **4** 5 6 **Medium weight** **A** 490 yds **B** 160 yds	 5.5mm/US 9, or size to obtain gauge, 60cm (24") or longer	**&** extra dpn crochet hook waste yarn
14½" high x 11½" wide after felting				

Entrée to Entrelac

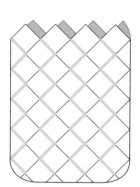

e   Work additional tiers.

d   *3D view* of Tiers 1 and 2.

c   *Rotate work* and
    complete Tier 2.

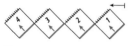

b   *Begin Tier 2.*

a   *Tier 1* Work 4 base rectangles.

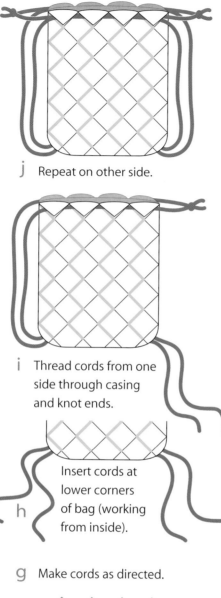

j   Repeat on other side.

i   Thread cords from one
    side through casing
    and knot ends.

    Insert cords at
    lower corners
    of bag (working
h   from inside).

g   Make cords as directed.

f   Fold down and tack
    each point for casing.

BROWN SHEEP COMPANY Nature Spun Worsted in colors N04W Z (A), and 308W (B)

Color sampler messenger bag

In this project the base bag is knit and felted, then the flap is picked up and knit. The entrelac flap of this messenger bag features a number of slip stitch color patterns each utilizing 3 colors. The placement of the colored units combined with alternating black tiers creates a mini canvas allowing each pattern to pop.

stitches

SEED STITCH **RS rows** [P1, k1] to end. **WS rows** [K1, p1] to end. *Note:* To maintain the pattern as stitch number changes, knit the purls and purl the knits.

DEC 1 IN PATTERN **RS rows** If next stitch should be knit, SSK; if next stitch should be purled, SSP. **WS rows** If next stitch should be knit, k2tog; if next stitch should be purled, p2tog.

INC 1 IN PATTERN If next stitch should be knit, increase by k&p into it; if next should be purled, increase by p&k into it.

SLIP STITCH PATTERNS All slip stitch patterns are worked as RR. Choose to use any combination of the slip stitch patterns provided. All slip stitch patterns are worked with 3 colors using only 1 color on each row.

notes

◆ *See page 152 for any unfamiliar techniques*

◆ *All left-slanting units are worked in Seed Stitch in color A; right-slanting units each feature a different slip stitch pattern.*

◆ *The bag uses some units which are hybrids of the basic units, for example an LSBT combines the features of both a Starting Triangle and a Join Base Triangle: on RS rows the unit works across existing stitches on the left needle, and at the end of WS rows increases are worked to grow the right side of the unit.*

◆ *Work all dec 1 and inc 1 joins and shapings in pattern.*

◆ *Work bag panels (page 114), then felt, before adding entrelac flap.*

For row-by-row instructions see page 158.

the UNITS

Base number
20 stitches

Join LBT

LET

LR

bo LTT

RR

Experienced

H × W × D

21" × 17½" × 2¾"
before felting
13¾" × 15" × 2½"
after felting

10cm/4"

24

18
over stockinette stitch,
before felting

1 2 3 **4** 5 6
Medium weight
A 925 yds
B, C, D 75 yds each

5.5mm/US
9, or size to
obtain gauge

steel crochet hook
(for picking up
stitches for flap)

&
Strap Homestead Heirlooms, Single Braided Handle, 45" × 1 7/8"

Contrast color pearl cotton for a temporary row marker

Entrée to Entrelac

LSTT

Cast on 1 next to last stitch worked. Work as for LST until 10 stitches from previous tier have been joined and 10 remain, end on RS row. Work rest of unit as for BO LTT.

LETT

With RS facing, PUK20 along edge of unit in previous tier.
Row 1 (WS) [K1, p1] 10 times.
Row 2 Work Seed Stitch to last 2 stitches, dec 1. **Row 3** Work to last stitch, turn work.
Row 4 Work 1 stitch in pattern, pass previously unworked stitch over (BO 1), work to last 2 stitches, dec 1. Repeat last 2 rows until 2 stitches remain, end with a RS row.
Next row (WS) K1. **Next row** SSK, pass unworked stitch over. Fasten off.

LEBT

Rows 1-19 Work as Join LBT to 10 unit stitches. **Row 20** (WS) Work Seed Stitch across stitches just worked. **Row 21** (RS) Work stitches just worked to last 2 stitches, dec 1 in pattern. Repeat Rows 20 & 21 until 1 stitch remains. **Next row** (WS) Work in pattern, fasten off.

Glow indicates a modified unit.

Entrelac Flap

With A and WS facing, and using steel crochet hook to pick up stitches through felted fabric, PUP90 across Back Panel bind-off and transfer to knitting needle. *Tier 1* Continuing with A, work LSBT, 2 Join LBT, LEBT. Cut yarn. *Tier 2* Work 3 RR in Dice, Linen, and Tweed patterns working Inc 1 or Dec 1 into pick-up row to correspond with stitch repeat. *Tier 3* With A, work LST, 2 LR, LET. Cut yarn. *Tier 4* Work 3 RR in Forest, Surprise, and Diagonal patterns. *Tier 5* With A, work LSTT, 2 Bo LTT, LETT. Cut yarn.

With A and WS facing, PUK60 on short side, 90 on long side, 60 on other short side of flap. Beginning with a knit row, work 4 rows stockinette stitch. Change to contrast color (B, C or D), purl 2 rows. Bind off, leaving 2-yard tail. Thread tail through tapestry needle and sew contrasting color to RS edge of bag, enclosing pick-up ridge.

Block flap. Attach strap to the top of the side panels.

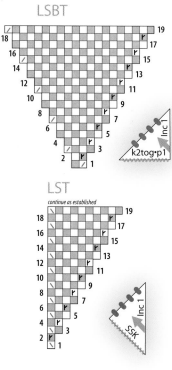

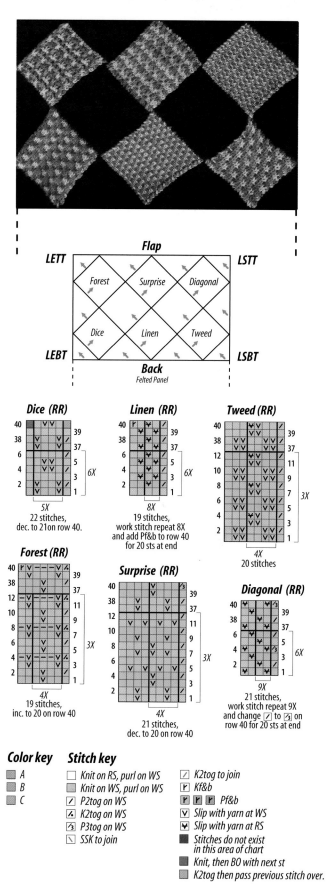

Front & Back panel

With A, cast on 80. Beginning with a WS row, work stockinette stitch for 125 rows. *Next row: Pick-up row* (RS) Hold strand of contrasting color pearl cotton with A, work 1 row; drop cotton. Work 5 rows in stockinette stitch.

Tuck row (RS) [With left needle, pick up purl bump 6 rows down on WS of Pick-up row; knit purl bump together with next stitch] across row; remove pearl cotton.

Work 17 rows in stockinette stitch. Repeat Pick-up row and Tuck row. Work stockinette stitch for 124 rows; bind off.

Side Panel

With RS facing, PUK9 along one bottom side edge of bag, between tuck rows. Work stockinette stitch for 125 rows, bind off. Repeat for other side panel.

Finishing

Sew edges of each side strip to front and back panels. Felt to measurements; shape and let air dry.

CASCADE YARNS Cascade 220 in colors 8555 (A), 8911 (B), 8903 (C) and 9467 (D)

Chullo sampler

A sampler hat is a good chance to explore your creativity. Each entrelac tier is worked in one color, but each unit uses a different pattern stitch — knitter's choice.

CASCADE YARNS Eco Alpaca in color 1516 (A), 1512 (B), 1511 (C)

stitches

TUCK With attached yarn, knit 4 rounds. **Joining round** Change to color of next tier, [with dpn, pick up purlwise bump from inside of hat 4 rounds directly below next stitch and knit it together with next stitch] repeat to end.

DEC 1 IN PATTERN RS rows If next stitch should be knit, decrease by SSK; if next stitch should be purled, SSP. **WS rows** If next stitch should be knit, decrease by k2tog; if next stitch should be purled, p2tog

notes

◆ *See page152 for any unfamiliar techniques.*

◆ *Project is knit in seamless entrelac with tuck ridges between each tier.*

◆ *Switch to dpns when stitches become too tight on circular needle.*

◆ *Because the stitches are on the needle after the tuck, no pick-up is necessary for the entrelac units.*

Hat

Hem With circular needle, waste yarn, and using temporary crochet cast-on, cast on 85 (102, 119). With A, join and knit 5 rounds. *Joining round:* Remove temporary cast-on a few stitches at a time, placing stitches on dpn. With B, and folding purl sides of fabric together [knit a stitch from circular needle together with a stitch from dpn] to end.

Entrelac Tiers *Work 5 units each tier, choosing stitch patterns as desired.* **Tier 1** With 10 (12, 14) base stitches, work 1 LR, joining to next 10 (12, 14) stitches (right ear flap); 1 LBT (center back); 1 LR joining to next 10 (12, 14) stitches (left ear flap); 1 LBT; 1 LBT (front). *Tuck ridge* With C, [k10 (12, 14), PUK10 (12, 14)] 5 times — 100 (120, 140) stitches. Work Tuck, changing to A on Joining Round. **Tier 2** [Work 10 (12, 14)-stitch RR, join to next 10 (12, 14) stitches] 5 times. *Tuck ridge* With B, [PUK8 (10, 12); k2tog, k6 (8, 10), k2tog] 5 times — 80 (100, 120) stitches. Work Tuck, changing to C on Joining Round. **Tier 3** [Work 8 (10, 12)-stitch LR, joining to next 8 (10, 12) stitches] 5 times. *Tuck ridge* With A, [k2tog, k4 (6, 8), k2tog; PUK6 (8,

CASCADE YARNS Eco Alpaca in color 1516 (A), 1512 (B), 1511 (C)

Experienced

S (M, L)

15 (18½, 22)"

10cm/4"

40

20

over Seed Stitch

1 2 3 **4** 5 6

Medium weight

A 35 (50, 80) yds
B 40 (55, 90) yds
C 45 (60, 95) yds

4mm/US 6, or size to obtain gauge, 40cm (16") or shorter

4mm/US 6, or size to obtain gauge set of 4 or 5

&

crochet hook waste yarn

the
UNITS

Base number
10 (12, 14) stitches

LR

Row 1 (RS) With attached yarn, work pattern of choice to last stitch, dec 1 in pattern to join (SSK or SSP). Row 2 (WS) Work pattern over base stitches. Repeat last 2 rows until all stitches from previous tier have been joined — base number of stitches.

RR

Row 1 (WS) With attached yarn, work pattern of choice to last stitch, dec 1 in pattern to join (p2tog or k2tog). Row 2 (RS) Work pattern over base stitches. Repeat last 2 rows until all stitches from previous tier have been joined — base number of stitches.

double join RR

Glow indicates a modified unit.

For row-by-row instructions see page158.

*Entrée
to
Entrelac*

Seed LBT

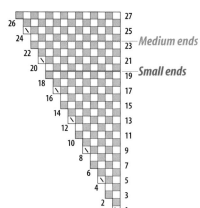

Medium ends

Small ends

Double Seed LBT

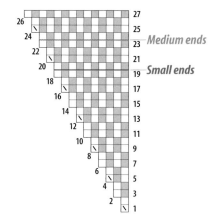

Medium ends

Small ends

Roman Rib LBT

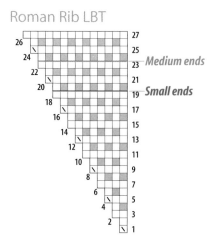

Medium ends

Small ends

10)] 5 times — 60 (80, 100) stitches. Work Tuck, changing to B on Joining Round. *Tier 4* [Work 6 (8, 10)-stitch RR, joining to next 6 (8, 10) stitches] 5 times. *Tuck ridge* With C, [PUK4 (6, 8); k2tog, k2 (4, 6), k2tog] 5 times — 40 (60, 80) stitches. Work Tuck, changing to A on Joining Round. *Tier 5* [Work 4 (6, 8)-stitch LR, joining to next 4 (6, 8) stitches] 5 times. *Tuck ridge* With B, [k0 (k2tog, k2tog), k4 (2, 4), k0 (k2tog, k2tog); PUK4 (4, 6)] 5 times — 40 (40, 60) stitches. Work Tuck, changing to C on Joining Round.

Crown

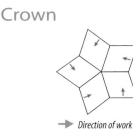

→ Direction of work

Tier 6 Work 4 (4, 6)-stitch RR; work 4 Double Join RR, binding off in pattern on last RR. Sew bound-off stitches to remaining edge of first RR.

Ties Cut four 3 (5, 6)-foot lengths of each color. Thread 4 strands of each color through point of ear flap to half-way point. Tightly braid for 4 (6, 8)" or to desired length. Tie with overhand knot and trim ends.

Chart Note
For Tiers 1 and 2 *For size S (M, L), work stitch pattern over 10 (12, 14) stitches from Row 1 to Row 19 (23, 27). For an LR, begin with Row 1; for a RR, begin with Row 2.*

As base number decreases, so will the number of pattern rows.

Braided Cable

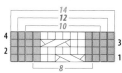

Moss

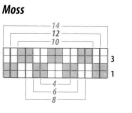

Column

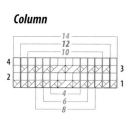

Seed

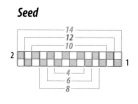

Double Seed

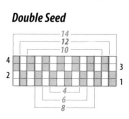

Twill

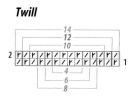

Twin Rib

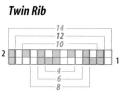

Welt

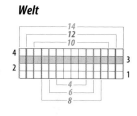

Horseshoe Cable

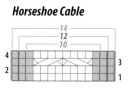

Roman Rib

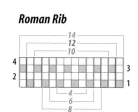

Mistake Rib

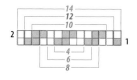

Stitch key
- ☐ Knit on RS, purl on WS
- ▨ Purl on RS, knit on WS
- ⧄ K2tog on RS, p2tog on WS
- ⧅ SSK
- ⓕ Knit into front & back on RS, purl into front & back on WS
- **2/2 LC** Slip 2 to cn, hold to front, k2; k2 from cn
- **2/2 RC** Slip 2 to cn, hold to back, K2; K2 from cn
- **1/1 RT** Skip first stitch. Knit into second stitch. Knit skipped stitch. Drop both from left needle

Cables & lace

Try a scarf, shawl, or throw depending on your committmnet to trying something new. The number of units per tier and the number of tiers define the size of your project. The lace pattern is a simple one row pattern with a reversible cable and seed stitch block. Note that the joins on the lace unit are unique to accommodate for the stitch pattern and the extra rib stitches in the middle.

stitches

LACE FAGGOTING *OVER AN ODD NUMBER OF STITCHES* **All rows** K1, [yo, k2tog] to end.

4/4 RC Slip 4 stitches to cable needle (cn) and hold to front, [k1, p1] 2 times; [k1,p1] 2 times from cn.

BIND OFF IN PATTERN
On last row of last unit in tier, bind off in pattern, binding last stitch over first pick-up stitch in next tier. For Cable RR, [k1, p1] 2 times, [k2tog] 4 times, [k1, p1] 2 times.

notes

◆ *See page 152 for any unfamiliar techniques.*

◆ *Note the special pickup used for each unit.*

◆ *Use cable cast-on throughout.*

◆ *When casting on for first unit of tier, begin LR or RR with Row 2.*

Lace Faggoting LR PUK1, [yo, PUK1] 6 times — 13 stitches. *Row 1 and all WS rows* K1, [yo, k2tog] 6 times. *Rows 2, 4, 6, 8, 18, 20, 22, 24* (RS) K1, [yo, k2tog] 5 times, yo, k3tog to join (last 2 stitches with stitch from previous tier) OR k2tog if not joining. *Rows 10, 12, 14, 16* K1, [yo, k2tog] 5 times, yo, k4tog to join (last 2 stitches with 2 stitches from previous tier) OR k2tog if not joining.

Reversible Cable RR With WS facing and picking up along edge of unit in previous tier, PUP1, [yo, PUP1] 11 times — 23 stitches. *Row 1* (RS) K1, p2tog, k2tog, p2tog, [k1, p1] 4 times, [k2tog, p2tog] 2 times—16 stitches. *Row 2* (WS) [P1, k1] 2 times, [k1, p1] 4 times, p1, k1, p1, k3tog to join (last stitch with 2 stitches from previous tier) OR k1 if not joining. *Row 3* [K1, p1] 2 times, 4/4RC, [k1, p1] 2 times. *Row 4 and all remaining WS rows* [P1, k1] 2 times, [k1 p1] 4 times, p1, k1, p1, k2tog to join (last stitch with stitch from previous tier) OR k1 if not joining. *Rows 5, 7, 9* [K1, p1] 8 times. Repeat Rows 3–10 once. Repeat Rows 3–8 once.

For row-by-row instructions see page158.

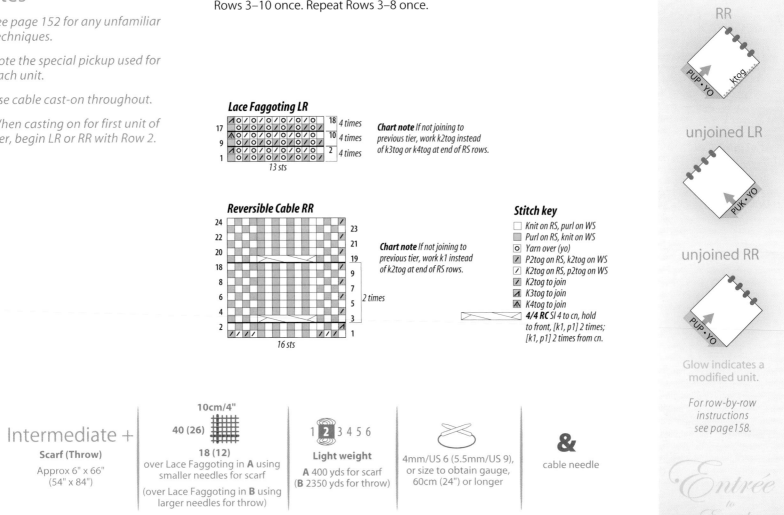

Lace Faggoting LR

17   18 *4 times*
9   10 *4 times*
1   2 *4 times*
13 sts

Chart note *If not joining to previous tier, work k2tog instead of k3tog or k4tog at end of RS rows.*

Reversible Cable RR
16 sts

Chart note *If not joining to previous tier, work k1 instead of k2tog at end of RS rows.*

Stitch key
☐ Knit on RS, purl on WS
▨ Purl on RS, knit on WS
◦ Yarn over (yo)
▨ P2tog on RS, k2tog on WS
▨ K2tog on RS, p2tog on WS
▨ K2tog to join
▲ K3tog to join
▲ K4tog to join
◁▷ **4/4 RC** *Sl 4 to cn, hold to front, [k1, p1] 2 times; [k1, p1] 2 times from cn.*

the UNITS

Base number
Lace 13 stitches
Cable 16 stitches

Work all right-leaning units as Reversible Cables RR and all left-leaning units as Lace Faggoting LR.

LR

RR

unjoined LR

unjoined RR

Glow indicates a modified unit.

Intermediate +
Scarf (Throw)
Approx 6" x 66"
(54" x 84")

10cm/4"
40 (26)
18 (12)
over Lace Faggoting in **A** using smaller needles for scarf
(over Lace Faggoting in **B** using larger needles for throw)

1 2 3 4 5 6
Light weight
A 400 yds for scarf
(**B** 2350 yds for throw)

4mm/US 6 (5.5mm/US 9), or size to obtain gauge, 60cm (24") or longer

&
cable needle

THROW

Note Use larger needle and B throughout.

Tier 1 Cast on 13. Work 1 Unjoined LR (knit last 2 stitches together on RS rows). **Tier 2** With WS facing, cast on 16. Work 1 RR; work 1 Unjoined RR (knit last stitch on WS rows). **Tier 3** Cast on 13. Work 2 LR; work 1 Unjoined LR. **Tier 4** Cast on 16. Work 3 RR; work 1 Unjoined RR. **Tiers 5–12** Repeat Tiers 3 & 4, working 1 more unit (LR or RR) each tier as shown on diagram. **Tier 13, 15, 17** Cast on 13. Work first LR; work 12 LR, binding off in pattern. **Tier 14, 16, 18** Work 12 RR; work 1 Unjoined RR. On Tier 18, bind off in pattern. **Tier 19** Work 12 LR, binding off in pattern. **Tier 20** Work 11 RR, binding off in pattern. **Tiers 21–30** Repeat Tiers 19 & 20, working 1 fewer unit each tier. Block.

ROWAN Cashsoft 4 Ply in color 435 (A) for scarf; Kidsilk Aura in color 767 (B) for throw (page 118).

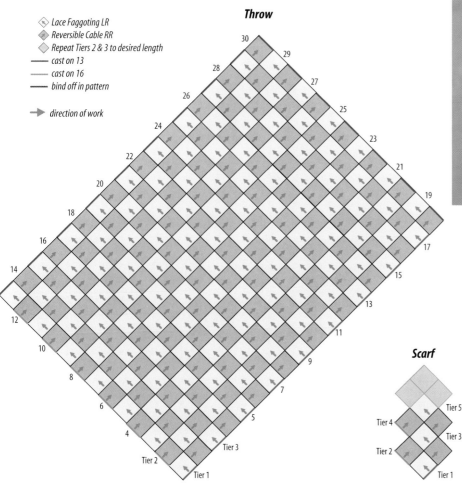

Throw

◇ Lace Faggoting LR
◈ Reversible Cable RR
◇ Repeat Tiers 2 & 3 to desired length
— cast on 13
— cast on 16
— bind off in pattern

➡ direction of work

Scarf

SCARF

Note Use smaller needle and A throughout.

Tier 1 Cast on 13. Work 24 rows in Lace Faggoting. **Tier 2** With WS facing, cast on 16. Work 1 RR; work 1 Unjoined RR, binding off in pattern. **Tier 3** Work 1 LR. Repeat Tiers 2 & 3 to desired length, binding off all stitches in pattern on last row. Block.

Made in easy-care linen, with A-line shaping in both the top and skirt, this pair is designed to be a wardrobe staple. The skirt features an elastic waistband and a main fabric made in a variation of twisted stockinette for additional elasticity. The top echoes the design elements in the skirt. The flounce at the bottom edge of both pieces becomes wider with each change in lace pattern.

notes

◆ *See page 152 for any unfamiliar techniques*

◆ *Skirt is knit in the round from the waist to the hem. Top is worked in both directions starting at the line of entrelac. Entrelac in both projects is knit seamlessly; cut yarn after each tier.*

◆ *To shorten skirt, work the second set of increase rounds closer together; to lengthen skirt, either increase the number of plain rounds between increases OR work additional plain rounds after the final increase round.*

◆ *Entrelac flounce is approximately 8" in length at shortest point.*

Flounce duo

Skirt

Waistband With waste yarn and using temporary crochet cast-on, cast on 145 (169, 193, 217, 241, 265). Knit 1 row. Beginning with a WS row, work 14 rows Twist Stitch. Join by slipping last stitch to left needle, k2tog; place marker (pm) for beginning of round. Work Round 1 of Twist Stitch; purl 1 round. Work 15 rounds of Twist Stitch.

Remove waste yarn and place stitches on smaller circular needle. Fold at purl ridge with slit on inside and hold 2 needles together. [Slip 1 stitch from back needle and 1 stitch from front needle purlwise to right needle; lift back stitch over front stitch and off needle] repeat for each pair of stitches.

Body Working in pattern as established, place markers (pm) as follows: work 18 (21, 24, 27, 30, 33), pm; work 36 (42, 48, 54, 60, 66), pm; [work 18 (21, 24, 27, 30, 33), pm] 2 times; work 36 (42, 48, 54, 60, 66) stitches, pm; work 18 (21, 24, 27, 30, 33) stitches to end of round. Work 6 rounds. ***Increase round*** * [Knit, yo, knit into next stitch, (KOK)], work to marker; repeat from * 5 times more — 12 stitches added. ***Marker shift round*** [Work to marker, remove marker, work 1 stitch, replace marker] working through back loop of each yo as you work around. Repeat last 8 rounds, 5 times more — 216 (240, 264, 288, 312, 336) stitches. Knit 14 rounds, work increase and Marker Shift round. Repeat last 16 rounds 5 times more — 288 (312, 336, 360, 384, 408) stitches.

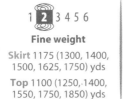

	Standard
C	**Skirt XS (S, M, L, 1X, 2X)**
B A	A 33 (37, 40½, 44½, 48, 51½)"
	B 25"
	Top XS (S, M, L, 1X, 2X)
	A 30 (34, 38, 42, 46, 50)"
	B 22½ (22¾, 23¼, 23½, 23¾, 24)"
	C 18 (19, 20, 20¾, 21½, 22)"

10cm/4"

36

26
over Twist Stitch

1 2 3 4 5 6
Fine weight

Skirt 1175 (1300, 1400, 1500, 1625, 1750) yds

Top 1100 (1250, 1400, 1550, 1750, 1850) yds

3mm/US 3, or size to obtain gauge
2.5mm/US 1
60cm (24") or longer

&

Skirt Only
1¼ yds of 1" non-roll elastic
markers
safety pins
crochet hook
waste yarn

join LBT

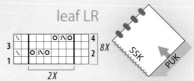

leaf LR

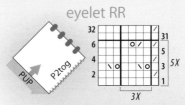

With RS facing, PUK16. Rows 1 & 3 (WS) P16. Row 2 (RS) K2, [k3, yo, sl 1, k2tog, psso, yo] twice, k1, SSK to join. Row 4 K2, [yo, sl 1, k2tog, psso, yo, k3] twice, k1, SSK to join. Repeat Rows 1–4 for a total of 32 rows.

eyelet RR

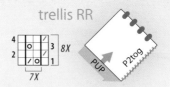

With WS facing, PUP16. Row 1 (RS) K16. Row 2 (WS) P15, p2tog to join. Row 3 K1, [yo, SSK, k2] 3 times, yo, SSK, k1. Row 4 P15, p2tog to join. Row 5 K16. Row 6 P4, [yo, p2tog, p2] twice, yo, p2tog, p1, p2tog to join. Repeat Rows 1–6 for a total of 32 rows, end on Row 2.

trellis RR

With WS facing, PUP16. Row 1 (RS) K1, [yo, k2tog] 7 times, k1. Rows 2 & 4 (WS) P15, p2tog to join. Row 3 K1, [SSK, yo] 7 times, k1. Repeat Rows 1–4 for a total of 32 rows.

purse LR

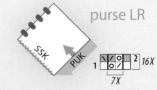

With RS facing, PUK16. **WS rows** P1, [yo, p2tog] 7 times, p1. **RS rows** P1, [yo, p2tog] 7 times, SSP to join. Work 32 rows.

Glow indicates a modified unit.

Entrelac Flounce – Work 12 (13, 14, 15, 16, 17) units as follows: **Tier 1** Work Join LBT. **Tier 2** Work Eyelet RR. **Tier 3** Work Leaf LR. **Tier 4** Work Trellis RR. **Tier 5** Work Purse LR, binding off stitches in pattern on last row of unit, and passing last stitch of unit over first stitch picked up on next unit.

Place safety pin at beginning of elastic; measure elastic around waist with a 1" overlap and mark with second safety pin. Use first safety pin to push elastic through waistband casing at split, temporarily securing elastic to skirt with second safety pin when it reaches the slit. Pin ends of elastic together, making sure it isn't twisted; try skirt on to check and adjust fit. Trim excess elastic and sew ends together; stitch slit closed. Wash garment before wearing to soften the fabric.

stitches

TWIST STITCH *OVER AN ODD NUMBER OF STITCHES*
RS rows K1, [k1 tbl, k1] around.
WS rows P1, [p1, p1 tbl] to last 2 stitches, p2.

TWIST STITCH IN THE ROUND *OVER AN EVEN NUMBER OF STITCHES*
Round 1 [K1, k1 tbl] around.
Round 2 [K1 tbl, k1] around.

PURSE STITCH *OVER AN EVEN NUMBER OF STITCHES*
All rows P1, [yo, p2tog] to last stitch, p1.

PURSE STITCH IN THE ROUND *OVER AN ODD NUMBER OF STITCHES*
Round 1 [Yo, p2tog] to last stitch, p1.
Round 2 [K2tog, yo] to last stitch, k1.

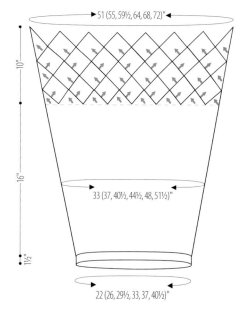

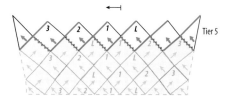
Tier 5

Tier 4

Tier 3

Tier 2

Tier 1

Stitch key

- ☐ Knit on RS, purl on WS
- ▨ Purl on RS
- ⊙ Yarn over (yo)
- ◪ K2tog on RS, P2tog on WS
- ◪ P2tog on RS
- ◪ K2tog to join on RS, p2tog on WS
- ◲ SSK on RS
- ◲ SSK to join
- ◪ SK2P
- ◪ SSP to join

——— picked-up stitch
〰〰 joined edge
——— bind off
◇ L last unit in tier
➡ direction of work

Top

Back With waste yarn and using temporary crochet cast-on, cast on 96 (108, 120, 132, 144, 156) stitches. Knit 1 row; beginning with Row 2, work Twist Stitch, increasing 3 (3, 5, 5, 7, 7) stitches evenly across first row — 99 (111, 125, 137, 151, 163) stitches. Work in pattern as established for 7 (7, 6½, 6½, 6¼, 6½)."

Shape Armhole Bind off 3 (4, 6, 8, 10, 13) stitches at beginning of next 2 rows. Decrease 1 stitch at each edge every RS row 2 (4, 5, 7, 10, 12) times — 89 (95, 103, 107, 111, 113) stitches. Work even until armhole measures 7½ (7¾, 8¾, 9, 9½, 9½)"; bind off in pattern.

Front Work as for Back through armhole shaping. Work even for 2¾ (3, 3¾, 4, 4½, 4½)" on next RS row, bind off center 31 (33, 33, 35, 37, 39) stitches. Place stitches of left shoulder on hold.

Working with attached yarn on right shoulder, decrease 1 stitch at neck edge every other row 14 (15, 16, 17, 18, 18) times. Work even to same length as back. [Bind off 4 (4, 5, 5, 5, 5) stitches at beginning of next WS row] 3 times. Bind off remaining stitches.

CLAUDIA HAND PAINTED YARNS Linen Sport weight in color Deep Blue

Place stitches of left front on needle, join yarn and repeat shaping at neck edge as for right front, reversing shaping by decreasing for neck at end of RS rows and binding off shoulder at beginning of RS rows. Seam front and back together at side and shoulder seams.

Neck edging With smaller needles and RS facing, PUK59 (63, 65, 69, 73, 75) stitches across back neck, 30 stitches along left front neck edge, 31 (33, 33, 35, 37, 39) stitches across center and 31 stitches along right front neck edge — 151 (157, 159, 165, 171, 175) stitches. Work around in Purse Stitch for 10 rounds; bind off in pattern.

Entrelac Flounce Remove waste yarn from Front and Back, placing 192 (216, 240, 264, 288, 312) stitches on needle. Work same as skirt flounce EXCEPT work 8 (9, 10, 11, 12, 13) units for each tier.

Sleeves With waste yarn and using temporary crochet cast-on, cast on 77 (87, 93, 105, 113, 121) stitches. Knit 1 row; beginning with Row 2, work Twist Stitch for 5".

Cap Bind off 3 (4, 6, 8, 10, 13) stitches at beginning of next 2 rows. Decrease 1 stitch each end every RS row 17 (23, 21, 27, 27, 28) times; every 4 rows 3 (1, 3, 1, 2, 2) times. Bind off 10 stitches at beginning of next 2 rows; bind off remaining stitches

Edging Remove waste yarn and place stitches on smaller circular needle. Beginning with a RS row, purl 1 row, decreasing 5 (7, 7, 9, 9, 9) stitches—72 (80, 86, 96, 104, 112) stitches. Work Purse Stitch for 1"; bind off in pattern. Seam underarm; set in sleeve cap. Wash garment before wearing to soften fabric.

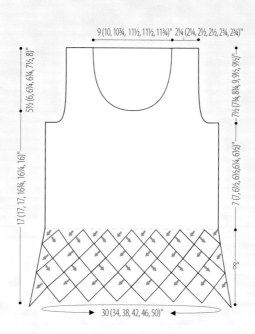

9 (10, 10¾, 11½, 11½, 11¾)" 2¼ (2¼, 2½, 2½, 2¾, 2¾)"

5½ (6, 6¼, 6¾, 7½, 8)"

7½ (7¾, 8¾, 9, 9½, 9½)"

7 (7, 6½, 6½, 6¼, 6½)"

17 (17, 17, 16¾, 16¼, 16)"

8"

30 (34, 38, 42, 46, 50)"

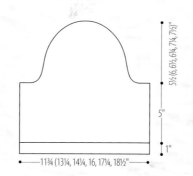

5½ (6, 6½, 6¾, 7¼, 7½)"

5"

1"

11¾ (13¼, 14¼, 16, 17¼, 18½)"

This modular pattern can be a pullover, a cardigan or a vest. Work the Entrelac Strip, Right Front Armhole Panel, and Back for all styles, then work either Pullover Front OR Cardigan Left Front and Right Front Opening Panel. Add sleeves if you like.

stitches

MOSS STITCH
OVER AN EVEN NUMBER OF STITCHES
Row 1 (RS) [K1, p1]. **Row 2** (WS) [K1, p1].
Rows 3 & 4 [P1, k1]. Repeat Rows 1-4.

WELT *6-ROW REPEAT*
Row 1 (WS) Knit. **Rows 2, 3, 6** Purl.
Rows 4 & 5 Knit. Repeat Rows 1-6.

DEC 1 IN PATTERN **RS rows** If next stitch should be knit, decrease by SSK; if next stitch should be purled, SSP.
WS rows If next stitch should be knit, decrease by k2tog; if next stitch should be purled, p2tog

notes

◆ *See page 152 for any unfamiliar techniques.*

◆ *Entrelac strip runs down center of Right Front; top of strip will be part of shoulder.*

◆ *Make note of how many rows are worked to ensure all pieces are the*

Father knows best

Pullover, cardigan, or vest

1 Argyle Panel

Tier 1 With B, work 3 Inc RBT. *Tier 2* With A, work LST, 2 LR, LET.

Tier 3

c
With RS facing and attached B, k6, PUK3 along side of LET9, and work 9-stitch Elongated RR. PUP3 on side of LR5; do not cut yarn.

b
With A, work LET9.

a
With B, work 1 RR. With WS facing, PUP3 on side of LR6; do not cut yarn.

` ` ` `	live stitches
` ` ` `	previously picked-up sts
———	pick-up stitches
⌇⌇⌇	joined edge
→	direction of work

Color key
- ▨ A
- ▢ B

f
With A, work LST, joining 3 stitches. Cut yarn.

e
With RS facing and attached B, k12, PUK3, and work 15-stitch Elongated RR. Cut yarn.

d
With A, work LET. Cut yarn.

Intermediate

Standard Fit
S (M, L, 1X, 2X)
A 40 (44, 48, 52, 56)"
B 24½ (24½, 24½, 29, 29)"
C 32 (34, 36, 36, 36)"
Argyle Reps 5 (5, 5, 6, 6)"

10cm/4"
26
18
over Moss Stitch

1 2 3 **4** 5 6
Medium weight
Cardigan A 950 (1050, 1300, 1425, 1550) yds
Vest: A 675 (750, 950, 1025, 1100) yds
B 145 (150, 175, 180, 190) yds for either

4.5mm/US 7,
or size to obtain gauge,
60cm (24") or longer

&
6 buttons
(cardigan only)

the
UNITS
Base number
3 stitches EXCEPT for
Elongated Rectangles

LR

LST

LET

RR

bo RTT

inc RBT

elongated RR

Glow indicates a
modified unit.

For row-by-row instructions, see page 158.

Tier 4 With A, work LST, 2 LR, LET. *Tier 5* With B, work 3 RR. Repeat last 4 tiers 4 (4, 4, 5, 5) more times or to desired sweater length, end on Tier 4. *Last Tier* With B, work 3 Bo RTT.

Block strip. Strip measures approximately 24½, (24½, 24½, 29, 29)". Measure 9 (10, 11, 12, 13)" from top, mark with stitch markers on either side for armhole.

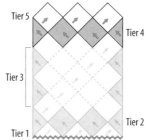

i

With B, work RR over 3 stitches. Cut yarn.

h

With A, work LST. Cut yarn.

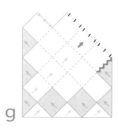

g

With B and beginning with Row 2, work 9-stitch Elongated RR, leaving last 3 stitches of 15-stitch RR on hold. Cut yarn.

Cardigan (Medium) TAHKI-STACY CHARLES, INC Donegal Tweed in colors 880 (**A**) and 894 (**B**)

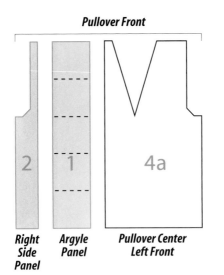

Pullover Front

Right Side Panel

Argyle Panel

Pullover Center Left Front

2 **Right Side Panel** With A, cast on 13 (16, 19, 22, 26). Work Moss Stitch to length of Argyle Panel from bottom to marker, end with a RS row. *Armhole shaping* **Next Row** (WS) Bind off 5 (6, 7, 9, 10), work to end. Dec 1 in Pattern at armhole every RS row 4 (5, 7, 8, 10) times — 4 (5, 5, 5, 6) stitches. Work even until piece is same length as Argyle Panel to shoulder. Bind off; block. With RS facing, sew to Argyle Panel.

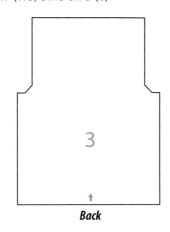

Back

3 **Back** With A, cast on 90 (100, 108, 118, 126). Work Moss Stitch until piece is same length as Right Side Panel to underarm, end with a RS row. *Armhole shaping* Bind off 5 (6, 7, 9, 10) at beginning of next 2 rows. Decrease 1 stitch at each end every RS row 4 (5, 7, 8, 10) times — 72 (78, 80, 84, 86) stitches. Work even until piece is same length as Argyle Panel. Bind off.

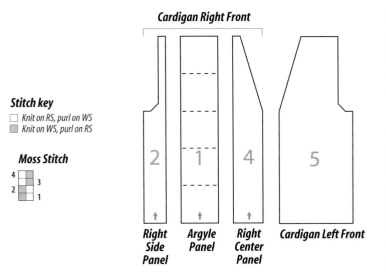

Cardigan Right Front

Right Side Panel

Argyle Panel

Right Center Panel

Cardigan Left Front

Stitch key
□ Knit on RS, purl on WS
■ Knit on WS, purl on RS

Moss Stitch

4 **Cardigan Right Center Panel** With A, cast on 17 (18, 20, 21, 22). Work Moss Stitch until piece is same length as Right Side Panel to underarm, end with a WS row. *Neck shaping* Dec 1 in Pattern at neck every 4 rows 13 (14, 15, 16, 16) times — 4 (4, 5, 5, 6) stitches. Work even until piece is same length as Argyle Panel, bind off. Sew to other side of Argyle Panel.

4a **Pullover Center/Left Front** With A, cast on 45 (49, 54, 58, 63), place marker (pm), cast on 17 (18, 20, 21, 22). Beginning with a WS row, work in Moss Stitch until piece is same length as Back to underarm, end with a WS row. *Right neck shaping* **Next Row** (RS) Work to marker, place stitches just worked on hold for Left Front. Remove marker. Dec 1 in Pattern at beginning of every 4 rows 13 (14, 15, 16, 16) times — 4 (4, 5, 5, 6) stitches. Work even until piece is same length as Back. Bind off. *Left armhole and neck shaping* Place held stitches on needle, attach yarn at neck edge, and work WS row. **Next Row** (RS) Bind off 5 (6, 7, 9, 10) for armhole, work to end — 40 (43, 47, 49, 53) stitches. Dec 1 in Pattern at armhole every RS row 4 (5, 7, 8, 10) times, AT SAME TIME Dec 1 in Pattern at neck every 4 rows 13 (14, 15, 16, 16) times — 23 (24, 25, 25, 27) stitches. Work even until piece is same length as Back. Bind off. Sew to other side of Argyle Panel.

5 **Cardigan Left Front** With A, cast on 45 (49, 54, 58, 63). Work Moss Stitch until piece is same length as Right Front to underarm, end with a WS row. *Armhole and Neck Shaping:* **Next Row** (RS) Bind off 5 (6, 7, 9, 10), work to end. Dec 1 in Pattern at armhole every RS row 4 (5, 7, 8, 10) times, AT SAME TIME Dec 1 in Pattern at neck every 4 rows 13 (14, 15, 16, 16) times — 23 (24, 25, 25, 27) stitches. Work even until piece is the same length as Right Front. Bind off.

128

Sleeve With B, cast on 42 (42, 44, 46, 52); work 6 rows of Welt pattern, cut B. Join A, and work Moss Stitch, increasing 1 stitch at each edge every 7 (6, 6, 5, 5) rows 13 (15, 18, 20, 21) times — 68 (72, 80, 86, 94) stitches. Work even until piece measures 18 (18½, 19½, 18¼, 17½)" or desired length to underarm. *Cap* Bind off 5 (6, 7, 9, 10) at beginning of next 2 rows. Decrease 1 stitch at each edge of every RS row 15 (11, 11, 9, 10) times, every 4 rows 3 (6, 7, 9, 9) times — 24 (26, 30, 32, 36) stitches. Bind off 8 (9, 9, 10, 11) at beginning of next 2 rows; bind off remaining stitches.

Finishing

Sew shoulder seams. Sew sleeves to Body or work Armhole bands for vest. Sew side seams.
Armhole band With B, PUK1 for each stitch, 9 for every 13 rows along armhole. Work 6-row Welt. Bind off.
Bottom band With B and RS facing, PUK180 (200, 216, 236, 252) along bottom. Work 6-row Welt. Bind off.
Cardigan bands Place markers along Left Front for 6 buttons, placing first marker 1" from bottom edge, last marker 1" below beginning of V-neck, and evenly spacing 4 more markers. With RS facing and B, PUK9 for every 13 rows along right center front, 40 (44, 49, 54, 60) along right neck, 26 (30, 30, 32, 32) across back neck, 40 (44, 49, 54, 60) along left neck, and 9 for every 13 rows along left center front. Work 6-row Welt, working 6 buttonholes along Left Front on Row 3, evenly spaced between 1" from bottom and beginning of V-neck shaping where marked. Bind off. Attach buttons on Right Front to correspond to buttonholes.

Pullover neck With RS facing and B, beginning at center front, PUK40 (44, 49, 54, 60) along right neck, 26 (30, 30, 32, 32) across back neck, 40 (44, 49, 54, 60) along left neck — 106 (118, 128, 140, 152) stitches. Working flat, work 6-row Welt. Sew selvedges along center front, crossing left over right.

15 (16, 17½, 19, 20½)"

6¼ (7, 7¾, 8½, 9)"

18 (18½, 19½, 18¼, 17½)"

9 (9, 9½, 10, 11)"

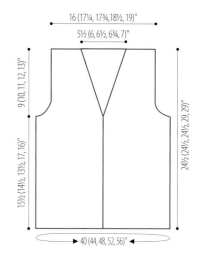

16 (17¼, 17¾, 18½, 19)"

5½ (6, 6½, 6¾, 7)"

9 (10, 11, 12, 13)"

24½ (24½, 24½, 29, 29)"

15½ (14½, 13½, 17, 16)"

40 (44, 48, 52, 56)"

Welt

			6		5
			4		3
			2		1

Stitch key
☐ *Knit on RS, purl on WS*
▨ *Knit on WS, purl on RS*

note

◆ *For pullover or vest armholes and bottom bands, all rows are RS.*

Large TAHKI-STACY CHARLES, INC Donegal Tweed in colors 833 (**A**) and 831 (**B**)

The original version of this project was made for my best friend's baby. Today's model uses short-rowed rectangles in the center of the bag to form a slit for a car seat belt.

Baby's first entrelac

Sleeves

With A and dpn, cast on 28 stitches and divide evenly between 4 needles. Join without twisting, mark beginning of round and work 7 rounds of k1, p1 rib, one in each color. **Tier 1** With 5 base stitches, work 4 Join LBT (1 unit on each needle). **Tier 2** Work 4 RR. **Tier 3** Increasing to 6 base stitches, work 4 LR. **Tier 4** Work 4 RR. **Tier 5** Increasing to 7 base stitches, work 4 LR. **Tier 6** *Underarm Rectangle* Work 1 RR with bind-off in center of previous tier. Place 3 remaining units on hold. Work second sleeve.

stitches

WORK UNIT WITH BIND-OFF
Bind off all stitches on last row of unit.

notes

◆ *See page 152 for any unfamiliar techniques.*

◆ *Work each unit in a different color, weaving ends as you go.*

◆ *To decrease base number: double decrease (p3tog or SSSK 1 stitch from unit with 2 stitches from previous tier) on first joining row and work 2 fewer rows.*

◆ *To increase base number: pick up an extra stitch AND work 2 more rows.*

◆ *The sample uses the colors in equal amounts, choosing at random and allowing no color to touch itself.*

Sleeve

Tier 6
Tier 4
Tier 2
Tier 5
Tier 3
Tier 1

▨ A		▨ A	
☐ B		▨ B	
		☐ C	
ᴵᴵᴵᴵᴵᴵᴵ live stitches		▨ D	
—— pick-up stitches		▨ E	
—— bind-off		▨ F	
—— temporary cast-on		▨ G	
⌇⌇⌇ joined edge			
◇◇ short-row slit			
◆ upper sleeve LR			
direction of work			

the UNITS

Base number
5 to 11 stitches

join LBT

LST

LR

LET

unjoined LR

RR

For row-by-row instructions see page 158.

Entrée to Entrelac

 **Experienced**

C
B — A

Loose Fit
0 – 6 mo

A 20"
B 19"
C 10½"

10cm/4"
34
22
over stockinette stitch

 1 2 **3** 4 5 6
Light weight
A-G 120 yds each
840 yds total

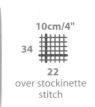
3.75mm/US 5, or size to obtain gauge, 60cm (24")

3.75mm/US 5, set of 5

&
crochet hook
waste yarn
9" zipper

130

SCHOELLER + STAHL Baby Merino in colors 3447 (A) and 4897 (B)

UNIVERSAL YARN Dolce Merino in colors 404, 407, 410, 411, 417, 420, 422

Body

Tier 3 Decreasing to 10 base stitches, work 10 LR. **Tier 4** Work 10 RR. **Tier 5** Work 10 LR.

3D view of Tiers 1 and 2.

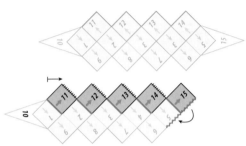

Removing waste yarn and joining to stitches from temporary cast-on, work 4 RR along bottom of Tier 1 rectangles, PUP11 and remove waste yarn from LR 5, placing stitches on left needle. Work RR, joining to live stitches from LR 5 — 110 stitches, 10 RR.

Tier 2 With WS facing, slip live stitches from last LR to right needle and PUP11 along its selvedge. Work 4 RR. PUP11 and remove waste from LR 1, placing stitches on left needle. Work RR, joining to stitches from temporary cast-on.

Tier 1, base rectangles [With waste yarn and temporary crochet cast-on, cast on 11. With main yarn, work Unjoined LR 5 times — 55 stitches, 5 rectangles.

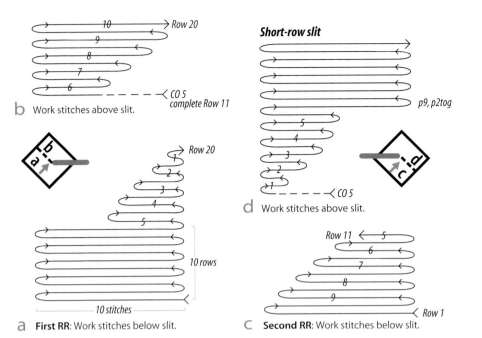

a **First RR**: Work stitches below slit.

b Work stitches above slit.

c **Second RR**: Work stitches below slit.

d Work stitches above slit.

Short-row slit

Begin Tier 6 Work 2 RR; work Short-row slit as follows:

a **First RR** Work RR through Row 10 (5 joins). *Row 11* (RS) K5. *Row 12* P4, p2tog to join. *Row 13* K4, leave 1 stitch unworked. *Row 14* P1, pass unworked stitch over stitch just worked (BO1), p2, p2tog to join. *Row 15* K3, leave 1. *Row 16* P1, BO1, p1, p2tog to join. *Row 17* K2, leave 1. *Row 18* P1, BO1, p2tog to join. *Row 19* K1, leave 1. *Row 20* P2tog, BO1, fasten off.

b *Complete Row 11* With RS facing and joining same color, cast 5 stitches onto right needle; k5. *Row 12* P6. *Row 13 and all RS rows* Knit stitches just worked. *Row 14* P7. *Row 16* P8. *Row 18* P9. *Row 20* P10 — RR complete. Cut yarn.

c **Second RR** With new color, PUP10. *Row 1* (RS) K10. *Row 2* (WS) P9, p2tog to join. *Row 3* K9, leave 1. *Row 4* P1, BO1, p7, p2tog to join. *Row 5* K8, leave 1. *Row 6* P1, BO1, p6, p2tog to join. *Row 7* K7, leave 1. *Row 8* P1, BO1, p5, p2tog to join. *Row 9* K6, leave 1. *Row 10* P1, BO1, p4, p2tog to join. *Row 11* K4; lift 2nd stitch on left needle over first to bind off; k1.

d *Complete Row 1* With attached yarn, cast 5 onto right needle. *Row 2* (WS) P1. *Row 3 and all RS rows* Knit stitch(es) just worked. *Row 4* P2. *Row 6* P3. *Row 8* P4. *Row 10* P5. *Row 12* P9, p2tog to join. *Row 14* P9, p2tog to join. *Rows 15-20* Repeat last 2 rows. Work 3 RR; repeat Short-row slit, steps a–d; work RR. *Tier 7* Decreasing to 9 base stitches, work 10 LR. *Tier 8* Work 10 RR.

Zipper Opening With RS facing, slip 2 units (18 stitches) from left needle to right needle; work is now directly over car seat slit. *Tier 9* Work LST, 9 LR, LET. *Tier 10* Decreasing to 8 base stitches, work 10 RR. *Tier 11* Repeat Tier 9. *Tier 12* Decreasing to 7 base stitches, work 10 RR. **Divide at Underarm** *Tier 13* Work LST; work 2 LR, binding off last LR. Work 5 LR, binding off last LR. Work 2 LR, LET.

Join Sleeves to Body Slip to first bound-off rectangle, 2 rectangles (14 stitches) from left to right needle. Sew underarm rectangle of one sleeve to bound-off stitches of body, seaming rows to stitches and stitches to rows. Slip remaining 21 sleeve stitches onto right needle. Slip to other bound-off rectangle, 4 rectangles (28 stitches) from left to right needle.

Sew second sleeve in place; slip remaining 21 stitches from sleeve onto right needle with body stitches. Slip 2 rectangles (14 stitches) from left to right needle — 98 stitches.

Yoke

Tier 14 Work 14 RR. *Tier 15* Decreasing to 6 base stitches, work LST, 13 LR, LET. *Tier 16* Work 14 RR, binding off last RR (center front). *Tier 17* Decreasing to 5 base stitches, work 13 LR, binding off last LR. *Tier 18* Decreasing to 4 base stitches, work 12 RR.

Hood

Tier 19 Increasing to 5 base stitches, work LST, 11 LR, LET. *Tier 20* Work 12 RR. *Tiers 21-26* Repeat last 2 tiers 3 more times. The next 2 tiers are sewn together to close the hood. When choosing colors, note where units will meet after seaming. *Tier 27* Work LST and 5 LR, all with bind-off; work 6 LR, LET. *Tier 28* Work 6 RR with bind-off.

Seaming Hood Fold hood in half at back, matching point A to valley A, B to B, and so on. Sew stitches to rows and rows to stitches.

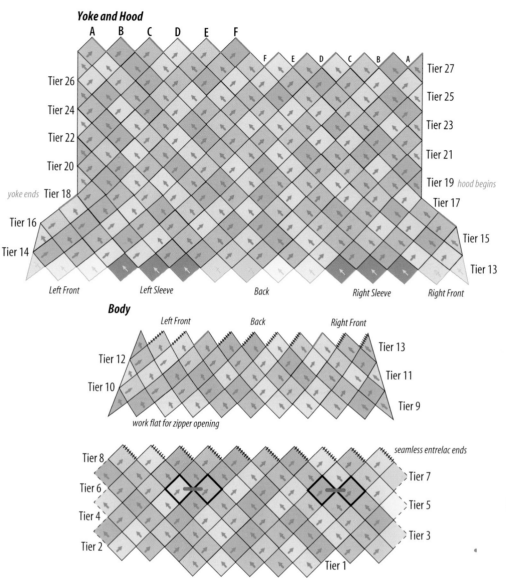

Yoke and Hood

Body

work flat for zipper opening

seamless entrelac ends

Finishing

Car Seat Slit With dpn, PUP15 along front bottom edge of slit; with new dpn, PUP15 along front top edge of slit. With same color and new dpn, PUK15 along back top edge of slit; with new dpn, PUK15 along back bottom edge of slit.

Holding front and back bottom edges together and top edges together, work 3-needle bind-off around slit. Fasten off.

Front Opening and Hood Edging PUK45 along right front, 10 along V-neck, 75 around hood, 10 along V-neck and 45 along left front. Work in k1, p1 rib for 4 rows, changing color every row and binding off in pattern on last row. Insert zipper from bottom of opening to top of neck; block.

Let's knit a gingham fabric and pair it with solid raglan style sleeves bring a baseball jersey to mind. Select your favorite team's colors and make one for the newest baseball (or softball) star in your family.

stitches

SEED STITCH
OVER AN EVEN NUMBER OF STITCHES
Row 1 [K1, p1] to end.
Row 2 [P1, k1] to end.

SEED STITCH
OVER AN ODD NUMBER OF STITCHES
Every row P1, [k1, p1] to end.

2X2 RIB
OVER A MULTIPLE OF 4 STS PLUS 2 FLAT
Every row P1, [k2, p2] to last stitch, k1.

notes

◆ *See page 152 for any unfamiliar techniques.*

◆ *Body is knit in seamless entrelac to armholes; fronts, back, and sleeves are worked flat.*

◆ *Entrelac units and sleeves are worked in Seed Stitch.*

◆ *Right-leaning units are worked in solid colors, changing colors every unit. Left-leaning units are worked with both colors, changing color every RS row.*

Baby gingham

Body

With A, cast on 160 (176, 192) stitches. Place marker (pm) for beginning of round and join. Work k2, p2 rib for 3 rounds, then 1 round B, 4 rounds A.

Tier 1 Work 20 (22, 24) LBT — 100 (110, 120) stitches. *Tiers 2 & 6* Begin with A and alternating colors across tier, work 20 (22, 24) RR. *Tiers 3, 5, 7* Work 20 (22, 24) LR. *Tiers 4 & 8* Begin with B and alternating colors across tier, work 20 (22, 24) RR.

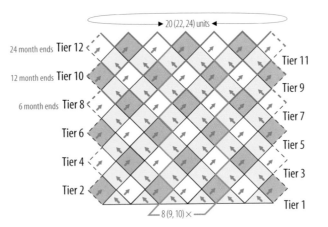

Color key
- ☐ A
- ☐ 2 rows A, 2 rows B
- ▨ B

llllll *live stitches*
——— *picked-up stitches*
——— *bind-off*
∿∿∿ *joined edge*
∧ *base number changes*
➡ *Direction of work*

Stitch key
- ☐ Knit on RS
- ▨ Knit on WS
- ⟋ K2tog on WS
- ⟍ SSK on RS
- ⊢ Inc1 right-slanting
- — Change color

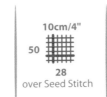

Advanced
Oversized
6 (12, 24) months
A 22 (24½, 27)"
B 9¼ (10½, 11¾)"
C 10½ (11½, 12¾)"

10cm/4"
50
28
over Seed Stitch

1 **2** 3 4 5 6
Fine weight
A 190 (220, 275) yds
B 300 (385, 465) yds

3mm/US 3, or size to obtain gauge, 40-50 cm (16-20")

the
UNITS
Base number
5 stitches

join LBT

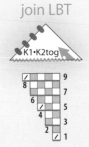

Row 1 With RS facing and new color, k2tog. **Row 2** (WS) K1. **Row 3** (RS) [K1, p1]. **Row 4** and *all WS rows* Work Seed Stitch. **Row 5** K1, p1, k2tog. **Row 7** [K1, p1] twice. **Row 9** [K1, p1] twice, k2tog. End on a RS row; do not turn work. cut yarn left at other end of needle.

LR

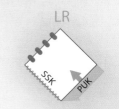

With RS facing and new color, PUK5. **Row 1** (WS) [K1, p1] twice, k1. **Row 2** (RS) Change color, [k1, p1] twice, SSK to join. Repeat last 2 rows 4 more times. Cut yarn left at other end of needle.

LET

Row 1 (RS) Change color, PUK5. **Row 2** and *all WS rows* Work Seed Stitch. **Row 3** and *all RS rows* Change color, work Seed Stitch to last 2 stitches, dec 1. Cut yarn and fasten off.

Entrée
to
Entrelac

LST

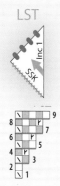

Row 1 (RS) With same color as attached, cast on 1 next to last stitch worked. SSK to join. Row 2 (WS) Inc 1. Row 3 Change color, p1, SSK to join. Row 4 and *all WS rows* Work Seed Stitch to last stitch, inc 1 in pattern. Row 5 and *all RS rows* Change color, work Seed Stitch to last stitch, SSK to join.

RR

With WS facing and new color, PUP5. Row 1 (RS) [P1, k1] twice, p1. Row 2 (WS) [P1, k1] twice, p2tog to join. Repeat last 2 rows 4 more times.

BO RTT

With WS facing and new color, PUP5. Row 1 (RS) [P1, k1] twice, p1. Complete triangle, maintaining Seed Stitch.

Glow indicates a modified unit.

For row-by-row instructions see page 158.

SCHOELLER & STAHL Baby Micro in colors 13447 (**A**) and 14897 (**B**)

Divide for Fronts and Backs

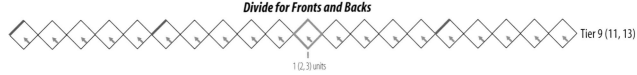

1 (2, 3) units

Tier 9 (11, 13)

12 MONTH ONLY: *Tiers 9, 10* Work as established. Bind off last unit of Tier 10.

24 MONTH ONLY: *Tiers 9–12* Work as established. Bind off last unit of Tiers 11 and 12.

Divide for Front and Back Tier 9 (11, 13) Work 5 LR, bind off last unit; work 10 (11, 12) LR, bind off last unit; work 5 LR, bind off last unit.

Work Tiers 10–15 (12–17, 14–19), following schematic for left and right front.

Back *Tier 10 (12, 14)* Working in established pattern, work one fewer unit each tier and bind off last unit, to Tier 15 (17, 19).

Final Tier Work 3 (4, 5) RTT.

Sleeves

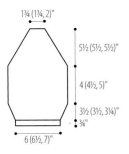

1¾ (1¾, 2)"
5½ (5½, 5½)"
4 (4½, 5)"
3½ (3½, 3¼)"
¾"
6 (6½, 7)"

With A, cast on 42 (46, 50) stitches. Work in k2, p2 rib, 3 rows A, 1 row B, 4 rows A.

Continue with B in Seed Stitch, increasing 1 stitch each edge every 4 rows 11 (11, 10) times — 64 (68, 70) stitches. Work even for 4 (4½, 5)".

Shape Raglan Cap Decrease 1 stitch each edge every 4 rows 8 (7, 7) times, every other row 18 (21, 21) times. Bind off in pattern.

Finishing

Seam raglan sleeve cap to body. Seam underarm.

Neck band With RS facing, A, and starting at center front, PUK 21 (28, 35) stitches along diagonal right neck edge, 16 (17, 16) stitches on vertical edge, 24 (32, 40) stitches on back neck, 16 (17, 16) stitches along vertical left edge, 21 (28, 35) stitches on diagonal neck edge to center front — 98 (122, 142) stitches. Work in k2, p2 rib for 2 rows; then, 1 row B, 2 rows A. Bind off in pattern. Stitch collar along center front edges, crossing left over right for a boy or right over left for a girl.

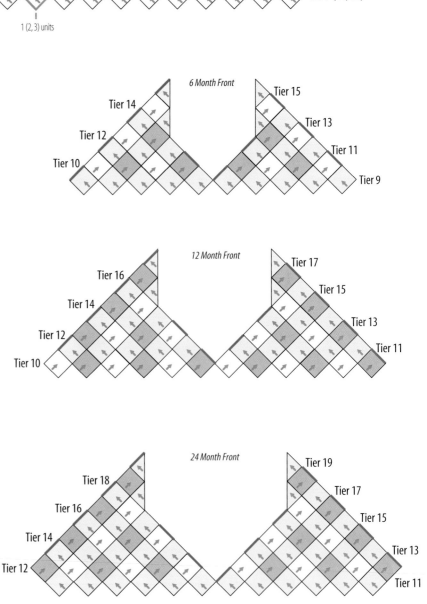

6 Month Front
Tier 14, Tier 15, Tier 12, Tier 13, Tier 10, Tier 11, Tier 9

12 Month Front
Tier 16, Tier 17, Tier 14, Tier 15, Tier 12, Tier 13, Tier 10, Tier 11

24 Month Front
Tier 18, Tier 19, Tier 16, Tier 17, Tier 14, Tier 15, Tier 12, Tier 13, Tier 11

Hearts 'n blocks

the
UNITS

Base number
15 stitches

LR

RR

dbl join LR

unjoined RR

For row-by-row instructions see page 158

Entrée to Entrelac

The entrelac cube, is an example of the 3-dimensional shapes that can be created. Many options are possible, I plan to create a garter stitch cube with embroider dots to look like a pair of fuzzy dice.

notes

- ◆ *See page 152 for any unfamiliar techniques.*
- ◆ *Use an empty dpn to pick up stitches at beginning of each side.*
- ◆ *At end of each side, leave stitches on hold on dpn. Reverse colors for second cube.*

Cube

Side 1 With waste yarn, A, and a temporary crochet cast-on, cast on 15. Work 31 rows in stockinette stitch, end with a RS row. Cut yarn. ***Side 2*** With WS facing and B, work 1 Unjoined RR (PUP15) along left edge of Side 1, end with a WS row. ***Side 3*** With WS facing and continuing with B, work RR, PUP along right edge of Side 2 and join to top of Side 1. Cut yarn. ***Side 4*** With RS facing and A, work LR, PUK along left edge of Side 3 and join to top of Side 2. Cut yarn. ***Side 5*** Remove waste yarn from cast-on and place stitches on dpn. With B, work Double-join LR, PUK along remaining edge of Side 2 and join on WS with top of side 4 and RS rows with bottom of Side 1: ***Row 1*** (WS) P14, p2tog to join with top of Side 4. ***Row 2*** (RS) K14, SSK to join.

Do not cut yarn.

Side 6 With RS facing and continuing with B, work Double-join LR, PUK along right edge of Side 1 and join on WS with top of side 4 and RS with top of Side 3: ***Row 1*** (WS) P14, p2tog to join with top of Side 5. ***Row 2*** (RS) K14, SSK to join.

Bind off all stitches in pattern on last row.

Finishing

Fill shape with poly stuffing. Seam closed, secure and hide tail.

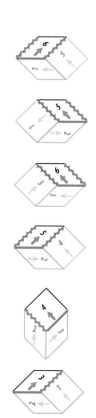

⁙⁙⁙⁙	*live stitches*
——	*picked-up stitches*
⩗⩗⩗⩗	*joined edge*
➞	*direction of work*

Intermediate

Cube Approximately 4" x 4" x 4"
(**Blanket**) 30" x 48"

10cm/4"
20 (16)
14 (8)
over stockinette stitch (over double knit one side only)

1 2 3 4 **5** 6
Bulky weight
Approximately 10–12 yds per side.
For 2 inverse cubes: A, B 60 yds each
(A, B 525 yds each)

5mm/US 8 (6mm/US10) or size to obtain gauge, set of 5

&
poly stuffing
waste yarn

Double knitting seems like a bit of magic. You work two colors, at the same time—each side in opposite colors. The heart motifs emphasize this point with red hearts in green squares on one side and green hearts in red squares on the other. Abracadabra!

stitches

DOUBLE KNIT JOIN PAIR With yarn held to back, slip first stitch as if to knit; slip second stitch to holder, hold to back. Slip 3rd stitch as if to knit, place held stitch back on left-hand needle. Work SSK with stitches on RH-needle; with yarn to front, p2tog stitches on LH-needle.

notes

◆ *See page 152 for any unfamiliar techniques.*

◆ *All units are worked in double knit, with yarns A and B. The yarns are held in back on knit stitches and in front on purl stitches; for each stitch pair (A, B), knit A first and purl B second or (B, A) knit B first and purl A second.*

◆ *At the beginning of each row, twist yarns to ensure the fabric does not separate at edge.*

◆ *When picking up stitches in double knit fabric, insert needle into center of last visible stitch on each side.*

◆ *Each square of chart represents 1 stitch pair and shows the color of the stitch on the facing side.*

Double knit baby blanket

Casting on Join A and B together with overhand knot. With A over thumb and B over index finger and alternately using knit and purl long-tail cast-on, cast on 90 — 45 stitch pairs. **Tier 1** Work 5 BT. **Tiers 2, 4** Work 1 stitch, 4 PR, ET. **Tier 3** Work [HR, 1 PR] twice, HR. **Tier 5** Work [PR, HR] twice, PR. **Tiers 6–16** Repeat Tiers 2-5 twice; 2 and 3 once; 2 once. **Tier 17** Work 5 TT. Bind off all stitches, maintaining stitch pair pattern.

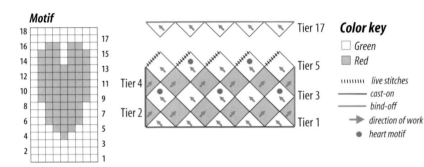

Motif

Color key

□ Green
▨ Red
〰〰〰 *live stitches*
——— *cast-on*
——— *bind-off*
➔ *direction of work*
● *heart motif*

Side A facing

1. Bring both yarns to back, k1 stitch from Side A with MC.

2. Bring both yarns to front, p1 stitch from Side B with CC (k1/p1 pair completed). Repeat Steps 1 and 2.

Changing colors in middle of row

K1 with MC, p1 with CC.

Side B facing

1. Bring both yarns to back, k1 stitch from Side B with CC.

2. Bring both yarns to front, p1 stitch from Side A with MC (k1/p1 pair completed). Repeat Steps 1 and 2.

For motif, k1 with CC, p1 with MC.

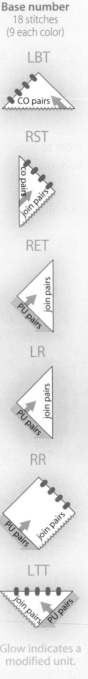

LBT

RST

RET

LR

RR

LTT

Glow indicates a modified unit.

For row-by-row instructions see page 158.

Entrée to Entrelac

Double Knit Units

Base Triangle (BT)

Row 1 (A, B) Work 1 stitch pair. **Row 2 and all even rows** (B, A) Work same number of stitch pairs on previous row. **Row 3** Work 2 stitch pairs. **Row 5** Work 3 stitch pairs. Continue adding 1 stitch pair every odd row to 9 stitch pairs, end on odd row. Do not turn work.

Starting Edge Triangle (ST)

Row 1 (A, B) Work 1 stitch pair. **Row 2** (B, A) Work same number of stitch pairs on previous row; cast on 1 B, A — 1 stitch pair added. **Row 3** Work to last stitch pair, Join Pair. Repeat last 2 rows until all stitches from previous tier have been joined, end on odd row.

Plain Rectangle (PR)

Pick up 9 stitch pairs, alternating PUK1 A on facing side, PUP1 B on reverse side. **Row 1** (B, A) Work 9 stitch pairs. **Row 2** (A, B) Work to last stitch pair, Join Pair. Repeat last 2 rows until all stitches from previous tier have been joined.

Ending Edge Triangle (ET)

Pick up 9 stitch pairs, alternating PUK1 A on facing side, PUP1 B on reverse. **Row 1** (B, A) Work 9 stitch pairs. **Row 2** (A, B) Work to last 2 stitch pairs, Join Pair — 1 stitch pair decreased. Repeat last 2 rows until 1 stitch pair remains. **Next row** K1 A; p1 B — first stitch pair for next tier.

Heart Rectangle (HR)

Work as for PR, following chart and working B, A for white squares and A, B for black squares on odd rows, and reverse on even rows.

Top Triangle (TT)

Pick up 9 stitch pairs, alternating PUK1 A on facing fabric, PUP1 B on reverse side fabric. **Row 1** (B, A) Work 9 stitch pairs. **Row 2 and all even rows** (A, B) Work to last stitch pair, Join Pair. **Row 3** Work 8 stitch pairs, leave last pair unworked. **Row 5** Work 7 stitch pairs, leave last 2 pairs unworked. Continue working 1 less stitch pair every odd row to 1 stitch pair. Turn work, Join Pair.

TRENDSETTER YARNS Blossom in color 14 (A) and color 19 (B)

Designing with entrelac

This final chapter, focused on designing with entrelac, contains only one design, but it is probably the most universal, classic design in the book, a long-sleeved, V-neck cardigan.

The cardigan could be made for a woman or a man, knit with whatever leftover yarns are laying around the house (as shown in the sample) or in a selected yarn or two, modified for lighter or heavier weight yarns—it is a true workhorse of a pattern. It is a jumping off point for starting to your own design in entrelac, and that is the reason it was saved for this chapter.

If you are reading this chapter, there is a strong possibility that you have already begun making design decisions: substituting yarns, working in different gauges, changing stitch counts, altering shapes. The All My Favorites Cardigan pattern contains most of the key entrelac design elements and is used as an example in the discussion that follows. So even if you are not going to knit the project, you will become familiar with it.

All my favorites

Entrelac is an outstanding vehicle for a stash garment. Like many of you, my stash has been accumulating since I became passionate about knitting—in my case about 20 years.

The key is that entrelac is forgiving, so consistent gauge is not an absolute requirement. This means that the finished item may not be exact either.

The pattern is in a classic cardigan style because I anticipate you will want to wear it often. As knitters, we each tend to be drawn to our favorite color, in our favorite weight, of our favorite yarns. This means that your left-over stash will often be composed of all your favorites making your new sweater a favorite, too.

All my favorites

Body

Yoke *Tier 1* [Cast on base number of stitches, work Unjoined LR] 6 times. *Tiers 2–9* Continue yoke following diagram through Tier 9.

Join Back to Fronts Arrange live stitches from Left Front, Back stitches from temporary cast-on, and live stitches from Right Front on needle. *Tier 10* Starting at right front, cast on base stitches. Work 10 RR, 1 Unjoined RR. *Tier 11* Cast on base stitches. Work 11 LR, 1 Unjoined LR. *Tier 12* Work RST, 11 RR, RET. *Tier 13* Work 12 LR. Repeat Tiers 12 and 13 until desired length ending with a right-leaning tier.

notes

◆ *See page 152 for any unfamiliar techniques.*

◆ *Stitches from final units of Tiers 3, 5, 7, & 9 are placed on hold.*

◆ *Work all cast-ons with waste yarn and using temporary crochet cast-on.*

◆ *This sweater is designed so one yarn is used per entrelac unit. Weave in ends as you go to minimize finishing at the end. Only a small amount of yarn is needed per unit, so save all the scraps. Work lighter weight yarns together as one to reach the gauge listed. Small variances in gauge per unit will only have a minor effect on the final project.*

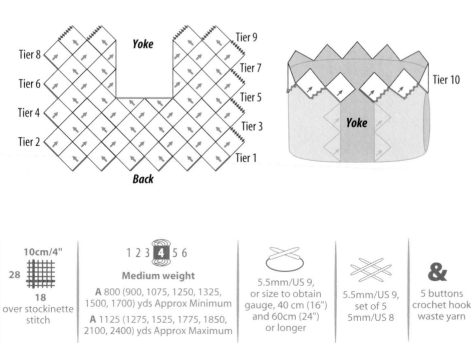

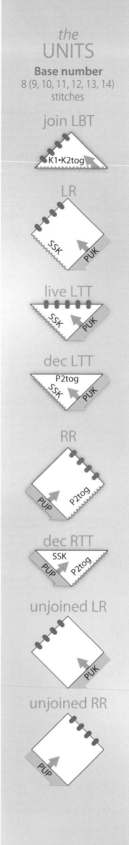

the
UNITS
Base number
8 (9, 10, 11, 12, 13, 14) stitches

join LBT

LR

live LTT

dec LTT

RR

dec RTT

unjoined LR

unjoined RR

For row-by-row instructions see page 158

Intermediate
Loose Fit

XS (S, M, L, 1X, 2X, 3X)
A 32½ (37, 41¼, 45½, 50, 54¼, 58½)"
B 21¾ (21½, 24, 26½, 25, 27, 29¼)"
C 27½ (29, 30, 30, 32, 32½, 33½)"

10cm/4"
28
18
over stockinette stitch

1 2 3 **4** 5 6
Medium weight
A 800 (900, 1075, 1250, 1325, 1500, 1700) yds Approx Minimum
A 1125 (1275, 1525, 1775, 1850, 2100, 2400) yds Approx Maximum

5.5mm/US 9, or size to obtain gauge, 40 cm (16") and 60cm (24") or longer

5.5mm/US 9, set of 5 5mm/US 8

&
5 buttons crochet hook waste yarn

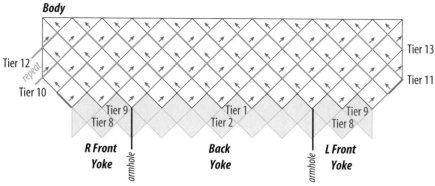

Body

Tier 12

repeat

Tier 10

Tier 13

Tier 11

Tier 9
Tier 8

Tier 1
Tier 2

Tier 9
Tier 8

R Front Yoke

armhole

Back Yoke

armhole

L Front Yoke

⁚⁚⁚⁚⁚ *live stitches*
——— *cast-on*
▬▬▬ *bind-off*
——— *picked-up stitch*
∿∿∿ *joined edge*
➡ *direction of work*

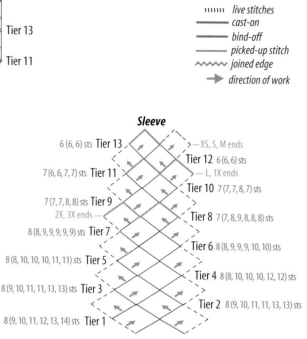

Sleeve

6 (6, 6) sts **Tier 13** — XS, S, M ends
Tier 12 6 (6, 6) sts
7 (6, 6, 7, 7) sts **Tier 11** — L, 1X ends
Tier 10 7 (7, 7, 8, 7) sts
7 (7, 7, 8, 8) sts **Tier 9**
2X, 3X ends — **Tier 8** 7 (7, 8, 9, 8, 8, 8) sts
8 (8, 9, 9, 9, 9) sts **Tier 7**
Tier 6 8 (8, 9, 9, 9, 10, 10) sts
8 (8, 10, 10, 10, 11, 11) sts **Tier 5**
Tier 4 8 (8, 10, 10, 10, 12, 12) sts
8 (9, 10, 11, 11, 13, 13) sts **Tier 3**
Tier 2 8 (9, 10, 11, 11, 13, 13) sts
8 (9, 10, 11, 12, 13, 14) sts **Tier 1**

Last Tier Work 12 Dec LTT.

Sleeves

Left Sleeve Place held stitches from Tiers 3, 5, 7, and 9 of yoke onto dpns, one unit per needle — Base × 4 units. ***Tiers 1–13 (13, 13, 11, 11, 8, 8)*** Work 4 units each tier from diagram.

Sleeve Cuff *Last Tier* Work 6 (6, 6, 7, 7, 8, 8)-stitch Dec LTT (LTT, LTT, LTT, LTT, RTT, RTT). With one yarn and smaller dpn, pick up and knit 36 (36, 36, 42, 42, 48, 48) stitches. Purl 5 rounds changing yarns each round. Bind off in purl.

Right Sleeve Remove waste yarn from first rectangle of Tiers 2, 4, 6, and 8 and place stitches for each rectangle on a larger dpn — Base × 4 units. Work same as Left Sleeve.

Finishing

Hem With one yarn, starting at left front corner, pick up and knit 144 (162, 180, 198, 216, 234, 252) stitches. Work in garter stitch for 10 rows, changing yarns every row. Bind off.

Button band and neck edging With one yarn, starting at right front corner, pick up and knit 3 stitches for every 2 triangle stitches, 1 stitch for every 2 rows of stockinette or garter, and 1 stitch for every stitch of stockinette around to left front corner. Work in garter stitch for 10 rows, changing yarns every row and placing buttonholes on Row 4 on right front beginning 1" from bottom edge and spacing the remaining 4 holes evenly to the beginning of the V-neck

143

Designing with entrelac

Challenges

Let's start with the reality that entrelac is a bias fabric. Those blocks are set on the diagonal and present unique design opportunities. Entrelac can stretch significantly without appearing distorted—much more than standard knit fabrics. Less ease is required because the fabric has more 'give.' With just one size, an entrelac garment can fit a wider range of bodies.

When you combine entrelac with standard knitting, you have to merge diagonal with vertical and horizontal edges. The triangle units used to bring entrelac back to square are not composed of a complete row or column of stitches but rather single stitches aligned from a series of rows. This means that the edge of a triangle has fewer stitches per inch than standard knitting of the same gauge and, of course, fewer rows per inch.

Throughout the book we increase 1 stitch for every 2 stitches whenever we go from standard knitting to entrelac or vice versa. The ratio of 3 to 2 seems to work in most cases. It has a lot to do with the Pythagorean theory— which we will discuss shortly.

Gauge

No knitting book would be complete without a section on gauge. But the diagonal nature of entrelac fabric requires a different approach to gauge. Along with different calculations, you have to accept that not all shapes and forms can be reasonably constructed.

In traditional knitting the question is, 'How many stitches will it take to get around the body?' When calculating the gauge, we work with stitches and rows stacked neatly and squarely within a predefined space. The number of stitches and rows within 4 inches or 10 centimeters can be broken down to single inches and centimeters. Then it's easy to multiply stitches per inch by your desired width. Length is usually easier; 'work to desired length,' allows great freedom in garment length.

You are probably familiar with this process and can comfortably punch out numbers on your calculator. But entrelac is a bit different. You have the confines of creating units that are basically twice as many rows as stitches; and those units are set on the diagonal, so you need to measure across a block from point to point for both height and width. Because you need to work with these units—we have that added variable. A bit tricky, but not a deal breaker. It is similar to working with a pattern repeat in a lace or cable patterns.

Now, the question becomes, 'How many units of what size do I need to get around a body?' Because entrelac is worked in units, garment size changes can be easily achieved by changing the base stitch count for the units, by adding or subtracting whole units, or, occasionally, by doing both. Calculating entrelac gauge is about determining the size and number of units needed in a garment. In fact, there are two ways to calculate entrelac gauge, the mathematical way and the knitterly way, with visual estimation. The mathematical way is my preference. From time to time, however, I check my mathematical calculations against the visual method and the differences are consistently tiny — close enough for knitting!

Calculating gauge starts the same way

The initial step to calculating entrelac gauge is the same: knit a swatch of a reasonable size in the yarn, needle, and pattern stitch of your choosing. In the case of entrelac, 'reasonable' is a few inches wider and longer than the anticipated size of the largest unit. The additional inches allow for measurements to be made in the middle of the fabric without distortion from

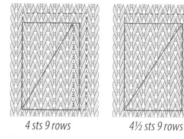 

4 sts 9 rows   4½ sts 9 rows   5 sts 10 rows

the edges, as well as the opportunity to measure a larger unit, should one be needed in the design.

It is important to remember that 'standard' entrelac units have twice as many rows as stitches. Therefore, an entrelac unit with 5 base stitches would have 10 rows. However, as a result of the joining process, each unit looses one row. And, when stitches are picked up along the selvedge edge, either a whole stitch or a half stitch is used up. Therefore, it is necessary to reduce the measurements by one stitch, vertically, and either one whole or one-half stitch, horizontally. It is important to note that both stitch and row gauge play a critical part in this calculation. If we look back at Morning, Noon and Night (page 84) we see that the stitch gauge for the Long Sleeve and Short Sleeve versions are within ¼ stitch per inch. However, their row gauges vary by 2 rows per inch. The resulting diagonal measurement of a 10-stitch unit in the Long Sleeve version is approximately 3.7" while the Short Sleeve version is approximately 3". Since it takes 10 units to get around the body in that pattern, it means the difference in row gauge has changed the finished bust measurement by 7".

Visual estimation

I start visually because to understand the math it helps me to *see* what is being calculated. Using pins, split ring markers, or some other method, mark a rectangle equivalent to the anticipated size of the entrelac unit being created, marking each corner.

Using a ruler, measure the diagonal distance between the markers. The resulting measurement will be the approximate height and width of each rectangular entrelac unit. Technically, this diagonal line will not fall in an exact vertical or horizontal position in the final entrelac fabric, but it acts like it does and averages out because the diagonal on adjacent units fall in the opposing angle, averaging out to a balanced fabric of units. This is just another example of the forgiving properties of entrelac.

Note your results (the diagonal measurement) and repeat the process for each size of unit required in the design. In some cases, only one unit size is used, but in other designs a number of different-sized units will be used.

The mathematical method

The Visualization and mathematical method work together. The mathematical method begins with a swatch, but it is only used to determine the number of stitches and rows per inch. It is important *NOT* to round to a whole number, but instead round to at least 1 or 2 decimal places.

If you didn't like math class — particularly geometry — this might not be the ideal method for you. However, the calculation is easy with the aid of a standard hand-held calculator. Even more helpful for the entrelac enthusiast, is a spreadsheet (with formulas) that does the math for you, all you do is enter is the stitch and row numbers. (Download a sample spreadsheet, visit my entrelac web site at www.nameofsite.com.)

Pythagorean Theorem

To calculate entrelac gauge mathematically, determine the diagonal length of the rectangle. Do this by applying the Pythagorean Theorem, which states: the short side of the rectangle multiplied by itself (AxA or A^2), plus the long side of the rectangle multiplied by itself (BxB or B^2), equals the diagonal measurement multiplied by itself (CxC or C^2). The formula looks like this: $A^2 + B^2 = C^2$

To calculate the diagonal measurement of a unit:

1 Determine the width of the rectangle by counting the stitches within the marked rectangle on your swatch and subtracting the subsequent pick-up (one whole or one-half stitch); divide that number by the stitch gauge; multiply the result by itself. This is A^2.

2 Determine the length of the rectangle by counting the rows within the rectangle and subtracting the subsequent join (one row); divide that number by the row gauge; multiply the result by itself. This is B^2.

3 Add the results of Step 1 and Step 2. This is C^2.

4 Use a calculator to determine the square root C^2. The result is the diagonal length of the unit.

As with visual estimation this process needs to be repeated for each size unit anticipated for the project. In my spreadsheet, I calculate the diagonal measurements with 3 assumptions: no stitch loss, one half stitch loss and a whole stitch loss. I do this for stitch counts from 4 to 30 stitches; this makes easy reference for blocks of many sizes. For almost all of my projects I use the numbers from the one-half stitch column, because that is my preferred method of picking up stitches.

Designing a sample project

You are now ready to design your own project. Besides picking a garment, you have made a choice of yarn, needle, stitch pattern; anticipated the size of units needed; and calculated the base number for those units.

To illustrate the possible design decisions and calculations, I will refer to a sample project — a long sleeve cardigan. (In fact, this is the design process I went through for the All My Favorites Cardigan.)

Start with diagrams

Diagrams are always a useful tool, but even more so when designing with entrelac. Over the years, I have discovered that diagrams are probably the best way to begin a design in entrelac.

I use 3 types for my entrelac designs:

- Generic graphic representation
- Directional representation
- 3-dimensional representation

The generic diagram is basically a sketch of the garment and is often all I have created before completing the gauge step. Diagrams do not have to be perfect or even highly-detailed; they need to be just accurate enough to help you visualize the final design. Use a generic diagram to determine the approximate size of the units and the type and placement of fabrics. At this stage, use the generic diagram to address details that may impact your design.

The directional diagram is used for understanding the direction of the various entrelac units. I use this diagram more than any other in the entrelac design process. The grid of square diamonds and right triangles, with arrows indicating the lean of a unit and the direction in which it is created. They are useful particularly in designing necklines, armholes, and other non-rectangular shapes. In most cases, I don't worry about drawing the units to scale, but use the diagram to note unit sizes and their tiers. A directional diagram along with a few notes is often sufficient for knitting an entire project.

A 3-dimensional model is the next level. The 3-dimensional model is made from pieces of grid paper that are cut and taped together to ensure that a great idea will actually work. In some cases, I use gingham fabric for the model; the fabric is flexible and the gingham pattern easily mimics a grid.

In the sample project, the generic diagram shows an all-over entrelac fabric with 5 or 6 units across the body, tapered long sleeves, a V-neck, and cardigan front. The directional schematic helps determine the construction of the garment. By building the yoke first, the sleeves can be started at the shoulders and worked down toward the wrist. The yoke can then be joined front to back and the remainder of the body knit down to the hem resulting in a completely seamless garment. This schematic is also used to refine the shaping of the V-neck. The 3-dimensional schematic verifies that all the pieces will come together resulting in an uninterrupted pattern throughout.

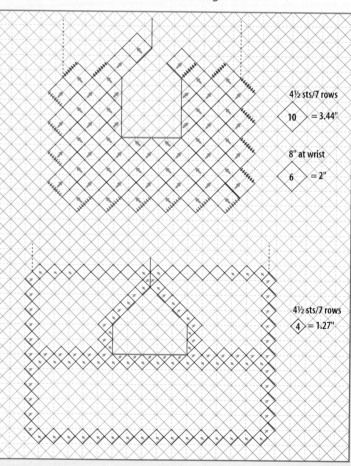

4½ sts/7 rows

10 = 3.44"

8" at wrist

6 = 2"

4½ sts/7 rows

4 = 1.27"

Directional diagram

147

The distinctive construction of entrelac fabric opens up a variety of ways to construct a project. Instead of choosing between bottom-up or top-down, the choice can be to knit in practically any direction…and do so without creating any obvious joins or seams. The complex nature of entrelac fabric presents some construction limitations, but honestly, I have yet to come across a problem that cannot be solved with a little creativity.

Merging and blending with standard knitting

A unique characteristic of entrelac is that the ratio of entrelac rows to stitches of transitional fabric is very consistent it can almost be applied universally as 2 stitches of a base or top triangle (since this is usually where the transition occurs) is usually equivalent to 3 stitches of the adjoining standard fabric worked at the same gauge.

Merging with standard knitting

You ask, 'But I do not want a garment of only entrelac? What now?' Great question especially because there are projects in the book that do this type of combination. But, more importantly if you plan to add button bands, arm bands, or sleeves you need this information as well and most projects have a finished edge that is not entrelac.

A unique characteristic of entrelac is that the ratio of entrelac rows to entrelac stitches are 2 to 1. You always join 2 rows to one stitch between units — be it decreases every other row, or picked up stitches every other row with half the amount of stitches.

Do you see something here? The 2 ends of a rectangle are stitches, plus every other row is joined to stitches from the previous tier, and the opposite selvedge will be a pick-up edge for stitches for a unit in the next tier. Every rectangle has a frame of the same number of stitches! That means each rectangle compacts into a square frame. And with the Pythagorean theory you get a square that works out to the ratio of Sides being 1X, and the diagonal is the square root of 2X which works out to a 1 to 1.4 ratio or approximately 2 to 3 which is perfect for knitting. The ratio is very important as long as you continually use yarns with the same gauge within a piece.

When you transition from standard fabric to entrelac, the process involves turning 3 stitches into 2 stitches or 2 joins (4 rows) — you could join, alternating 2-stitch with 3-stitch decreases, where only 1 stitch from the unit is joined alternately with 1, then 2 of the standard fabric.

Going from entrelac to standard knit will involve increasing 1 stitch for every 2. This can be accomplished in a few ways — picking up 3 stitches for every 2 stitches along the top ending triangle, or base triangle. pick up stitch for stitch (the bans number) and then increasing 1 between pairs of stitches.

Along the edge triangles one would picking up 3 stitches for every 4 rows along the edge of a beginning or ending triangle. Another option is to pick up a stitch in each decreased increased stitch and increase between pairs of stitches to get that 2 to 3 ratio.

This information enables you to pick up the proper amount of stitches for along the triangle hypotenuse so that you aren't blindly guessing and hoping for edge treatments that do the job.

This 45° and 90° grid works well for entrelac.

For free download of this grid go to KnittingUniverse.com/entrelac

Entrée
to
Entrelac

Project Yarns

CLAUDIA HAND PAINTED YARNS *Linen* (100% linen; 100g; 270yd)

KOIGU WOOL DESIGNS *KPPPM* (100% Merino Wool; 50g; 175yds)

KOLLAGE YARNS *Luscious* (63% Cotton, 37% Nylon elastic; 100g; 345yds)

MALABRIGO *Lace* (100% Baby Merino Wool; 50g; 470yds)

ROWAN *Pure Wool 4 Ply* (100% Super Wash Wool; 50g; 174yds)

SKACEL/SCHOELLER+STAHL *Baby Micro* (46% Superwash Wool, 46% Microfiber, 8% Acetate; 25g; 107yds)

BERROCO YARNS, INC. *Ultra Alpaca Light* (50% Superfine Alpaca, 50% Peruvian Wool; 50g; 144yds)

BERROCO YARNS, INC. *Bonsai* (97% Bamboo, 3% Nylon; 50g; 77yds)

BERROCO YARNS, INC. *Pure Pima* (100% Pima Cotton; 50g; 115yds)

BROWN SHEEP CO. INC. *Lanaloft Sports Weight* (100% Wool; 50g; 145yds)

PLYMOUTH YARNS *Grass* (65% Cotton, 35% Hemp; 50g; 115yds)

SKACEL/SCHULANA *Merino Cotton 135* (53% Merino Wool, 47% Cotton; 50g; 148yds)

UNIVERSAL YARN *Dolce Merino* (50% Merino, 50% Microfiber; 50g; 126yds)

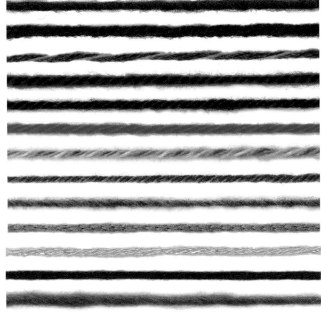

BROWN SHEEP CO. INC. *Lana Loft Worsted* (100% Wool; 50g; 145yds)

BROWN SHEEP CO. INC. *Shepherd's Shades* (100% Wool; 100g; 131yds)

BROWN SHEEP CO. INC. *Serendipity Tweed* (60% Cotton, 40% Wool; 100g; 210yds)

BROWN SHEEP CO. INC. *Nature Spun Worsted* (100% Wool; 100g; 245yds)

CASCADE YARNS *Eco Alpaca* (100% Natural undyed Alpaca; 100g; 220yds)

CASCADE YARNS *220* (100% Peruvian highland wool; 100g; 220yds)

JOJOLAND *Rhythm* (100% Wool; 50g; 110yds)

JOJOLAND *Rythmn Superwash* (100% Wool; 50g; 110yds)

KNIT ONE, CROCHET TOO *Paintbox* (100% Wool; 50g; 100yds)

KNIT ONE, CROCHET TOO *Wick* (53% Soy, 47% Polypropylene; 50g; 120yds)

KOLLAGE YARNS *Temptation* (65% Bamboo, 27% Cotton, 8% Nylon; 50g; 90yds)

KOLLAGE YARNS *Cornucopia* (100% Corn; 35g; 100yds)

LORNA'S LACES *Bullfrogs & Butterflies* (85% Wool, 15% Mohair; 113g; 190yds)

Yarn weight categories

Yarn Weight

1	**2**	**3**	**4**	**5**	**6**
Super Fine	*Fine*	*Light*	*Medium*	*Bulky*	*Super Bulky*

Also called

Sock Fingering Baby	Sport Baby	DK Light- Worsted	Worsted Afghan Aran	Chunky Craft Rug	Bulky Roving

Locate the Yarn Weight and Stockinette Stitch Gauge Range over 10cm to 4" on the chart.
Compare that range with the information on the yarn label to find an appropriate yarn.
These are guidelines only for commonly used gauges and needle sizes in specific yarn categories.

Stockinette Stitch Gauge Range 10cm/4 inches

27 sts to 32 sts	23 sts to 26 sts	21 sts to 24 sts	16 sts to 20 sts	12 sts to 15 sts	6 sts to 11 sts

Recommended needle (metric)

2.25 mm to 3.25 mm	3.25 mm to 3.75 mm	3.75 mm to 4.5 mm	4.5 mm to 5.5 mm	5.5 mm to 8 mm	8 mm and larger

Recommended needle (US)

1 to 3	3 to 5	5 to 7	7 to 9	9 to 11	11 and larger

LOUET *MerLin Worsted* (70% Merino Wool, 30% Wet Spun Linen; 100g; 156yds)

MALABRIGO *Worsted* (100% Merino Wool; 100g; 210yds)

MOUNTAIN COLORS *4/8's Wool* (100% Wool; 100g; 250yds)

MUENCH YARNS *Touch Me* (72% Rayon Microfiber, 28% Wool; 50g; 61yds)

PRISM ARTS, INC *Neat Stuff* (Rayon, Cotton, Nylon, Kid Mohair, Wool, Alpaca, Poly; 85-113g; 150yds)

PRISM ARTS, INC *Frost* (100% Nylon; 42.5g; 90yds)

ROWAN *Kidsilk Aura* (75% Kid Mohair, 25% Silk; 25g; 82yds)

SKACEL/ZITRON *Opus 1* (100% Wool infused with Aloe Vera and Jojoba oils; 100g; 208yds)

TAHKI STACY CHARLES, INC./ TAHKI YARNS *Donegal Tweed* (100% Pure New Wool; 100g; 183yds)

TRENDSETTER YARNS *Tonalita* (52% Wool, 48% Acrylic; 50g; 100yds)

5
Bulky

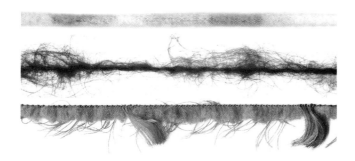

KNIT ONE, CROCHET TOO *PJ's* (100% Polyester; 50g; 88yds)

MOUNTAIN COLORS *Mohair* (78% Mohair, 13% Wool, 9% Nylon; 100g; 225yds)

TRENDSETTER YARNS *Blossom* (73% Nylon, 27% Viscose; 50g; 90yds)

Techniques

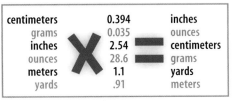

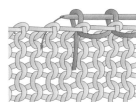

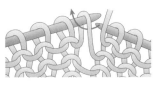

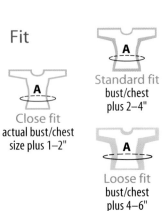

TECHNIQUES

Specifications
at a glance

Use the charts and guides below to make educated decisions about yarn thickness, needle size, garment ease, and pattern options.

centimeters	**0.394**	**inches**
grams	0.035	ounces
inches	**2.54**	**centimeters**
ounces	28.6	grams
meters	**1.1**	**yards**
yards	.91	meters

Conversion chart

Equivalent weights

¾	oz	20 g	
1	oz	28 g	
1½	oz	40 g	
1¾	oz	50 g	
2	oz	60 g	
3½	oz	100 g	

Needles/Hooks

US	MM	HOOK
0	2	A
1	2.25	B
2	2.75	C
3	3.25	D
4	3.5	E
5	3.75	F
6	4	G
7	4.5	7
8	5	H
9	5.5	I
10	6	J
10½	6.5	K
11	8	L
13	9	M
15	10	N
17	12.75	

Sizing

Measuring

A Bust/Chest
B Body length
C Center back to cuff
arm slightly bent

BASICS

Yarn over (yo)

Between knit stitches
Bring yarn under the needle to the front, take it over the needle to the back and knit the next stitch.

Between purl stitches
With yarn in front of needle, bring it over the needle to the back and to the front again; purl next stitch.

On next row
Knit or purl into front of yarn-over unless instructed otherwise. The yarn-over makes a hole and adds a stitch.

Knit through the back loop (k1 tbl)

1 With right needle behind left needle and right leg of stitch, insert needle into stitch…

2 …and knit.

Purl through the back loop (p1 tbl)

1 With right needle behind left needle, insert right needle into stitch from left to right…

2 …and purl.

Pick up & knit

With right side facing and yarn in back, insert needle from front to back in center of edge stitch, catch yarn and knit a stitch. (See stockinette above, garter below.)

Pick up & purl

With wrong side facing and yarn in front, insert needle from back to front in center of edge stitch, catch yarn, and purl.

Measure around the fullest part of your bust/chest to find your size.

Children	2	4	6	8	10	12	14
Actual chest	21"	23"	25"	26½"	28"	30"	31½"

Women	XXS	XS	Small	Medium	Large	1X	2X	3X
Actual bust	28"	30"	32–34"	36–38"	40–42"	44–46"	48–50"	52–54"

Men	Small	Medium	Large	1X	2X
Actual chest	34–36"	38–40"	42–44"	46–48"	50–52"

Fit

Close fit
actual bust/chest size plus 1–2"

Standard fit
bust/chest plus 2–4"

Loose fit
bust/chest plus 4–6"

CAST-ONS

Temporary crochet cast-on

1 With waste yarn and leaving a short tail, make a slipknot on crochet hook. Hold hook in right hand; in left hand, hold knitting needle on top of yarn and behind

hook. With hook to left of yarn, bring yarn through loop on hook; yarn goes over top of needle, forming a stitch.

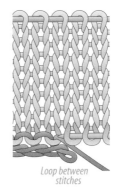

2 Bring yarn under point of needle and hook yarn through loop forming next stitch. Repeat Step 2 until 1 stitch remains to cast on. Slip loop from hook to needle for last stitch.

Picking up loops from a temporary cast-on

Loop between stitches

Temporary cast-ons use waste yarn to hold the loops that form between stitches under the needle. When this waste yarn is removed, these loops can be placed on a needle and worked into.

There will seem to be 1 fewer loops than cast-on stitches. Pick up the last loop in the loop between the last stitch of the first row of knitting and the first stitch of the second row of knitting.

Cable cast-on

1 Start with a slipknot on left needle (first cast-on stitch). Insert right needle into slipknot from front. Wrap yarn over right needle as if to knit.

2 Bring yarn through slipknot, forming a loop on right needle.

3 Insert left needle in loop and slip loop off right needle. One additional stitch cast on.

4 Insert right needle **between** the last 2 stitches. From this position, knit a stitch and slip it to the left needle as in Step 3. Repeat Step 4 for each additional stitch.

Long-tail cast-on, knit

Make a slipknot for the initial stitch, at a distance from the end of the yarn, allowing about 1½" for each stitch to be cast on.
1 Bring yarn between fingers of left hand and wrap around little finger as shown.

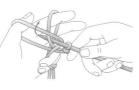

2 Bring left thumb and index finger between strands, arranging so tail is on thumb side, ball strand on finger side. Open thumb and finger so strands form a diamond.

3 Bring needle down, forming a loop around thumb.
4 Bring needle **under** front strand of **thumb loop**…

7 Slip thumb out of its loop, and use thumb to adjust tension on the new stitch. One knit stitch cast on.

Repeat Steps 3–7 for each additional stitch.

5 …up **over index finger yarn**, catching it…

6 …and bringing it **under** the front of **thumb loop**.

Long-tail cast-on, purl

1–3 Work as Steps 1–3 of long-tail cast-on, knit.
4 Bring needle **behind yarn** around index finger, **behind** front strand of **thumb loop**…

5 …up **over index finger yarn**, catching it…

6 …and bringing it **in front of** thumb loop…then backing it out **under thumb loop** and **index finger yarn**.

7 Slip thumb out of its loop, and use thumb to adjust tension on the new stitch. One purl stitch cast on.

Repeat Steps 3–7 for each additional stitch.

INCREASES

Knit into front and back (kf&b)

1 Knit into the front of next stitch on left needle, but do not pull the stitch off the needle.
2 Take right needle to back, then knit through the back of the same stitch.

3 Pull stitch off left needle. Completed increase: 2 stitches from 1 stitch. This increase results in a purl bump after the knit stitch.

Purl into front and back (pf&b)

1 Purl into front of next stitch, but do not pull stitch off needle.
2 Take right needle to back, then through back of same stitch, from left to right…

3 … and purl.

4 Pull stitch off left needle. Completed increase: 2 stitches from 1 stitch. This increase results in a purl bump before the stitch on the right side.

Inc 1 (knit into back of yarn over)

Insert right needle through back loop of yarn-over strand on left needle and knit.

The yarn over twists for a left-slanting increase.

BIND-OFFS

Bind off knitwise

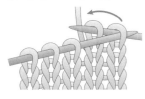

1 Knit 2 stitches as usual.
2 With left needle, pass first stitch on right needle over second stitch…

… and off needle: 1 stitch bound off (see above).
3 Knit 1 more stitch.
4 Pass first stitch over second. Repeat Steps 3–4.

Bind off purlwise

Work Steps 1–4 of Bind off Knitwise EXCEPT, **purl** the stitches instead of knitting them.

Fasten off

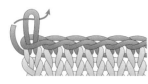

Work bind-off until only 1 stitch remains on right needle. If this is the last stitch of a row, cut yarn and fasten off stitch as shown above. Otherwise, this is the first stitch of the next section of knitting.

3-needle bind-off

Bind-off ridge on wrong side
1 With stitches on 2 needles, place **right sides together**. * Knit 2 stitches together (1 from front needle and 1 from back needle, as shown); repeat from * once more.
2 With left needle, pass first stitch on right needle over second stitch and off right needle.

3 Knit next 2 stitches together.
4 Repeat Steps 2 and 3, end by drawing yarn through last stitch.

Bind-off ridge on right side
Work as for ridge on wrong side, EXCEPT, with **wrong sides together**.

DECREASES

K2tog

1 Insert right needle into first 2 stitches on left needle, beginning with second stitch from end of left needle.

2 Knit these 2 stitches together as if they were 1.
The result is a right-slanting decrease.

P2tog

1 Insert right needle into first 2 stitches on left needle.

2 Purl these 2 stitches together as if they were 1.
The result is a right-slanting decrease.

K3tog

1 Insert right needle into first 3 stitches on left needle, beginning with third stitch from tip.
2 Knit all 3 stitches together, as if they were 1.
The result is a right-slanting double decrease.

SSK

1 Slip 2 stitches **separately** to right needle as if to knit.

2 Slip left needle into these 2 stitches from left to right and knit them together: 2 stitches become 1.

The result is a left slanting decrease.

SSSK

Work same as **SSK** EXCEPT:
1 Slip **3** stitches….
2 Slip left needle into these 3 stitches… 3 stitches become 1. The result is a left-slanting double decrease.

P3tog

1 Insert right needle into first 3 stitches on left needle.
2 Purl all 3 stitches together, as if they were 1. The result is a right-slanting double decrease.

SSP

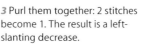

1 Slip 2 stitches **separately** to right needle as if to knit.

2 Slip these 2 stitches back onto left needle. Insert right needle through their 'back loops,' into the second stitch and then the first.

3 Purl them together: 2 stitches become 1. The result is a left-slanting decrease.

SK2P, sl 1-k2tog-psso

1 Slip 1 stitch knitwise.
2 Knit next 2 stitches together.
3 Pass the slipped stitch over the k2tog: 3 stitches become 1; the right stitch is on top.
The result is a left-slanting double decrease.

SSSP

Work same as **SSP** EXCEPT:
1 Slip **3** stitches….
2 Slip these **3** stitches… into third stitch, then second, and then first.
3 … **3** stitches become 1. The result is a left-slanting double decrease.

MISC

I-cord

Make a tiny tube of stockinette stitch with 2 double-pointed needles:
1 Cast on 2 or 3 sts.
2 Knit. Do not turn work. Slide stitches to opposite end of needle. Repeat Step 2 until cord is the desired length.

Twisted cord

1 Fold strand in half and knot cut ends together.
2 Place knotted end over a door knob or hook and index finger in folded end, then twist cord tightly.

3 Fold cord in half, smoothing as it twists on itself. Pull knot through original fold to secure.

Overhand knot

1-row buttonhole

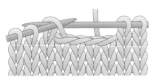

1 (Right-side row) Bring yarn to front and slip 1 purlwise. Take yarn to back and leave it there. * Slip next stitch, then pass previously slipped stitch over it; repeat from * for each buttonhole stitch. Put last slipped stitch back onto left needle.

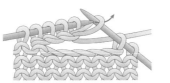

2 Turn work. Bring the yarn to back and cable cast on as follows: * Insert right needle between first and second stitches on left needle, wrap yarn as if to knit, pull loop through and place it on left needle; repeat from * until you have cast on 1 stitch more than was bound off.

3 Turn work. Bring yarn to back, slip first stitch from left needle, pass extra cast-on stitch over it, and tighten.

eyelet buttonhole

Row 1 (Right-side) SSK, yarn over (as shown). *Row 2* Purl into yarn-over.

Inserting zipper

Although the knitted fabric has stretch, the zipper does not, and the 2 must be joined. Follow these steps for a smooth installation:

1 Measure the length of the opening. Select a zipper that length or a bit longer.
2 Pre-shrink your zipper in the method you will use to clean the garment. Wash and dry or carefully steam it (you don't want to melt the teeth if they are plastic or nylon).
3 Place the zipper in opening, aligning each side. Allow extra length to extend beyond opening.
4 Pin in place. Be generous with the pins, and take all the time you need. Extra care taken here makes the next steps easier.
5 Baste in place. When you are satisfied with the placement, remove the pins.
6 Sew in the zipper, making neat, even stitches that are firm enough to withstand use.
7 Sew a stop at end of zipper and clip excess off if necessary.
8 If the zipper extends beyond the opening, trim extra length.

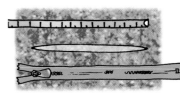

Measure

Pin

Baste

Sew

Short rows, wrap & turn (W&T)

Each short row adds 2 rows of knitting across a section of the work. Since the work is turned before completing a row, stitches must be wrapped at the turn to prevent holes. Wrap and turn as follows:

Knit side
1 With yarn in back, slip next stitch as if to purl. Bring yarn to front of work and slip stitch back to left needle (as shown). Turn work.
2 With yarn in front, slip next stitch as if to purl. Work to end.

3 When you come to the wrap on a following knit row, hide the wrap by knitting it together with the stitch it wraps.

Purl side
1 With yarn in front, slip next stitch as if to purl. Bring yarn to back of work and slip stitch back to left needle (as shown). Turn work.
2 With yarn in back, slip next stitch as if to purl. Work to end.

3 When you come to the wrap on a following purl row, hide the wrap by purling it together with the stitch it wraps.

Seam stitches to rows

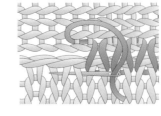

Pick up 2 row bars (as shown) for every cast-on stitch.

Intarsia

Color worked in areas of stockinette fabric: each area is made with its own length of yarn. Twists made at each color change connect these areas.

Right-side row

Wrong-side row

Interlocking the colors

Work across row to color change, pick up new color from under the old and work across to next color change.

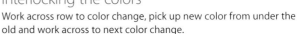

CROCHET

Half double crochet (hdc)

1 Insert hook into a stitch, catch yarn, and pull up a loop. Chain 2 (counts as first half double crochet).
2 Yarn over, insert hook into next stitch to the left (as shown).

Catch yarn and pull through stitch only; 3 loops on hook.
3 Catch yarn and pull through all 3 loops on hook: 1 half double crochet complete. Repeat Steps 2–3.

Chain stitch (ch st, ch)

1 Make a slipknot to begin.
2 Catch yarn and draw through loop on hook.

First chain made. Repeat Step 2.

Slip stitch (sl st)

1 Insert the hook into a stitch, catch yarn, and pull up a loop.

2 Insert hook into the next stitch to the left, catch yarn and pull through both the stitch and the loop on the hook; 1 loop on the hook. Repeat Step 2.

FELTING

Felting by machine

Protect your washer from excess fiber; place each item to be fulled into a zippered pillow protector or fine mesh bag. Set washer for hot wash, low water level and maximum agitation. (Using the rinse and spin cycles is not recommended as they may set permanent creases.) Add a small amount of mild detergent, and two old towels (non-shedding) or pairs of jeans for abrasion. Check on the progress every few minutes. Every time you check the progress, pull the item into shape. Reset the washer to continue agitation if necessary. When you are happy with the size, remove from washer. Rinse thoroughly in warm water. Roll in towels to remove as much water as possible. try on, pull into shape and finished dimenions, then stuff and let dry.

1 Place in mesh bag (or pillowcase).

2 Place in washer (with hot water and soap) and agitate…

…checking progress every few minutes.

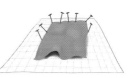

3 Roll in towel to remove excess moisture.

4 Shape and stuff with plastic bags or wadded paper to dry.

ABBREVIATIONS

CC contrasting color
cn cable needle
cm centimeter(s)
dec decrease
dpn double-pointed needle(s)
g gram(s)
" inch(es)
inc increase
k knit
LH left-hand
M1 Make one stitch (increase)
m meter(s)
mm millimeter(s)
MC main color
oz ounce(s)
p purl
pm place marker
psso pass slipped stitch(es) over
RH right-hand
RS right side(s)
sc single crochet
sl slip
SKP slip, knit, psso
SK2P slip, k2tog, psso
ssk slip, slip, knit these 2 sts tog
ssp slip, slip, purl these 2 sts tog
st(s) stitch(es)
tbl through back of loop(s)
tog together
WS wrong side(s)
wyib with yarn in back
wyif with yarn in front
x times
yd(s) yard(s)
yo yarn over

Working from charts

Charts are graphs or grids of squares that represent the right side of knitted fabric. They illustrate every stitch and the relationship between the rows of stitches.
Squares contain knitting symbols.
The key defines each symbol as an operation to make a stitch or stitches.

The pattern provides any special instructions for using the chart(s) or the key.
The numbers along the sides of charts indicate the rows. A number on the right side marks a right-side row that is worked leftward from the number. A number on the left marks a wrong-side

row that is worked rightward. Since many stitches are worked differently on wrong-side rows, the key will indicate that. If the pattern is worked circularly, all rows are right-side rows and worked from right to left.
Bold lines within the graph represent repeats. These set off a group of

stitches that are repeated across a row. You begin at the edge of a row or where the pattern indicates for the required size, work across to the second line, then repeat the stitches between the repeat lines as many times as directed, and finish the row.

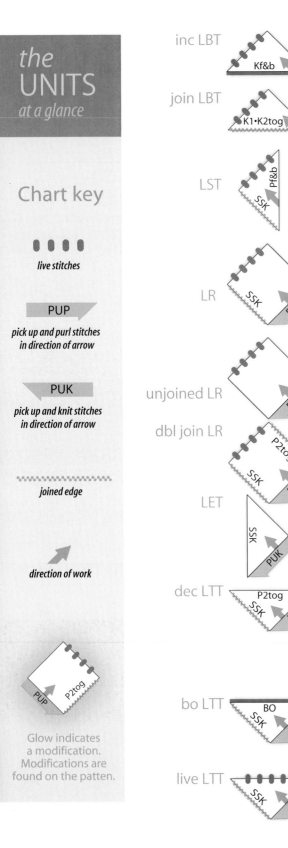

Chart key

live stitches

PUP

pick up and purl stitches
in direction of arrow

PUK

pick up and knit stitches
in direction of arrow

joined edge

direction of work

Glow indicates
a modification.
Modifications are
found on the patten.

inc LBT

join LBT

LST

LR

unjoined LR

dbl join LR

LET

dec LTT

bo LTT

live LTT

LBT Left-leaning Base Triangle

Increase LBT With RS facing, cast on 1. *Row 1* (WS) P1 (cast-on stitch). *Row 2* (RS) Knit in front and back of stitch (kf&b). *Row 3* Purl stitches worked on previous row. *Row 4* Knit to last stitch, kf&b. Repeat last 2 rows to base number of stitches, end with a RS row.
Join LBT *Row 1* (RS) K1 (existing stitch). *Row 2 and all WS rows* Purl stitch(es) worked on previous row. *Row 3* Knit stitch(es) worked on previous row, k2tog (2 existing stitches). *Row 5* Knit stitches worked on previous row, k1 (existing stitch). Repeat last 4 rows to base number of stitches, end with a RS row.

LST Left-leaning Starting Triangle

With WS facing, cast on 1 next to last stitch worked in previous tier. *Row 1* (RS) SSK to join (cast-on stitch with stitch from previous tier). *Row 2* (WS) Pf&b. *Row 3* Knit to last stitch of unit, SSK to join. *Row 4* Purl to last stitch, pf&b. Repeat last 2 rows until all stitches from unit in previous tier have been joined, end with a RS row—base number of stitches.

LR Left-leaning Rectangle

With RS facing, pick up and knit base stitches along edge of unit in previous tier (PUK). *Row 1* (WS) Purl base stitches. *Row 2* (RS) Knit to last stitch of unit, SSK to join (last stitch with stitch from previous tier). Repeat last 2 rows until all stitches from unit in previous tier have been joined—base number of stitches.
Unjoined LR PUK OR knit into cast-on stitches and work same as LR EXCEPT *Row 2* (RS) Knit. Repeat last 2 rows until unit has twice as many rows as base stitches.
Double-join LR Work same as LR EXCEPT. *Row 1* (WS) Purl to last stitch of unit, p2tog to join (last stitch with stitch from adjacent left-leaning unit).

LET Left-leaning Ending Triangle

With RS facing, pick up and knit base stitches along edge of unit in previous tier (PUK). *Row 1* (WS) Purl stitches worked on previous row. *Row 2* (RS) Knit to last 2 stitches, SSK. Repeat last 2 rows until 1 stitch remains. *Next row* (WS) P1, fasten off.

LTT Left-leaning Top Triangle

Decrease LTT With RS facing, pick up and knit base stitches along edge of unit in previous tier (PUK). *Row 1* (WS) Purl base stitches. *Row 2* (RS) Knit to last stitch of unit, SSK to join (last stitch with stitch from previous tier). *Row 3* Purl to last 2 stitches, p2tog. Repeat last 2 rows until all stitches from unit in previous tier have been joined and 1 stitch remains. Purl this stitch together with last stitch of Row 1 as you work on next unit OR fasten off on final unit of tier.
Bound-off LTT Work same as Decrease LTT EXCEPT *Row 3* Purl to last stitch. *Row 4* K1, pass previously unworked stitch over (BO 1), knit to last stitch of unit, SSK to join with previous tier. Repeat last 2 rows. Fasten off last stitch or bind off over first stitch on Row 2 of next unit.
Live-stitch LTT Work same as Decrease LTT EXCEPT *Row 3* Purl 1 stitch fewer than worked on previous row. If desired wrap next stitch, then turn work. When all stitches from unit in previous tier have been joined, base number of stitches remain on needle.-

Icons always show the right-side of the fabric — perfect if you knit in both directions (see pages 2–4).

RBT Right-leaning Base Triangle

Increase RBT With WS facing, cast on 1. *Row 1* (RS) K1 (cast-on stitch). *Row 2* (WS) Purl in front and back of stitch (pf&b). *Row 3* Knit stitches worked on previous row. *Row 4* Purl to last stitch, pf&b. Repeat last 2 rows to base number of stitches, end with a WS row.
Join RBT *Row 1* (WS) P1 (existing stitch). *Row 2 and all RS rows* Knit stitch(es) worked on previous row. *Row 3* Purl stitch(es) worked on previous row, p2tog (2 existing stitches). *Row 5* Purl stitches worked on previous row, p1 (existing stitch). Repeat last 4 rows to base number of stitches, end with a WS row.

RST Right-leaning Starting Triangle

With RS facing, cast on 1 next to last stitch worked in previous tier. *Row 1* (WS) P2tog to join (cast-on stitch with stitch from previous tier). *Row 2* (RS) Kf&b. *Row 3* Purl to last stitch of unit, p2tog to join. *Row 4* Knit to last stitch, kf&b. Repeat last 2 rows until all stitches from unit in previous tier have been joined, end with a WS row — base number of stitches.

RR Right-leaning Rectangle

With WS facing, pick up and purl base stitches along edge of unit in previous tier (PUP). *Row 1* (RS) Knit base stitches. *Row 2* (WS) Purl to last stitch of unit, p2tog to join (last stitch with stitch from previous tier). Repeat last 2 rows until all stitches from unit in previous tier have been joined — base number of stitches.
Unjoined RR PUP OR purl into cast-on stitches and work same as RR EXCEPT *Row 2* (WS) Purl. Repeat last 2 rows until unit has twice as many rows as base stitches.
Double-join RR Work same as RR EXCEPT *Row 1* (RS) Knit to last stitch of unit, SSK to join (last stitch with stitch from adjacent right-leaning unit).

RET Right-leaning Ending Triangle

With WS facing, pick up and purl base stitches along edge of unit in previous tier (PUP). *Row 1* (RS) Knit stitches worked on previous row. *Row 2* (WS) Purl to last 2 stitches, p2tog. Repeat last 2 rows until 1 stitch remains. *Next row* (RS) K1, fasten off.

RTT Right-leaning Top Triangle

Decrease RTT With WS facing, pick up and purl base stitches along edge of unit in previous tier (PUP). *Row 1* (RS) Knit base stitches. *Row 2* (WS) Purl to last stitch of unit, p2tog to join (last stitch with stitch from previous tier). *Row 3* Knit to last 2 stitches, SSK. Repeat last 2 rows until all stitches from unit in previous tier have been joined and 1 stitch remains. Knit this stitch together with last stitch of Row 1 as you work on next unit OR fasten off on final unit of tier.
Bound-off RTT Work same as Decrease RTT EXCEPT *Row 3* Knit to last stitch. *Row 4* P1, pass previously unworked stitch over (BO 1), purl to last stitch of unit, p2tog to join with previous tier. Repeat last 2 rows. Fasten off last stitch or bind off over first stitch on Row 2 of next unit.
Live-stitch RTT Work same as Decrease RTT EXCEPT *Row 3* Knit 1 stitch fewer than worked on previous row. If desired, wrap next stitch, then turn. When all stitches from unit in previous tier have been joined, base number of stitches remain on needle.

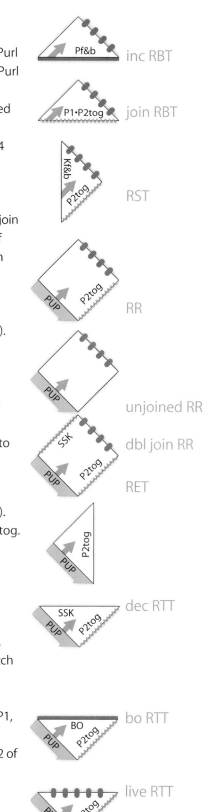

inc RBT

join RBT

RST

RR

unjoined RR

dbl join RR

RET

dec RTT

bo RTT

live RTT

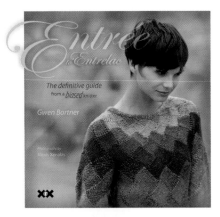

It was hard to choose.

Any large project is rarely accomplished by just one individual, and that is certainly true in the case of a book. There are many people for which I am grateful (more than I can hope to list), but the following are the major players in this adventure.

First, I acknowledge my parents, Lloyd and Donna Hall, for their unending love, support, and encouragement — but, especially my mom, who patiently taught me to knit when I was young and continues to knit samples for me. To Pat Sanguinetti, the yarn shop owner I knew, who had no idea what she started when she dropped a blob of knitting in front of me and said, "I bet your mathematical mind will understand this entrelac thing." Many thanks to my first knitting buddies, Pam Haurlan and Bev Jensen, who helped me through the process of getting my first entrelac design published way back when.

I am thankful for the encouragement of customers, students, and the folks at XRX who thought not only that it was time for a good book on entrelac, but also that I should be the person to write it. Thank you to generous vendors who supplied yarn for the many projects and to my sample knitters—without whom this book would be many more years in the making. Thank you Sally Black, Maryanne Cleary, Kim Dominic, Beverly Jensen, Lora Karaim, Clara Masessa, Kellie Nuss, Sarah Peasley, and Sammi Sherwin.

Last, but certainly not least, many thanks to all the folks at XRX (and I really mean everyone) who worked tirelessly on this project. Of particular note are Beth for her tech editing skills and continued friendship, Natalie and the whole production department for the beautiful book layout, design skills, and fabulous graphics; Alexis and his photo crew for the beautiful photos; Rick, Karen, Kristi, and Sue for all the editorial support; Ginger, Kellie, and Sarah for the 'final set of eyes'; and most importantly, Elaine for shepherding me through this process, pushing me to be my best and becoming a friend along the way.

My deepest gratitude is for my husband, Arlis, who is infinitely supportive, amazingly patient with my crazy schedule, and my greatest gift from God. Arlis, I love you very much.

Writing a book has been an adventure and adventures make life worth living. Thank you all for being a part of it.

—*Gwen Bortner*